The Little Platoon

'To be attached to the sub-division, to love the little platoon we belong to in society, is the first principle (the germ as it were) of public affections, the first link by which we proceed towards a love to our country.'

Edmund Burke, 1790

The Little Platoon

*Diplomacy
and the Falklands Dispute*

MICHAEL CHARLTON

Basil Blackwell

Copyright © Michael Charlton 1989

First published 1989

Basil Blackwell Ltd
108 Cowley Road, Oxford, OX4 1JF, UK

Basil Blackwell Inc.
432 Park Avenue South, Suite 1503
New York, NY 10016, USA

British Library Cataloguing in Publication Data

Charlton, Michael, *1927–*
The little platoon: diplomacy and the Falklands Dispute
1. Falkland Islands. Policies of British
government, history
I. Title
997′.11
ISBN 0–631–16564–9

Library of Congress Cataloging in Publication Data

Charlton, Michael.
    The little platoon: diplomacy and the Falklands dispute / Michael Charlton.
    p. cm.
    Includes index.
    ISBN 0–631–16564–9
    1. Falkland Islands – History. 2. Great Britain – Foreign relations – Argentina. 3. Argentina – Foreign relations – Great Britain. 4. Falkland Islands War. 1982 – Diplomatic history.
5. Oral history. I. Title.
F3031.C48   1989
997′.11–dc 19   88-7578
                                                                 CIP

Typeset in 10½ on 12 pt Ehrhardt
by Joshua Associates Ltd, Oxford
Printed in Great Britain by
T.J. Press (Padstow), Padstow, Cornwall

Contents

163846

Preface

The contributors to this oral history of British diplomacy are those who created and conducted British policy over the Falkland Islands from the time it once again became an active issue in the 1960s. They are the senior officials of the Foreign Office and Ministry of Defence who were principally concerned and the successive foreign secretaries and other British ministers to whom they gave advice. In addition, there are their counterparts, at relevant periods, in the United States and in Argentina. Lastly, there are the admirals – who had the last word.

Understandably overlooked in the popular acclaim for a brilliant feat of arms, the least known aspect of the Falklands conflict remains these many years of diplomacy which preceded it. They are its greater fraction. As we shall see, when Parliament hastily assembled on the morning of 3 April 1982, stirred by the rapid impulse of an unpredicted war, that thoughtful custodian of institutional memory, the Librarian of the House of Lords placed on the reading tables photocopies of Dr Samuel Johnson's thunderous pamphlet concerning the Falklands in 1771 – following shortly on the first time Britain made preparations to fight over those desolate and distant islands. It has indeed been a long struggle. The reading tables that day were a reproof to successive modern Parliaments that had been repetitively dismissive of the charged nature of the Falklands dilemma. An understanding of the final miscalculations by Britain and Argentina is hardly possible without a knowledge, given here at first hand, of how the search for a tolerable *modus vivendi* in the South Atlantic was pursued over such a long period.

Clausewitz, the philosopher of war, made it his purpose to develop a concept of war that could be thought out with lucidity. He 'rejected theories which failed to take account of the singularity of each combination of events, or which were contrary to the nature of things, like those which failed to recognize the role of emotion, of military virtues and passions'[1] – in short, the human side of war. Diplomacy, the antecedent to war (although, happily, not always so) confronts the same complexity, and the Foreign Office certainly found the Falklands an uncommon combination. At the time of the Falklands War, as in the days of the first Elizabeth, which followed the loss of Calais and the continental possessions – the first British Empire – Britain was a small country, enmeshed in internal difficulties and with slender resources. Ministers were bent upon retrenchment at home and abroad. Then, as now, it was a nation for which no cheap and easy answers were available.

Among the huge frescos at the top of the entrance staircase to the Foreign Office is 'Britannia Sponsā'. What appears, from a distance, to be the victim of a mass violation reveals herself to be, on closer inspection, Britannia betrothed or, as the legend continues, 'The Seafarers claim Britain as their Bride.' The breakdown of policy over the Falklands, among the last offspring of this union, illuminated many things as, beyond these frescos, a generation of officials had tried to take account of Britain's reduced circumstances and the end of the colonial era. Not the least were Britain's view of herself in the world, and the revival of the old argument between the continental commitment and the maritime schools of strategy. The Falklands is the story of a nation that could not make up its mind.

The interviews in this book were recorded in the autumn of 1985 and the spring of 1986 in Britain, Argentina and the United States, and originally broadcast as a series of eight programmes for the BBC's Radio Three. Without the constraints of time in broadcasting, it has been possible to expand substantially the use of the recorded material for this book. The participants were given notice of the areas of questions in advance of the interviews to enable them, where possible, to refresh their memories from their papers or personal diaries of the time. The questions and answers in the following pages were those recorded at the time, 'on the spot'. No subsequent alterations have been made, other than those minor instances where the conventions of the spoken word need clarification in print.

Much thanks is owed, on several counts. First, of course, it is owed to the distinguished contributors themselves, who gave their time and searched their memories for the BBC. My thanks go also to George

---

1 Raymond Aron, *Clausewitz* (Routledge & Kegan Paul, 1976).

Fischer, the Head of Talks and Documentary programmes, to Ian McIntyre, the Controller of Radio Three who commissioned the original BBC broadcasts, and to their Producer, my colleague Cathy Wearing, for all her help.

Michael Charlton
Broadcasting House, London

The Contributors

ADMIRAL GUALTER ALLARA   Argentine Navy. Minister in military government, 1977; in command of aircraft carrier *Veinticinco de Mayo*, and commander of Task Force 79, during Falklands war.

RT HON. JULIAN AMERY MP   Minister of state, Foreign Office, 1972–4.

SIR JOHN BIGGS-DAVISON MP   Vice-chairman of the Conservative Parliamentary foreign and Commonwealth affairs committee.

RT HON. SIR BERNARD BRAINE   Parliamentary under-secretary of state for Commonwealth affairs, 1962–4; Conservative front-bench spokesman on Commonwealth affairs, 1967–70.

REAR-ADMIRAL CARLOS BUSSER   Argentine marines. Planning Staff and operational commander of the Argentine landing on the Falkland Islands in 1982.

RT HON. LORD CALLAGHAN MP   Secretary of state for foreign and Commonwealth affairs, 1974–6; prime minister, 1976–9.

DR OSCAR CAMILION   Argentine foreign minister, March–December 1981.

HUGH CARLESS   Head of Latin American department, Foreign Office, 1973–7; minister and chargé d'affaires, Buenos Aires, 1977–80; ambassador to Venezuela, 1982–5.

RT HON. DAME BARBARA CASTLE   Chairman of the Labour Party, 1958–9; minister of overseas development, 1964–5; minister of transport, 1965–8; secretary of state for employment, 1968–70; secretary of state for social services, 1974–6.

RT HON. LORD CHALFONT   Minister of state, Foreign Office, 1964–70.

RT HON. SIR FRANK COOPER   Assistant under-secretary of state, Air

Ministry, 1962–4; assistant under-secretary of state, Ministry of Defence, 1964–8; permanent under-secretary, Ministry of Defence, 1976–82.

DR NICANOR COSTA MÉNDEZ   Argentine minister of external relations and religion, 1966–9 and 1981–2.

ROBERT 'ROBIN' EDMONDS   Head of Latin American department, Foreign Office, 1966–8; under-secretary, Foreign Office, 1969–73.

THOMAS O. ENDERS   American diplomat. Assistant secretary of state for inter-American affairs, State Department, 1981–3.

LORD GREENHILL   Assistant under-secretary of state, Foreign Office, 1964–6; deputy under-secretary of state, Foreign Office, 1966–9; permanent under-secretary of state, Foreign Office, and head of the Diplomatic Service, 1969–73.

ROBERTO GUYER   Argentine diplomat since 1956. Former professor of international law, University of Buenos Aires. Various senior posts in the Argentine Ministry of Foreign Affairs; UN under-secretary general for political affairs, 1971–8; Argentine ambassador to the Hague; Argentine ambassador to Federal Republic of Germany, 1978–84.

GENERAL ALEXANDER HAIG   Commander-in-chief of US European Command, 1974–9; supreme Allied commander, Europe, 1979; US secretary of state, 1981–2.

HON. HENRY HANKEY   Head of American department, Foreign Office, 1956; assistant under-secretary of state, Foreign Office, 1969–74.

SIR NICHOLAS HENDERSON   Assistant under-secretary to Ernest Bevin, 1944–7; ambassador to Poland, 1969–72; ambassador to Federal Republic of Germany, 1972–5; ambassador to France, 1975–9; ambassador to the US, 1979–82.

WILLIAM HUNTER CHRISTIE   Author of *The Antarctic Problem* (Allen & Unwin, 1951); former diplomat, British Embassy, Buenos Aires; a founder of the Falkland Islands 'lobby'.

JEANE KIRKPATRICK   American diplomat. Professor of political science, Georgetown University, 1978–80; American ambassador to the UN, 1981–5.

ADMIRAL SIR HENRY LEACH   Chief of the Naval Staff and First Sea Lord, 1979–82.

ADMIRAL LORD LEWIN   Chief of the Naval Staff and First Sea Lord, 1977–9; chief of the Defence Staff, 1979–82.

RICHARD LUCE MP Parliamentary under-secretary of state, 1979–81; minister of state, Foreign Office, 1981–2.

RT HON. SIR JOHN NOTT MP Minister of state, Treasury, 1972–4; secretary of state for trade, 1979–81; secretary of state for defence, 1981–3.

RT HON. SIR MICHAEL PALLISER Head of Planning Staff, Foreign Office, 1964; private secretary to prime minister, 1966; ambassador to European communities, 1973–5; permanent under-secretary of state, Foreign Office, and head of the Diplomatic Service, 1975–82.

SIR ANTHONY PARSONS Under-secretary, Foreign Office, 1971–4; ambassador to Iran, 1974–9; UK ambassador to the UN, 1979–82; special adviser to the prime minister on foreign affairs, 1982–3.

JAVIER PÉREZ DE CUÉLLAR Peruvian diplomat. Secretary general of the UN since 1982.

RT HON. LORD PYM Secretary of state for defence, 1979–81; leader of the House of Commons, 1981–2; secretary of state for foreign and Commonwealth affairs, 1982–3.

EDWARD 'TED' ROWLANDS MP Parliamentary under-secretary of state, Welsh Office, 1969–70; Parliamentary under-secretary of state, Foreign Office, 1975–6; minister of state, Foreign Office, 1976–9.

LORD SHACKLETON Deputy leader of the House of Lords, 1967–8; Lord Privy Seal, 1968; leader of the House of Lords, 1968–70; opposition leader of the House of Lords, 1970–9.

RT HON. PETER SHORE Deputy leader of the House of Commons, 1969–70; secretary of state for trade, 1974–6; secretary of state for the environment, 1976–9; opposition spokesman on foreign affairs, 1979–80.

SIR IAN SINCLAIR Assistant legal adviser, Foreign Office, 1960–4; legal counsellor, Foreign Office, 1967–71; second legal adviser, Foreign Office, 1973–5; legal adviser, Foreign Office, 1976–84; legal adviser to the UK at numerous international conferences, including the Geneva conference on Indo-China, 1954, and to the UK delegation at Brussels on negotiations for entry into the EEC, 1961–3.

RT HON. LORD STEWART MP Secretary of state for Foreign Affairs, January 1965–August 1966; first secretary of state, 1966–8; secretary of state for economic affairs, 1966–7; secretary of state for foreign affairs, 1968–70.

ADMIRAL HARRY TRAIN US Navy. Supreme Allied commander Atlantic (SACLANT) at time of the Falklands war.

GENERAL VERNON WALTERS   Roving US ambassador for special missions; interpreter for Presidents Truman, Eisenhower and Nixon; deputy director, Central Intelligence Agency, 1972–6; US ambassador to the UN since 1985.

CASPAR WEINBERGER   US secretary of health, education and welfare, 1973–5; secretary of defence, 1981–7.

SIR ANTHONY WILLIAMS   Head of Chancery, Moscow, 1965–7; head of Imperial Defence College, 1968; political counsellor, Washington, 1969–70; ambassador at Phnom Penh, 1970–3; ambassador to Libyan Arab Jamahariya, 1977–9; ambassador to Argentina, 1980–2.

1

Bin Ends of Empire

The war that Britain fought for the Falkland Islands in 1982 is now installed as one of the more remarkable episodes in recent military history. To fight an unexpected war eight thousand miles away from home and win, against superior modern arms, is by any judgement an extraordinary achievement. The first surprise had been that it was fought at all. The Falklands proved to be a lesson in the tremendous consequence of inconsequence.

Since the end of the Second World War, a notable accomplishment of British statecraft has been peaceful disengagement from empire. Why Britain tripped up over the Falklands, why Parliament would not permit the settlement which successive governments recommended, is the task of this history to explore with those ministers and their senior advisers in Whitehall who, over many years, made the decisions which shaped British policy and diplomacy.

Writing of the contemporary revolution he detested, with its spirit of contempt for prescriptive rights, and its destruction of nation and tradition, Edmund Burke said that 'to be attached to the sub-division, to love the little platoon we belong to in society, is the first principle (the germ as it were) of public affections, the first link by which we proceed towards a love to our country.'[1] The Falkland Islanders were, indeed, a very small platoon. In going to war, Burke's first principle, that democracy begins with small cases which cannot be overlooked, was shown to lie at the foundation of British sympathies and patriotism. In reality, the Falklands war was a question of domestic British politics.

The first foreign secretary who had to deal with the Falklands as an active modern issue was **Michael Stewart** in the Labour Government of the 1960s. At Westminster, on the eve of the Falklands war in 1982, he was reminded of just how long-standing a dispute it has been. In his

1 *Reflections on the Revolution in France* (1790).

eighty-first year, and a pensioner, Lord Stewart recalled this bipartisan legacy in British politics, which is now more than two centuries old.

I remember going to the House of Lords for the debate on the Saturday, an unusual thing in itself, and immediately after the Argentines had occupied the Falklands. The library had dug out a piece that Dr Johnson had written, in 1771, advocating, I think, that we abandon our claim to Spain, and saying it wasn't worth arguing about.

What impact did that make on you?

I'm afraid I made the uncharitable reflection that Dr Johnson after all was an old Tory drawing a pension from a Tory government!

As you say, he thought it was not worth going to war over?

Yes. Johnson, and the issue of going to war, reminded me, you know, of another of the eighteenth-century settlements. Corsica was for the first time given to France, and the Corsicans resented this bitterly. Boswell had visited Corsica and he wrote a book about it that caught the popular imagination. There were tremendous outbursts of feeling about our allowing France to take Corsica, and some Cabinet Minister remarked, 'Well, we really cannot go to war with France because Mr Boswell has written a book!'

Lord Stewart brings to mind for us a period of irregular British spirit and vigour abroad. In the 1760s the British had captured Havana and ransomed Manila. Spain responded with a claim to exclusive possession of the Falklands, and a Spanish expedition from Buenos Aires expelled the British. The news raised a general indignation in England. Both sides prepared for war. Two million pounds was added to the Royal Navy's estimates. Spain gave way and, in return for the restoration of Havana and Manila, ceded all of Florida to Britain, and the right to cut timber in Honduras, but *without* any acknowledgement of British right to the Falklands. In arguing that the colony in the Falklands was not worth a contest, Dr Johnson wrote, 'That of which we were almost weary ourselves we did not expect others to envy, and therefore supposed that we would be permitted to reside in Falkland's Island, the undisputed lords of tempest beaten barrenness.'[2]

In those sentiments, set down in 1771, is the seed of the Falklands war in the 1980s. There was, said Johnson, 'a general error running through the British argument; that its tiny settlement was not only lawful but unquestionable'. He considered the question of sovereignty to be

2 *Thoughts on the late Transactions respecting Falkland's Islands* (1771).

inexplicable and endless. As indeed it has proved to be – the current dispute involving Argentina's right to inherit the Spanish claim originating in the 1830s.

Therefore, not at all times has the British title to the Falkland Islands been thought sound in Britain itself. To what extent has Britain's modern diplomacy, beginning in the 1960s, incorporated such doubts? The custodians of the immensely complex history of the rival claims are the Foreign Office lawyers. Among them it is a matter for careful utterance. A Foreign Office senior legal adviser who has been directly involved with the question is **Sir Ian Sinclair**.

Clearly over the years since the dispute first arose in 1833 there had been a whole series of lengthy historical and legal researches made into the question of our title. We had reached the conclusion that our case was a strong case. So I don't think that our diplomacy as such was, strictly speaking, affected by any doubts as to the strength of our title.

None the less, we find this in minutes of proceedings of the Foreign Affairs Select Committee of the House of Commons in April 1983. It was in the Chairman's draft report concerning policy over the Falkland Islands, and it says, 'Although your Committee believes that the historical evidence is finely balanced, we are obliged to conclude that the weight of the evidence argues in favour of the view that Argentina's claim to the Falkland Islands is, or at least to East *Falkland was, at the time of the British occupation in 1833, of greater substance than has been credited by official United Kingdom government sources. We are supported in this conclusion',* it said, 'by the doubts on this subject repeatedly expressed by British officials during the first half of this century.'[3]

That, as you say, relates to a draft report and I believe it was not in fact incorporated into the final report. As to the question of doubts which may have been expressed by officials from time to time, it is inevitable in a matter such as this, involving consideration of complex historical and factual questions, that doubts may have been expressed from time to time by officials. It depends very much on the time at which they were expressed. The law has developed over the years. Anything, for example, prior to 1928 would not have taken account of a major arbitration in that year, bearing upon the question of 'acquisitive prescription' in the Palmas arbitration. Anything prior to that certainly has to be considered in that light.

How significant is it that neither Argentina nor Britain in modern times has sought to refer this question to the International Court or other forms of arbitration?

3 Author's emphasis.

It is a very sensitive issue politically in both countries. No question about it. For Argentine public opinion it is a matter of national honour. In terms of British public opinion there is the question, which surfaced very quickly in 1982 of course, about the wishes of the Falkland Islanders themselves. It is, very simply, whether given those considerations this is a matter which is suitable to go to international judicial settlement. Certainly, in addition to the question of historic title, there is now the pervasive influence of the principle of self-determination.

It is suggested that the crucial period is between the Spanish settlement of East Falkland in 1811, and the British occupation of the islands in 1833. How, in terms of international legal attitudes, do we emerge from that?

As far as the historic title is concerned, that is the question of claims based upon the concept of 'early settlement', that period is, of course, of very considerable significance.

The Spaniards abandoned their settlement in 1811. For a period of at least nine years, the Islands were virtually uninhabited, apart from the few visits of sealers and whalers, from North America mainly, who put into anchorages in the Falklands primarily to take on water. In that period of nine years when the Islands were uninhabited, they were subject to no form of government whatsoever. Then, there is the later period, from 1820 onwards.

In 1824, M. Vernet, an adventurer of French ethnic origin, but settled in Hamburg, started to try and begin a settlement on the Falklands. He did not succeed. His first effort was unsuccessful. He tried again, a few years later, in 1826. Now comes the crucial question you referred to. That is, the extent to which, let us say from 1826 until 1831, there had been sufficient state activity, *by Argentina*, in relation to the Falklands, to warrant a strengthening of such title as they claim to have on the basis of inheritance from Spain.

We have looked pretty carefully at the evidence relating to that period. We are convinced that the amount of activity by M. Vernet initially was in his private capacity. He paid no taxes, and he received no assistance from the government in Buenos Aires until 1829, when he was formally appointed Governor of the Falkland Islands, by decree, in Buenos Aires. That, of course, was one to which we made an immediate protest, reverting to the fact that the Islands were British.

It is suggested by Argentina, and some sympathetic to her claim, that there was a 'secret promise' at the time we nearly went to war with Spain over the Falklands in the 1770s; that Britain agreed that if her presence, which had been removed by Spain, was restored in the Islands, we would not in the end maintain it; and that there was this 'secret promise' given by the Prime Minister, Lord North?

Yes. I believe this partly derives from a book published by Professor Julius Goebel, of the Yale School of Law, in 1928. Now, frankly, when this allegation was first made by Argentina in 1833, Lord Palmerston, who was the foreign secretary at the time, caused a search to be made throughout the whole of the archives of the Foreign Office to see whether any evidence existed of this so-called, alleged, 'secret promise'. He discovered no evidence inviting the certainty that the secret promise was made. Here again, the situation is one of a conflict of evidence. Whether, or how far, it is relevant to the matter is another question.

Does documented evidence exist anywhere else for the assertion made about a secret promise, even if Lord Palmerston's searches of the foreign office archives in London did not disclose one?

If such evidence existed, it has never been shown to us.

What, in essence, do we dispute about this interpretation of history, going back to the 1770s and the 1820s and '30s? Why do we regard our title to the Falkland Islands as cured?

Could I put it this way? Our title to the Falkland Islands is based on early settlement; that is to say, the events from 1764 up until 1833. But, to the extent that there *could* be any question raised about the strength, or conclusiveness, of that title, of course our title is re-inforced by the fact that we have been in continuous peaceful possession, occupation and administration of the Islands since 1833. This is the doctrine that we international lawyers refer to rather peculiarly as 'acquisitive prescription'. It's not unlike the concept of adverse possession in English property law. If there is a doubt as to the title, or if title may originally have been invested in somebody else – which I don't concede – then the fact that you have been in continuous, peaceful occupation, and possession, and been administering the territory for a lengthy period of years, will cure any so-called or alleged defect in the title.

Is our title to the Falklands based upon 'acquisitive prescription' in the broadest terms as good, shall we say, as the title the United States has to San Francisco?

I think you have to consider the whole historical progression. We claim title on the basis of early settlement, but *reinforced* by this concept of acquisitive prescription. I was asked by the Foreign Affairs Committee of the House of Commons if our title to the Falklands was as secure as our title to the City of London, which is very similar to the question you've just put to me. All I can say as a lawyer, and I am cautious, is that one really cannot compare the two. Clearly, as regards sovereignty over the Falkland Islands there is a dispute; but we are convinced of the strength of our title.

*Argentina, at intervals down the years, has often protested and from the very
early history of this dispute. Is that persistent protest enough to prevent the
ripening, or maturing, or curing of our title over all the years since 1833?*

It would not be, on our analysis of the situation, sufficient to do that.
In any event, we would not take the view that the concept of acquisitive prescription could not operate, even in circumstances where
protests had been made. Particularly, if those protests had not been
accompanied by anything more than the mere fact of protest.

*In your long experience of giving legal advice to the Foreign Office, historically
speaking, how does the Falkland Islands compare with other classical disputes? Is
there a particularity about it?*

That it is a dispute of very long standing. A formal dispute in effect
since 1833, but then the background to *that* dispute reaching back to
events in the middle of the eighteenth century. That is what gives it its
particularity.

As Sir Ian Sinclair makes clear, Britain has its own view of the matter.
That view is disputed by Argentina. Power, rather than legal argument,
proved decisive in the early history. It did so again in 1982.

Not for the first time these drenched, symbolic islands, where it
rains for an average of two hundred and forty days a year, have marked
a sea-change for the British as a nation state. In the eighteenth century,
as we have seen, they were an issue of pride and vanity which
dramatized the rise of Britain as a maritime world empire. And, as
Britain has moved out of the old order which it dominated, to return to
the general life of Europe, the Falkland Islands have emerged from
their solitude once more, to demonstrate painful ambiguities in British
policy.

By the 1960s, in a world ordered by the ballistic missile, the strong-
holds of a former British naval supremacy, from the Falklands to Hong
Kong to Aden and Gibraltar, were the last of a vintage, the 'bin ends' of a
vanishing empire. The head of the Foreign Office towards the end of the
1960s was **Sir Denis Greenhill** – Lord Greenhill today.

The thing you have to remember all the time is that there was a great
need for economy in defence spending. The advice of the chiefs of
staff, consistently, all through the discussions of the Falkland Islands,
was that these islands are not defensible, and that we have got much
more important things to do. People were talking about withdrawing
from the Gulf, the Middle East, and all that sort of thing. There, as
you know, British interests were immeasurably greater than in the
Falkland Islands. So, people really felt the need, and certainly the

Ministry of Defence was pressing to be relieved of the responsibility of protecting all these left-overs from the break up of the British Empire.

May I read to you something which a great Foreign Secretary, Lord Curzon, wrote in 1907? He said, 'When India has gone, and your great colonies have gone too, do you suppose that we can stop there? Your ports, and your coaling stations, your fortresses and dockyards, your Crown Colonies and Protectorates will go too. For, either they will be unnecessary, as the toll gates and barbicans of an empire that has vanished, or they will be taken[4] *by an enemy who is more powerful than you are.' Did the Foreign Office consider that Lord Curzon's prophecy must become the foundation of the advice it gave to Ministers?*

I don't think we had Lord Curzon's words on the wall, but I think that was the obvious conclusion. As far as I was concerned, I always tried to ensure that the little island colonies that had been left over were well administered, and well supported, and a credit to our colonial tradition. But that required money. It was a very unpopular idea to lavish money on these islands. And so on, and so on. I think that what Lord Curzon said was very far-seeing. He was absolutely right.

Lord Curzon, of whom it was said that 'his cold eye danced in order to get warm', had, therefore, lit up the future. By the 1960s, given Britain's relative weakness, among the difficulties for the Foreign Office in being 'far-sighted' was the moral dimension to Labour's foreign policy.

Just as Ernest Bevin, of strong heart and strong opinion, was convinced when he was foreign secretary that Labour had captured the moral leadership in world affairs, so those who followed after him in the Labour Government of the 1960s were resolved to support the international order of the United Nations. That meant forgoing purely national advantage in accepting its verdicts. As the Foreign Office saw it, the process of 'decolonization' was allied to an, at times, conflicting determination to stand by 'the little platoon' and minorities in the 'left-overs' of empire. At a time of declining strength, the difficulty in formulating policy arose if doing so meant trouble with other countries. **Michael Stewart** was, twice, Labour's foreign secretary in the 1960s.

I never really put our decision to stand by the Falkland Islanders in the same sort of box as our position east of Suez. The question east of Suez was, 'Are we going to go on maintaining responsibilities towards countries which are independent, and which are not British possessions?' The question of the Falklands, and of Gibraltar, was, what are we going to do with a territory which *is* a British possession, and the

4 Author's emphasis.

inhabitants of which want it to *go on* being a British possession? We
played this game of imperial snatch in the eighteenth and nineteenth
centuries, which left us all kinds of odd bits of territory, to which the
answers are never the same in each case. We are in the process now
of disembarrassing ourselves of Hong Kong. The situation is rather
different there, because it was perfectly clear that by a particular
date we should cease to have any legal right to be there. That was
not so with Gibraltar or the Falklands. So, are we to say that
because Britain is obviously not as great a power, in the whole
category of powers, as it used to be – are we to say, that as a result of
that, we abandon every responsibility we have? Well, I hope *not*,
that's all.

*That's what you felt, over the Falklands, in the 1960s? It was this moral
responsibility to a minority?*

Yes. Yes. These were our fellow subjects. We could not transfer them
against their wishes. And there you were. You see, it seems to me that
a country that's become really adult, and lived in the twentieth
century, would not *make* demands of this kind on territory. Canada
does not demand that those two little islands in the river St Lawrence,
which are French possessions . . .

Miquelon and St Pierre?

Yes, Miquelon and St Pierre. You see, there, Canada could put up as
good a case for having them as the Argentines can for the Falklands. It
doesn't *do* it, because, what is the point? What advantage? Why try to
make people do something they obviously don't want to do? Merely,
as far as I can see, for vanity. The French don't demand the Channel
Islands, which are much nearer to France than they are to Britain.

Although there have been times when they did?

I was always very careful never to produce that argument in case it put
ideas into General de Gaulle's head.

Lord Stewart's belief that a mature political society would not make
adolescent territorial demands, of the kind that Argentina insisted upon
over the Falklands, conforms to Labour's evangelical support in the
1960s of the moral example enshrined in the United Nations charter.
This devotion to 'rule by example' must be seen as among the factors
which led Britain to take insufficient account of Argentina's obsession
with the Falklands. It was an oversight common to both the major
political parties.

At the same time, the Labour Government of the 1960s had a strong
commitment to anti-colonialism. The extent to which this became a

controlling factor when it was decided to cede to Argentina sovereignty over the Falklands, under certain conditions, is confirmed by the Foreign Office minister who had responsibilities for the Falklands during this period, **Lord Chalfont**.

> There was, first of all, the Labour Party's general, philosophical, and ideological view of colonialism. The belief that our sovereignty over the Falkland Islands was a residuum of a colonial empire which was being, and ought to have been, liquidated. But the second thing, I think, was a very clear, and quite hard-headed, realization of the conflict between good relations with Argentina (and the necessity of recognizing and reconciling the claims of self-determination of the Falkland Islanders) and the legalities of our claim to sovereignty. I think that what happened was that a Labour government which had, of course, undeniably, a kind of anti-colonial ideology would have come down in favour of the idea that this was a matter for negotiation and ought to be negotiated as soon, and as effectively, as possible.

Lord Chalfont sets out the roots of British policy by the time Argentina had successfully raised the future of the Falklands to the level of an international dispute, by securing United Nations backing for her claim in 1965. At this early stage, the reservations Lord Stewart has expressed over 'abandoning the tiny minority of Falklanders against their wishes' were not uppermost in the minds of ministers, or their advisers. From the outset, in the 1960s, there was always the wider British interest dominating official attitudes to the Falklands, described by the former head of the Foreign Office, **Lord Greenhill**.

> At the back of everybody's mind there was the necessity to get a solution to the problem of the Falkland Islands. I think people were surprised really when it sort of blew up. But they did not, at that time, believe that it would have been impossible to reach a solution. Everybody thought, in my view quite rightly, that here are a small number of people, equal to a sort of Cornish fishing village, or a medium-sized comprehensive school. They cannot be an obstacle, provided they were properly treated, to our relations not only to the Argentine, but to the whole of Latin America. We had this – we saw it later at the time of the Falklands war – hostility against this country from the whole of Latin America. It was detrimental to trade and to everything else. We were beginning to be capable of trading on a scale which, immediately after the Second World War, we could not possibly have contemplated. The Latin American countries themselves were growing in size and importance.

Michael Stewart *did* see the importance of Latin America. His own visit there was part of a policy to re-establish our position in that whole area. He was very far-seeing in wanting to pursue that.

The Foreign Office advice, therefore, was that Britain still had a role to play in Latin America, following a very long period of neglect. The belief that this advice was sound had been encouraged by a remarkable creative success for British diplomacy – the Antarctic Treaty.

The main operational effects of this Treaty, ratified in 1961 by twelve nations including the USA, the USSR and Argentina, were to suspend all territorial claims and disputes involving Antarctica, the last continent. This treaty stood as a symbol holding out the possibilities of a new internationalism in foreign policy. It was also, and first and foremost, the carefully thought-out response by the Foreign Office to the intense overlapping rivalries in the area. Of these rivalries, the principal one to be surmounted was the territorial rivalry between the British and the Argentines. The head of the Latin American desk in the Foreign Office in the early 1960s was **Robin Edmonds**.

My own view is that to understand the mood and the ideas with which the British Government entered into the negotiation with Argentina over the Falklands in 1966, you have to go back to the entry into force of the Antarctic Treaty, in 1961. The basic concepts of the Treaty were the brainchildren of three very gifted British officials. The people who sat around the tables in Whitehall originally, having these very remarkable ideas, did have at the back of their minds after Suez that things could not go on forever as they had.

The Antarctic Treaty was of fundamental importance in relation, not just to the Falklands dispute, but to *all* our territorial disputes then outstanding. These, if I may remind you, were the dispute with Guatemala, over what was then called British Honduras and is now called Belize, and, not by any means to be ignored, there was the Venezuelan claim to one third of the whole territory – down to the Essequibo River – of British Guiana, which was then coming up for independence, and is Guyana today.

The point about the Antarctic Treaty I would like to make, and which I think will strike historians in the future, was that the British and the Argentines drew more or less diametrically opposite conclusions from the fact that they had been able – both of them – to sign this very, very difficult treaty. For their part, the Argentines took a very deep breath and said, 'OK. We've signed this treaty in which we have agreed for thirty years, and maybe beyond to, in quotes, "freeze our sovereignty".' That is Article 4 of the Antarctic Treaty. 'But', they said, 'we are not, in doing this, going to give up, in any way, our claim to the Malvinas' – what we call the Falkland Islands.

This was made very clear to me in a rather surprising place, namely the Island of Tahiti. The very first Antarctic Treaty Consultative Meeting was held in Canberra. They were held in alphabetical order, 'A' for Australia. Anyway, there was a strike, so that neither my Argentine opposite number, nor I, could travel home westwards. So we went east about. This involved us in a miraculous few hours' stop in Tahiti. My Argentine opposite, Roberto Guyer, an intrepid driver, hired a rather ancient Renault and rushed round the island. Mercifully we stopped, I think it was at Venus Point, and he chose this remarkable scene to say, 'Robin, I want you to know one thing. We're *not going to give up* the claim to the Falklands.' In my memory, that is the first time that I realized this was so.

Now for the British. The lesson that the *British* drew from the signature of the Antarctic Treaty was that if a problem as complex and as vast as *that* one could be solved with application, good will and reasonable intelligence, then, given time, the other equally difficult disputes elsewhere in Latin America – difficult because they involved actual inhabitants – could be solved.

The Falkland Islands were very much on the back burner in those days. Much to the fore was the Guatemalan claim to Honduras, and increasingly, from about 1961 or '62 onwards, the Venezuelan claim to one third of the territory of British Guiana.

During those first meetings with Argentine diplomats, how conscious were officials like yourself in the Foreign Office that there was an emotional content in this dispute over the Falklands? That, as they saw it, they were not so much making a claim to the Falklands but reviving *a claim of very long standing?*

We were aware that there was a strong emotional content. But again, there was a strong emotional content in the Guatemalan claim to Belize, and indeed the Venezuelan claim to a third of Guyana which was seriously advanced. At that time the Argentine claim seemed to be a comparatively *moderate* one.

I think one also has to remember that the Argentines, if not literally, are our oldest friends in the subcontinent. They were in many ways our best friends. It was natural, as part of this revived effort in Latin America, to invite to London President Arturo Frondisi, one of the first Latin American heads of state to come here. After all, the Argentine Republic, in terms of its infrastructure, was very largely the creation of British investment. There was the meat trade and everything else that went on. Everything was in full swing in those days. It added up to a very extensive fund of goodwill towards the Argentines – at the beginning. I am talking of course before 1968. After 1968 everything was totally different. I seem to remember that some other departments were sceptical of our efforts. Indeed, at some meetings our only ally was the Bank of England who, surprisingly and quite rightly, took the view that it is sometimes better not to have all one's eggs in one basket.

When Roberto Guyer said to you in Tahiti, 'I want you to understand we will never', despite the Antarctic Treaty, 'give up our claim to the Falklands, to the Malvinas', can you remember what answer you returned?

If I had answered it, I suppose I would have said, 'Oh, come off it, Roberto', or something like that. Or I might have said, 'Well, if we really bend our minds to it perhaps, in due course, we can think of some civilized solution.' Because, one can't emphasize too strongly, it was absolutely natural to British officials well into the 1960s to think that because of their traditions, and the fact that they had solved or attacked so many intractable problems, that really anything was worth a go. There was a certain negotiating hubris, *negotiator's* hubris perhaps is the right phrase, of which I was certainly as representative as anybody else, I'm afraid.

If there was a 'negotiator's hubris', as the head of the Latin American department in the mid-1960s, Robin Edmonds, suggests, which was sustained by the successful creation of the Antarctic Treaty, it did not endure.

In December 1965, Argentina won a spectacular success at the United Nations with the passing of Resolution 2065. This called upon Britain to settle the Falklands issue. It was put forward in the guise, and the emotional context, of decolonization. Britain did not vote against this resolution and so was obliged to discuss sovereignty over the Falklands with Argentina.

From the British point of view, 'decolonization' was preparing peoples for independence, a task which Britain performed some forty times. But in the case of the Falklands independence was considered rhetorical nonsense. The Islands did not *want* independence, and were too small to maintain it if they had.

With Resolution 2065, for the first time the Foreign Office officials had begun to feel the heat blowing in their faces over the Falklands. A former head of the Latin American desk, and under-secretary in the 1960s, regarded by colleagues as the principal architect of the Antarctic Treaty, was the Honourable **Henry Hankey**.

Resolution 2065 was really a tremendous landmark in this whole affair. Up to that time the dispute had been dragging on for years. It had got a bit worse during Peron's time, but after they had succeeded in banging the colonial drum hard enough at the United Nations, they got a largely 'Third World' majority in favour of this recommendation that we and the Argentines should negotiate a friendly settlement. A settlement in which the interests of the Islanders would be taken account of, but not their wishes. They never stopped after that, at every possible moment, to pester us for immediate further negotiations on the subject of sovereignty.

The position immediately afterwards was quite dangerous in many ways. There were two weird incidents where private Argentine citizens made incursions into the Islands of one kind and another.

Like 'Operation Condor', in 1966, when a group of Argentinians landed a DC4 airliner at Port Stanley – a symbolic 'seizure' of the Islands?

That's right. And there was an understandable fear that if we did not respond in some way to what was, after all, a resolution of the United Nations of which we were a member, it would be impossible to contain what might turn into a much bigger explosion. It was certainly realized, in official circles, that there might be an *official* Argentine 'follow-up'. I don't think people thought seriously that this would take the form of an invasion. There are many other ways of tweaking the lion's tail. However, it would have been embarrassing. That is why, in 1967, the Labour Government and George Brown decided to take what was really a startling step forward. They were prepared, in a document called a 'Memorandum of Understanding', to offer to cede sovereignty if the Argentines would concede the necessary safeguards for the islanders.

The apprehension of danger, in the Foreign Office, was not confined to the British interest in Latin America and Antarctica. Britain was overstretched, and at risk, in all the oceans, not the South Atlantic alone.

Just how numerous the possibilities of suffering 'embarrassment' were seen to be, and how much the Foreign Office felt compelled to take account of them in advising retrenchment, the permanent undersecretary of the period, **Lord Greenhill**, reminds us.

It was facing facts. Supposing some of the disputed islands in the Pacific had been taken over by the Chinese, or the Russians, and the Argentinians *had* been contemplating taking over the Falklands, how could we possibly have dealt with that situation? My own feeling was that we would be subjected to the most terrible international humiliation. You see, various things happened. Like Anguilla, which made us look ridiculous really.

Where we flew out a detachment of the metropolitan police, and had them going around knocking on doors in support of the civil power and to restore authority, British rule, in Anguilla in the Caribbean?

Yes. It would have been ludicrous if all these places started being snapped up by people who had claims against them.

I believe that our peaceful disengagement from empire was a great achievement, and that we were extraordinarily lucky that we were not more actively challenged whilst this disengagement was going on. One kept one's fingers crossed all the time that one would be able to achieve it; and be able to get settlements in these territories which were being turned loose, which would be satisfactory not only to the people in the territories, but would not provoke *trouble*. What was our motive for trying to get the Antarctic Treaty? It was the desire to get the international politics of the Antarctic on one side, and hand the problem over to the scientists. From the time that I was in Whitehall, from 1964 onwards, the Antarctic Treaty was regarded as an *achievement*. It had got international activity in the Antarctic going on constructively and peacefully. Penguins were being looked after, seals were being looked after, instead of people quarrelling about their claims to the territory. It was regarded as an achievement. Indeed it was.

However, was it a wholly atrophied memory, in the minds of British policy makers, that at another time Britain had taken a quite different view of the possibilities of Antarctica? I'm thinking of Leo Amery, when he was Secretary of State for the Colonies, in the twenties, who saw Antarctica as the 'last continent', which Britain had, almost single-handedly, opened up, enduring much hardship in the process. Therefore we should make a commitment, and exploit such riches as were there. To what extent was that in our minds when drawing up the Antarctic Treaty?

It was certainly in *some* people's minds. However, the main fact was, and people knew it, that attitude, and that policy, depended on a strong defence capability. For Britain to behave in that way, in the 1960s and '70s, was impossible.

Official feeling in this decade of the 1960s was clearly strong that Britain could not support a policy backed by force so far from home and, further, that the importance of the Falklands had become greatly diminished. In the world of modern strategic weapons the Islands did not count for much. The transfer of sovereignty away from Britain involved no great strategic or economic loss. None the less, questions over resources in the Antarctic were still an influence on policy. In any negotiation over the Falkland Islands, the foreign secretary of the period, **Lord Stewart**, had this important caveat.

We felt that, if we had, as it were *given way* over the Falklands, that would be followed, inevitably, by attempts to squeeze us out of our rights in Antarctica as well. But the argument was not, as a rule, pushed that far. We had of course certain rights in Antarctica already. All these had been frozen in the famous Antarctic Treaty. It was very important we should not be jockeyed out of our potential rights there. We felt, therefore, that a *surrender* on the Falklands would have been a jolt in the wrong direction.

It would seem to be with a rather muffled candour that Britain began to negotiate sovereignty over the Falklands with Argentina. Following the watershed of Suez in 1956, the world east of Suez was now seen as precarious for Britain – a world in which the Foreign Office, like the Bank of England, thought it prudent not to have all Britain's eggs in one basket. This was the impulse behind the renewed effort being made, by the Foreign Office, in these years to revive the withered British interest in South America, and in Argentina in particular.

The largest British community living abroad in any one city lived in Buenos Aires. There had been a close relationship all through the last century. With strong support from the Bank of England, great importance was attached to the expansion of trade with Argentina. That, in turn, meant lowering the temperature over the Falklands.

Remarkably, for a power with the maritime reach and imperial tradition of the United Kingdom, Michael Stewart's visit, in 1966, was the first ever made by a British foreign secretary to Latin America. It conveyed to the Argentines the impression that the British national interest transcended the Falklands issue. The minister of state at the time was **Lord Chalfont**.

Michael Stewart's visit is absolutely crucial to this whole argument. When he came back, he wrote a report in which he underlined the deficiencies in our relationships with Latin America, and the importance, as he saw it, of our relations with Latin America both in the political and in the commercial sense. I think it is true to say that that kind of report was in the back of people's minds when they came to consider the future of the Falkland Islands. I would not have said that it was decisive in those discussions. It had a kind of background influence on people's thinking.

But the need to develop a positive relationship with Latin America made the interests of the Falkland Islanders subordinate to that aim?

I think that is true. The foreign policy interests of the United Kingdom then, as I believe now, are linked to good relations with many of the countries in Latin America. Argentina is certainly one of those countries and probably one of the most important. There are various reasons why we should have close, and friendly, relations with Argentina. To some extent this is irrespective of what kind of regime is in power there; although the arguments change depending on whether you have a military dictatorship or a parliamentary democracy. Argentina is important in the context of our relations with the Americas overall. It has always been a perception of foreign policy experts, including those in the Foreign Office, that those relationships are more important than the perceptions of a small number of inhabitants of the Falkland Islands. The views of two thousand, or more, inhabitants of the Falklands should not be allowed to distort our foreign policy any more than the inhabitants of Wales or Scotland.

When it comes to first-hand recollections, there is an elusive, clearly 'sensitive', period in the 1960s. Michael Stewart served two terms as foreign secretary. From the end of 1966, the ebullient figure of George Brown sat in Lord Palmerston's chair – until he resigned in 1968, whereupon Stewart was reincarnated as foreign secretary. It was Palmerston who, in the 1870s, had laid down what was the guiding principle for British policy overseas – that Britain had no need of vast imperial possessions, 'any more than any rational man with an estate in the north of England, and a residence in the south, would wish to possess all the inns on the great north road'.[5] Twenty-five years later, by the turn of the century, opposition to the Palmerstonian doctrine of imperialism, in the form of colonialism, had taken root, and it became the tail that wagged the Whitehall dog.

It was during George Brown's time as foreign secretary, in 1967, that the British Government, for the first time, stated formally to Argentina that they would be prepared to give up sovereignty over the Islands, under certain conditions. Lord Stewart told me he felt that George Brown 'was more willing to consider the transfer of sovereignty than I would have been'.

As we shall see, it is known that George Brown made an impression on Argentine thinking when he discussed the Falklands with Nicanor Costa Méndez. The latter was Argentina's foreign minister in the 1960s, and would hold the post a second time in 1981–2, at the time of the Falklands war.

The head of the Latin American desk of the Foreign Office, when George Brown became foreign secretary, towards the end of 1966, was **Robin Edmonds**.

5 Quoted in Anthony Nutting, *The Scramble for Africa* (Constable, 1970), p. 60.

With all respect to Michael Stewart, for whom I, as all of us, had a great affection, it looked as though, in George Brown, we had, for the first time for some time, a foreign secretary who would have political 'clout' in Cabinet. It sounds rather like 'chalk and cheese', but some of us did, vaguely, hark back to the days of Ernest Bevin, and his 'I won't 'ave it!', and all that.

It did not, alas, quite work out like that. As far as Latin America is concerned Brown made it very clear that in general, and not just in relation to Latin America, he intended to be an activist foreign secretary in the Palmerstonian sense. He changed the portrait in the foreign secretary's office. He removed George III, and he put Palmerston in his place in his office, over the fireplace. That was rather symbolic. He thought of Palmerston as an energetic figure on the world stage, cutting a dash, which indeed is what George Brown wanted to do and tried to do. In particular, of course, he tried to do it over Europe. His natural reaction to a negotiation already in progress, and within the broader context which I have tried to stress from the outset, would have been, 'Well, let's have a go!'.

Settle it?

If possible.

The difficulties which George Brown's initiative over the Falklands occasioned the Labour Cabinet in 1968, when the secret diplomacy surfaced, are noted in irritated asides during the last half of that year in the diary-keeping of two significant ministers, Richard Crossman and Barbara Castle. **Barbara Castle** makes it plain that sympathies in that Cabinet were lacking for George Brown's forceful style as foreign secretary.

There comes a moment in government when you are beset by all sorts of major difficulties, both economic and political. Along comes an incident, affecting a tiny group of people, which can overthrow a government, or throw out of gear its economic planning. You get a feeling of absolute exasperation. We needed the Falklands issue as much as we needed a hole in the head! There does tend to be an irritation against a minister who leads his government into a situation in which it faces a united attack in Parliament. Why did he have to go buzzing around like this stirring things up? Harold Wilson assured us that it was all a legacy of George Brown, when he was foreign secretary. 'He started it!', Harold said, as if to say, you know, that explains a lot!

It does if your diary entry for 5th December 1968 can be taken as sufficient explanation of what happened, because you raise that very point. 'Glorious little

incident on the Falkland Islands at Cabinet', you tell us. 'Dick Crossman wanted
to know how did we get started on this ridiculous thing at all when, it was quite
clear, we could not reach agreement with the Argentine on conditions acceptable
to ourselves? Once again the Foreign Office officials have been going beyond
their remit. Harold informed us this was part of the George Brown legacy.
It was he who had started the overtures without even consulting the Prime
Minister. We were all rather cross about the unnecessary storm having been
raised and agreed with Harold when he said we had got to avoid getting into
these side rows during the next two years.'[6]

I think the Foreign Office, with a lot of good sense on its side, felt this
was an issue that ought to be got out of the way. At an earlier Cabinet
meeting, when we had been told about this joint 'Memorandum of
Understanding' with the Argentine government, which said attention
would be paid to the *interests* of the Falkland Islanders, it was I who
wished to insert *views* instead of *interests*. Michael Stewart said, 'Oh
no. The Argentine government would not touch a joint memorandum
on that basis.' So then, there was talk as to whether one unilateral
statement safeguarding the paramountcy of the Islanders' views
should be published as a United Nations document, side by side with
the Memorandum of Understanding. Michael Stewart came back to
us and said the Argentines would not sign a Memo, even if our unilateral document was merely published side by side with it. I think
then we gradually began to lose sympathy with the attitude of the
Argentine government. They were obviously not willing to help us go
gradually, step by step. I think my mood changed then. We said,
'Right! If they say that then nothing goes.'

By 1967, however, the whole web of factors was in place which led
British ministers to agree to their dramatic step forward: offering to give
up the Islands if a settlement could be reached.

United Nations Resolution 2065 had called upon Britain and
Argentina to resolve their dispute, 'having regard to the *interests* of the
islanders'.[7] These were the terms to which Britain was now a party in
trying to reach an agreement with Buenos Aires. The wording is of the
greatest importance. To negotiate on the basis of *interests* rather than
wishes meant seeking a compromise.

Alun Chalfont was the Foreign Office minister in the Wilson
government who conducted these first negotiations.

6 Barbara Castle, *The Castle Diaries, 1964-70* (Weidenfeld & Nicolson 1984),
p. 566.
7 Author's emphasis.

'The "interests" of the Islanders' was the key phrase. At that stage we all realized, or thought we realized, that *we* were the people who could decide upon the interests of the Islanders, not so much the Islanders themselves.

Into the making of that decision had gone all the considerations of how important the Falkland Islands were in our overall foreign policy. The main one was that, in any kind of negotiations about future sovereignty over the Islands, it was the interests, underline *interests*, of the Islanders that should be taken into consideration. Much later all this came to be changed. We moved to other formulations, until we finally arrived at a position at which, in effect, the Islanders had a veto over a most important area of foreign policy.

Self-determination for the Falklanders was not your first thought, nor that of the Foreign Secretary?

No indeed. That's true. Certainly, the basic idea was that here was an island which was far closer to Argentina than it was to us. In future, it might have its interests more closely identified with those of Argentina than the United Kingdom. The question of self-determination came very low down on the list of the priorities of the Labour Government of the time. The idea was that, sooner or later, we would *have* to discuss with Argentina the question of sovereignty. It was also accepted that, sooner or later, sovereignty would have to be transferred to Argentina. The question was, how quickly and with how much political difficulty could this be achieved.

The accommodation we were trying to reach was quite simple. We wanted to agree that we had to settle, definitively, the question of sovereignty. There was no question then, there is no question now, at least in *my* mind, that sovereignty is an issue. You have got to talk about it. We were ready to agree that, in the context of some final settlement, Argentina's claim to sovereignty *would* be agreed. It was only a question of date, and the sort of processes, and phases, which would be necessary to reach that end.

These first negotiations with Argentina, exploring the implementation of United Nations Resolution 2065, were neither confirmed by the Government, nor discussed in Parliament, until 1968. By that time they had been in progress for some two years. The highly charged nature of issues involving 'kith and kin', making ministers and officials all too well aware of the likely outcry had there been a 'megaphone' diplomacy, is something which Lord Chalfont readily acknowledges determined the Foreign Office ministers to proceed as unobtrusively as possible.

Absolutely. But this is a function of the whole business of secret diplomacy. What we were engaged in, at that time, was a highly sensitive set of negotiations with Argentina. And it was in the interests of the success of those negotiations that they were, by definition, secret and confidential. I don't think there's anything devious about this. Had they become known, they would have been the subject of pressures in the press, and from pressure groups in Parliament and outside Parliament. There are occasions when international negotiations *should* be carried on in secret. These *were* secret negotiations. It was not until I went to the Falkland Islands in 1968 that they became fully known, although perhaps rumoured abroad before that.

Once we had taken the plunge over sovereignty, weren't there only two possibilities? Either, that we were stringing Argentina along, in effect, by holding out the prospect of an end to the negotiations which could not be realized, or that the negotiations would put the Islanders in some sort of 'nutcracker'?

I would agree, as a sort of intellectual analysis of the position. What we were really determined to do at that time was to arrive at an agreement with Argentina. We decided that it was in the interests of our overall foreign policy aims. It may sound patronising and it may sound paternalistic, but we had decided that it was also in the long-term interests of the people of the Falkland Islands. I'm not quite sure that I'm entirely happy with the nutcracker analogy! When I went there in 1968, it was to try to persuade the Falkland Islanders that it *was* in *their interests*, in the long term, that there should be this kind of agreement with Argentina.

Argentine hopes were running high in consequence. Britain was about to impale itself on the Falklands hook over the vital distinction between the interests and wishes of the inhabitants. **Michael Stewart** returned as foreign secretary, following George Brown's resignation in March 1968. His own more flexible approach, when contrasted with Lord Chalfont's carrying into effect of George Brown's line, shows clearly in exchanges about the crucial question of 'interests' and 'wishes'.

You can't separate the two entirely. The moment you talked of the *wishes* of the Islanders, it was quite clear what the answer was going to be. There was no possible evidence at all to think that the Islanders wanted the transfer of sovereignty. Neither, I think, was there any real evidence to show that it would be in their *interests*. To put people under a form of government that they will heartily detest from the start, it's rather difficult to argue that that is in their interests.

Can we be in much doubt that, when you first entered upon these negotiations with Argentina, we would have liked to dispossess ourselves of these 'orphans of empire', especially when we derived so little economic benefit from them?

Only in the sense that if the Islanders themselves had wanted that, we certainly should not have obstructed it. We had no desire to hold on to the territory against their will. Equally we, quite certainly, were not going to hand them over to Argentina against their wishes, particularly as it was then a dictatorship. There was no getting away from this. The idea of parting with a British possession to a foreign country that they did not want to go to was bad enough in itself; that it should be a dictatorship made it worse.

However, while the opinion of the Islanders proved obdurate, that was not the hope (less certainly the expectation) of ministers and their officials, in the summer and autumn of 1968, as the outline of an agreement with Argentina emerged from these negotiations which had been begun by Michael Stewart himself. Stewart and his ministerial colleagues were all reluctant, at this stage, to give the Islanders a veto over any agreement.

There was no sense of crisis. **Lord Chalfont** remembers relations with the Argentine foreign minister, Dr Costa Méndez (foreign minister again when war broke out in 1982), as 'calm and relaxed'.

There was certainly no sense of crisis. This was regarded then as a *long-term* problem, I might say. Both sides realized this was not going to be solved overnight. When we agreed, and I quote now from the Memorandum of Understanding, that there would, one day, be a 'final settlement which would recognize Argentina's sovereignty over the Islands from a date to be agreed', we were all looking ahead *decades*, not years. It was all very relaxed; a normal, civilized, and long-term diplomatic negotiation.

At the time, Nicanor Costa Méndez seemed to me to be an extremely sophisticated, certainly well-informed, and very intelligent politician and statesman, who was certainly not a rabid nationalist. He wanted to solve this problem, and he wanted to solve it in a way that would be acceptable to both our countries, and incidentally to the people of the Falkland Islands. What he was doing at that time was trying to maximize the Argentinian position in the negotiations. He realized that we had, in the British Government, a tendency to wish to divest ourselves of what was becoming an embarrassing encumbrance to our foreign policy. I don't think there's any point, you see, in trying to conceal this. One has gone on long enough saying

that the interests, and the wishes, of these gallant people of the
Falkland Islands are 'paramount' etcetera, etcetera. The simple fact
of the matter is, and Costa Méndez realized this as well as we did in
the United Kingdom, that you really cannot, in the long run, conduct
the foreign policy of an important international power according
entirely to the interests, and certainly not to the wishes, of a couple of
thousand inhabitants of some islands in the South Atlantic.

The draft Memorandum of Understanding reached, in August 1968, by
the ministers and officials of both Britain and Argentina was taken out to
the Falkland Islands by Alun Chalfont in November of that year.

Lord Chalfont thus became the first British minister ever to visit the
inhabitants in their remote and gloomy solitude. Once there, he was
struck by the combination of that isolation and their dependence on
Britain, eight thousand miles away. The recommendations of that
Memorandum of Understanding were intended to mark a turning point
in the history of the Falkland Islands. However, history as **Lord
Chalfont** found, has a habit of going straight on.

I travelled all over the Islands, to the farms and the outlying settlements in the Falklands. The Memorandum of Understanding that I
was taking to them was roughly on these lines: that Argentina, and
Britain, had a common objective, which was to settle amicably, but
finally, the dispute over sovereignty – taking into account the
'interests' of the population, not the 'wishes', the crucial word. I told
them we had agreed that the two governments would make early
progress with practical measures to improve communications, and
movement, between the mainland and the Islands. This was
supposed to be a way of preparing the ground for the transfer of
sovereignty. The date was to be agreed as soon as possible after the
two governments had resolved, what was called, 'the present
divergence between them'. Then, the UK agreed that it would
consider the 'interests' of the Islanders in the context of the kind of
guarantees which Argentina would offer about the future life of the
Islanders.

The Memorandum of Understanding, of course, had still not been
considered by Parliament in Britain. It was a Memorandum on the
basis of which we were to negotiate a final agreement with Argentina
and would subsequently be a matter for decision by the British
Parliament.

The time-scale in the Memorandum of Understanding is quite
interesting. It set a date not less than four years and not more than ten
years after the signature of the Memorandum. That was the sort of

time-scale we were talking about. We were saying that if, at the end of ten years, nothing had been resolved, then it was time to get together and ask why. If you were to ask me what I thought was a reasonable time-scale, I was personally thinking, although this never came up in the negotiations, of something like twenty-five years. Within a generation. I thought that if, in 1967 and 1968, we could have arrived at an agreement which covered twenty-five years then, during that time, we could have done all that was needed in terms of communications between the Islands, exchange of educational facilities, and so on, which would have made a transfer of sovereignty acceptable to the Islanders. While this was never formalized, in writing, undoubtedly in my discussions with the Argentine government this was an understanding with which they were prepared to go along.

What warnings did you give them in the Islands, during your visit, in 1968?

I made it quite clear, to everybody I spoke to, that what we were talking about was a future, an indeterminate future perhaps, but a future in which sovereignty would be handed over. I made it clear to them that this would have a certain impact on their lives, but that what we were, I think, quite entitled to say at that time, was that the impact would not be as dramatic, or as appalling, as some of them seemed to think. Here they were within close reach of Argentina which had an extremely admirable educational system, with whom there could be exchanges of cultural visits, of tourism, and so on.

And in which there were large British minorities living.

Large British minorities living in Argentina, certainly.

Their response to all that being what?

The response was one of scepticism, to put it mildly. The view was quite simply, and I thought somewhat simplistically, 'We are British. We are not interested in your plans for any future world in which we should become Argentinians. We are British, that's all there is to it, and will you please take that message back to your masters in London.'

You also went to Buenos Aires. Did that modify or alter your opinion?

No. My discussions with Costa Méndez were such as to convince me the line we were taking was the right one. They had a claim to sovereignty which we might not be prepared to accept in legalistic terms but, in realistic terms, for the future of our relations with Argentina and the future prosperity of the people of the Falkland Islands, it seemed to me we were on the right track. What I discussed with the government in Argentina simply reinforced that.

In your long and detailed report you uttered what was to be a prophetic warning. 'Unless sovereignty is seriously negotiated', you said, 'and ceded, in the long term we are likely to end up in a state of armed conflict with Argentina.' What made you think that would be the outcome?

I had come to the conclusion that Argentina took the question of sovereignty over the Islands very seriously – partly because of a sense of national pride, partly because of a sense of geographical reality. Here are these islands off the coast of Argentina. There was some argument that they might have a historical claim to them. As someone who had spent his whole life in the world of strategy, and military policy, it seemed to me inevitable. I saw at the time, as I said in my report, although I didn't know how prophetic it would be, that sooner or later, unless we came to some diplomatic conclusion with them, they would take advantage of their proximity and perhaps be forced by internal political difficulties to choose the only alternative there is to a political settlement, which is military action.

It was indeed the trumpet of a prophecy. By September 1968, agreement having been reached at official level that 'the Government of the United Kingdom would recognize Argentina's sovereignty from a date to be agreed', statements to this effect were read in both Houses of Parliament in December.

The result was dramatic. Waves of hostility overwhelmed both Chalfont who spoke for the Labour Government in the Lords, and Michael Stewart, the foreign secretary, at the dispatch box in the Commons. Chalfont says he was 'quite unprepared for the degree of passionate opposition there was, extending even to *any* negotiation with Argentina'. British policy over the Falklands crumbled when, in the Commons, the same implacable wall confronted **Michael Stewart**.

I concluded from that I think what I had already known; that the idea of actually transferring sovereignty would be extremely unwelcome to Parliament. The phrase was that sovereignty was to be transferred 'at a date to be agreed'. That still left it for us to say 'yes' or 'no'. We had not given any commitment that our answer would be 'yes'.

It is in consequence of this drubbing, if I may put it like that, which the Government had in the House of Commons over this issue, in December 1968, that you informed the House that 'The Government are', and I'm using your words, 'very conscious of the close ties between the Island population and the United Kingdom, and their loyalty to the Crown, and it is for this reason that the Government have insisted on the paramountcy of the Islanders' wishes.' That is the first time this famous word 'paramount' appears, I think. Can you recall how you thought about that word, and the implications of it?

It meant to me what I'd always considered to be the essential feature of the whole situation. Whatever international law practice may have been in the past, I do not think, in the twentieth century, you go handing people over to a government that they will detest, and which can put up no case in law for the territory either. There were a number of people in Parliament who either were, or claimed to be, very gravely alarmed at the possibility of our handing over the Islands. There was never any justification, I may say, for that alarm but I thought it was my duty in this adjournment debate to put the matter beyond doubt. That is, we were not going to hand over the Islands against the wishes of the inhabitants.

Yet, on the other hand, you refused to remove sovereignty from the agenda. It was that question that was exciting the opposition in Parliament.

Yes. The point there was that if we had refused, if we'd taken sovereignty off the agenda, we should have found ourselves unable to talk to the Argentines about *anything*. That would not have been convenient. We were quite prepared to go on discussing sovereignty but what we had to say about it remained the same.

It's recorded that you told the Argentine ambassador of the time, Eduardo McLoughlin, that 'given the political storm in the House of Commons the Government could not be seen to be taking action against the Falkland Islanders'. Now McLoughlin then said to you, 'Well, who am I negotiating with, Her Majesty's Government, or the Islanders?' To which, it is said, you replied, 'That's unanswerable!' He clearly infers that the Islanders have been given a veto over the British Government's policies as long as you're sticking to this word 'wishes' as opposed to 'interests'?

Yes, I suppose that you can put it that way. It *is* giving them a veto. But what else would one say? How would one justify handing over two thousand people against their wishes? Absolutely one hundred per cent against their wishes. What is more, something which could not be demonstrated as being in their *interests* either. And again, the population of Britain, once they were aware of the issue, was not in the least in favour of giving the Falklands away to the Argentines. Why should they?

By the end of 1968 British diplomacy, whose objective was to induce the unwilling to accept the unavoidable, had reached a classical impasse. A central block had been reached in the House of Commons with the entrenchment of the Islanders' wishes and, above all, the promise that those wishes were paramount. In other words, the population of the Islands now had the right of veto.

As a consequence of this long and patient negotiation in the 1960s, how close had Britain and Argentina been to the reality of an agreement? **Henry Hankey** was the under-secretary of state in the Foreign Office, supervising Latin American policy, at the end of the 1960s.

I think they were miles away from it! I don't think there was any question of it. That is what made the Argentines so annoyed; because, I think they realized, as soon as we were absolutely stuck tight on saying the Islanders' 'wishes' must be respected, that we were pulling their legs. They knew perfectly well the Islanders were not going to agree.

Do you recognize the atmosphere of the time in what Barbara Castle, who was a minister at the Cabinet on December 11th 1968, which took the decision to side- track the sovereignty issue, said: 'I thought to myself, it's a classic case of these so- called moral issues one can't win. Which should be our parliamentary priority, to defend to the last ditch the rights of a small group of people who want to be Britishers, or to do nothing which would increase our defence expenditure?' Mrs Castle puts it her way, but it is a dilemma which has never been resolved.

It's never been resolved. I think that it could have been resolved perhaps later, in various ways, if the explosion had not been so big at the start. It could have been resolved, I suppose, if the Falklanders had been prepared to consider all sorts of strange ideas which were in the air, like accepting resettlement outside somewhere. But nobody wanted to push them. Chalfont was accused, I think very unfairly, of trying to push them along. After a bit it became almost impossible to say *anything* to the Islanders because you risked being accused of trying to throw the game away. So, it has something of the elements of a Greek tragedy about it.

To continue Henry Hankey's metaphor, those elements were a noble ideal, and a chorus in Parliament in support of a commitment which successive British governments were never quite willing to pay for.

The Cabinet meeting of 11 December 1968 had decided what Michael Stewart would be allowed to say to the House of Commons. At this meeting the Foreign Secretary was compelled to withdraw the paper of his draft agreement with Argentina. This paper said that 'sovereignty would be transferred at a date to be agreed.' Barbara Castle recorded in her diary that day, 'One by one we all turned upon him.' Whereupon, as we have heard, the foreign secretary conceded his vital qualification in the House of Commons – the paramount right of the Falkland Islanders to say 'No'.

Looking back, in great wisdom, what was it **Lord Stewart** would wish to add?

It is a disappointment, of course, if you've put a paper to the Cabinet, asked them to adopt a particular point of view, and they turn it down. Of course this is bound to happen to every Cabinet minister at some time. Quite frankly I did not regard it as one of the major problems that I was engaged with, so I put up with my defeat on this rather philosophically. The Cabinet took the plain British man in the street's view about the Falkland Islanders – more plainly and definitely than I did, because they, unlike me, had not been sort of 'soaked' in the Foreign Office atmosphere.

You mean that the Foreign Office pressure was there all the time, that this is something we ought to settle?

Yes. In a sense, Foreign Offices *always do* want to settle that kind of thing. The Foreign Office did not prophesy that it would come to a war between us if we did not settle it, and it never occurred to me to put that forward, therefore, as an argument, to the Cabinet. It would not have convinced them if I had, I think! They would never have believed it possible.

Yet, as we have seen, Lord Chalfont, in his report following what had been the first ever ministerial visit to the Falklands, *had* warned of the dangers of conflict, which only shows that warnings take a while to sink in and can sink too far.

Lord Stewart is surely right to remind us of the lowly priority the Falkland Islands had in the immense overall global adjustments being made by Britain at this time and how, in between crises, they would drop out of sight. But the ferocity with which Michael Stewart had been assailed in Parliament seared itself into the collective memory of the officials in Whitehall – among them, the head of the Latin American department of the Foreign Office in the 1960s, **Robin Edmonds**.

He was howled down on the floor of the House, this gentle, kind, humane man. Howled down by members, and nobody, no member of Parliament in any party, and above all not in his own party, ever forgot that. That is why I regard December 1968 as an absolute watershed. From then on, in my view, in this country the Falkland Islands issue became primarily an issue of *domestic* politics. Previously we had regarded it, rightly or wrongly, as largely a *foreign policy* issue with, of course, like every foreign policy issue, some overtones of domestic politics. Not much, however. From then on it was exactly the other way round – a domestic policy issue with foreign policy overtones. Therefore if ever the chips were down again on the 1968 model – which of course they were, in the House of Commons, in 1982 – once again the Islands would become more or less like a village in Kent. There is no other comparison to be made. Not an issue of foreign affairs.

However often the writer of a minute, or memorandum, or the draft of a Cabinet paper in the Foreign Office on the Islands, in that short period of three years when I was under-secretary in the seventies, however often such a document might kick off with this reminder that this was a very odd kind of foreign policy question, and really a domestic policy question, nevertheless in practice you had to deal with it as though it were wholly a foreign policy issue. It was rather like what I think some German philosopher in the nineteenth century called 'Die Philosophie der als Ob', the philosophy of 'as if'. The whole thing was rather as if it were foreign policy, but it was *not*, and people knew that. None the less, you had to try to go on and deal with it as though it were an ordinary question.

Robin Edmonds lays the Foreign Office finger on the paradox that ministers and governments would not resolve. For the diplomat the philosophy of 'as if', with its view of history running counter to the facts, was a bad habit of the politician. If only, it has been remarked, Good King Wenceslas had looked out on a thaw!

As the decade of the 1970s began, the challenge of the Falklands for British diplomacy grew more menacing.

2

Islands Surrounded by Advice

By the end of 1968, British policy over the Falklands lay in ruins. The secret diplomacy, ending in a carefully prepared 'understanding' with Argentina, had aroused a violent reaction in Parliament. From this point forward, it became a *public* policy, with the Islanders themselves having to be consulted at every step. The 'understanding', reached at official level in the course of 1968, had provided for Britain to transfer sovereignty following a transitional period, which British ministers thought could be as long perhaps as twenty-five years, before a final settlement. Unable to pass either the Commons or the Cabinet, the sovereignty issue, although it was not withdrawn from the agenda, had then been driven off the negotiating table in a manner so emphatic that it left ministers, and their Foreign Office advisers, somewhat dazed.

In December 1968, a categorical assurance had been extracted from the foreign secretary, Michael Stewart, in the House of Commons, that the wishes of the two thousand Islanders were *paramount*. In practical terms this gave the Falkland Islanders the right to veto future directions of British policy. It became, as it has remained, the central block in the Falklands issue.

As the Foreign Office surveyed its unclimbable molehill in the South Atlantic in the aftermath of these events in the 1960s, the under-secretary superintending British policy in Latin America, and therefore Argentina and the Falklands, was **Henry Hankey**.

It was a complete breakdown. The Argentines were sore and irritated at our failure to come any way to meet them at all. They felt that it was just dangling something in front of them, and then snatching it away; to offer sovereignty on an unacceptable condition. About that time the Ministry of Foreign Affairs in Buenos Aires sent over a couple of splendid people to plead with us. They said that, in Buenos Aires, they, in the Ministry of Foreign Affairs, dreaded an escalation of this dispute into something which could be much worse. Unfortunately, they said, their views were not shared by the Ministry of Defence and by other people in Buenos Aires. Therefore, if we could not come up with some basis for discussion they feared it would be impossible to keep things quiet. They could not answer for the consequences. They were rather menacing really, rather aggressive. They annoyed us really quite considerably. We had several very informal talks with these two chaps, and I think it was then that we said almost in exasperation, 'After all, why do you come to *us* always? Why don't *you* do something about it? The Falkland Islanders hate you, and fear you. You insist on regarding them as Argentine citizens. They have to have an Argentine passport in order to visit your country. They live a very uncomfortable life in many ways, isolated as they are. If you could woo them, as it were, by cutting off some of these restrictions which hem them in, and make their life tolerable, who knows? Eventually, if you're prepared to keep up some kind of friendly relationship perhaps for a generation, you might find that they'll think it'll be a very good idea to become Argentine citizens, because they will know they can also remain British citizens, as we have dual citizenship.'

It may have been a coincidence that, some time after that, it became possible for us to negotiate with them a whole series of agreements which were called the Communications Agreements. They covered the provision of air transport into the islands; a special 'white card' by which the Islanders could travel to the Argentine, and Argentines, using the same white card, could travel to the Islands. There were agreements about education. There were about five of these agreements in all. This made a great difference.

As the decade of the 1970s began, the Foreign Office can hardly be accused of an insufficiency of ideas. It would be said of these years immediately ahead that the Falklands were 'islands entirely surrounded by advice'.[1]

The Communications Agreements embodied the Foreign Office conviction that the rational answer to the problem lay in the Falkland Islanders accepting the fact that their growing proximity to Argentina, and now their economic future, made them more dependent on Buenos Aires than it did on Britain. The permanent under-secretary, the head of the Foreign Office, at this time was **Lord Greenhill**.

One felt that if we got a Communications Agreement, which we saw as initial steps towards a solution of the problem, people would see

1 Bon mot attributed to Lord Shackleton.

the mutual benefits which would flow from it, and that would, in the end, make a final solution easier to reach.

It was the indirect approach, leaving the hard part till last, the sovereignty issue?

Yes, yes.

What the Americans call 'winning the hearts and minds'?

I suppose you could put it like that. People thought that the Communications Agreement would bring home to *both* sides the advantages of an understanding and the advantages of cooperation, and that gradually they would then be ready to consider something more dramatic.

Would it be true to say that, with the Communications Agreement, we made a 'confidential ally' of Argentina? We were asking them to recognize, following Stewart's and Chalfont's 'roughing-up' in Parliament, that the issue of sovereignty had to be put on the back burner for a bit, but we would proceed along these lines? It was then they went along with us, complying with our wishes?

Well, you have got to have mutual confidence if an agreement is going to be reached. We were, all the time, trying to get a mutually satisfactory agreement.

The rivers of ink which had flowed in support of rival claims to sovereignty were temporarily diverted by the new activity of the Communications Agreements. The crucial issue, sovereignty, was deliberately avoided. The Islanders were to be coaxed out of their vulnerable isolation. The apathy of a stagnant, if not sterile, community with a falling birth-rate was to be exposed to more intimate contacts with Argentina.

The response to the invitation from the Foreign Office to 'woo the islanders' although conducted by Argentina, in **Henry Hankey**'s description, 'with the clumsiness of Bottom', began well enough.

Having told the Argentines in 1968 that we would cede sovereignty if the islanders wanted it, the whole purpose of our approach was to say, 'Make them want it! We can't make them want it. We are not going to put on any pressure. If we start putting pressure on them it will work in the other direction for all we know. You have seen what happened and it's time for *you* to do something.' Well, they *did* do something. It all worked like a charm in the beginning. It was quite remarkable. The Islanders actually went. They made friends in the British community in Buenos Aires; they sent their children to schools there; they had fresh vegetables. They went across to Bahia Blanca and were able to meet some of the people of Scottish and Welsh descent

who had settled in Patagonia and lived perfectly happily there un-
interrupted by the Argentines. Anyway, the Argentines are rather an
urban people who don't really like going and living in wild places.
The Falklanders could see that there would not be much disturbance
of their way of life in the Falklands. It *began* well.

It may be felt that official reasoning behind the Communications Agreements was rooted in assumptions which conformed, in part, to Dr
Johnson's portrait of the austerity of life on the Falklands in the
eighteenth century, when the tiny British settlement was 'shrinking from
the blast', as he put it, 'and shuddering at the billows'.

It was hoped the Islanders would be attracted by the prospects of
greater comforts and wider opportunities, and in consequence be more
yielding over the eventual political implications. In these Communications Agreements, which ushered in the 1970s, almost every provision
was calculated to diminish the former dependence of the Falkland
Islands on Britain. Britain herself did not fully comply with the terms
and conditions of the Agreements in this respect. The Islands had a sea
link to Montevideo in Uruguay which was withdrawn and not replaced
by Britain. This left the Islanders dependent on communications with
the mainland of Argentina. Foreign Office officials, like Lord Greenhill,
disavow any Machiavellian intention: the Foreign Office was under
pressure from the Treasury to reduce expenditure, and money ear-
marked for the old sea service failed to get over the Treasury hurdle.

The head of the Latin American desk in the Foreign Office at the time
the Communications Agreements were being put into effect was **Hugh
Carless**.

Those agreements of course were of political, as well as economic,
importance. If you looked at them in an economic or commonsensical
kind of way they were providing services for the Islanders at the most
economic rate. These services were air travel, education, health in
critical cases, and the supply of fuel oil, which would either have had
to be delivered to the Islands from Europe, eight thousand miles
away, or from mainland Argentina, which was three hundred miles
away. The same applied to the construction of the airstrip, and then a
permanent airport, at Port Stanley. Was a contractor to be sent out
from Britain, or was a local contractor to be used? It seemed common
sense that a local contractor should be used. But, of course, the
political effect was to reduce the independence of the Islands and
make them more dependent on Argentina. In these practical ways
British sovereignty was being reduced. The Islanders liked some of
the services that they received from Argentina. The younger people,

for example, enjoyed the very good English language schools in Buenos Aires. Psychologically, the Islanders realized that they *were* becoming more dependent on Argentina, and the more gifts the Argentines thrust on them, the less they liked them.

This meant that the political ends which the Communications Agreements were designed by Britain and Argentina to secure stayed out of reach. Like the bar of a high jump which rose as soon as it was cleared, the 'paramount wishes' of the Islanders, upheld by their supporters in Parliament, could not be surmounted.

The policy of trying to overcome the Islanders' resistance to a change in the status quo, by forging new links between Argentina and the Falklands, had survived the fall of the Wilson Government and was being carried out under the Conservative Government led by Edward Heath, elected in 1970. In 1972 a change of ministers brought a change of emphasis.

Julian Amery, whose father, Leo Amery, had been a master imperialist as Secretary of State for the Colonies after the First World War, and had wished to include Antarctica in the British imperial design, was now the minister with responsibility for the Falklands. Julian Amery's senior policy adviser was the head of the Foreign Office, **Lord Greenhill**.

I can remember that, as you would expect, Mr Amery took a great interest in the subject for what were, in a way, sentimental reasons. He has a great sense of history, comes from a highly political family, and he did take a greater interest in the subject than some other ministers had done.

Would you say that Julian Amery took a different view of Lord Curzon's 'barbicans and toll gates of empire'? Was he, in effect, asking you, 'Is it true these places cannot be defended – let me have your views?'?

Yes. I remember him saying to me once, 'I was always told never to give up any real estate, and', he said, 'that's a rule that I've always followed.' He did take the line that it was a mistake to *give up* any real estate. I don't think he meant that it was a mistake to give up any real estate if you have got a satisfactory agreement, but don't go rushing in and *giving* things away. Argentine attitudes were changing and they were forcing the pace really.

The regret I have about the whole thing, from the time I started to deal with it, is that more care was not taken to get the problem understood by ministers, and the possible developments that had to be anticipated, dealt with, preferably in *advance*.

By asking Lord Greenhill, in effect, for a thoughtful pause in such progress as was being made over the Falklands dispute, **Julian Amery** challenged what had been underlying assumptions of British policy. Amery was concerned by the extent of the Argentine interest. After taking soundings in Madrid, a visit he made to Argentina left him with some vivid impressions of the then chaotic state of Argentine politics. However, in Amery's judgement, there was no hint during this visit that Argentina felt it worth raising the Falklands issue to the level of crisis.

It so happened that at the time I was minister of state,[2] it became apparent that General Perón, who was then living in exile in Madrid, was about to come back to power. I asked our ambassador in Madrid, Sir John Russell, to have a talk with the General, and discuss with him generally Anglo-Argentine relations. After a few days he telegraphed back that he had been to see the General in his villa in Madrid, and they'd had an hour and a half's conversation. As far as I can recall the telegram there was one paragraph in which the General had said that, of course, there was the problem of the Falklands, which must be cleared up one day, but it gave me the impression there was no great hurry about it.

Then General Lanusse, who was the Dictator of the Argentine at the time, decided to resign, and there were elections. Dr Campora, the first dentist who ever became a head of state – a rather good qualification, he knew how to draw teeth – became president. I went out to Buenos Aires to represent the Queen at the inauguration of President Campora. In his speech, which lasted two and a half hours, General Campora spent, I should have thought, four or five minutes on the Falklands, simply saying the Argentine had a claim which must be dealt with in due course.

Then the official guests were all bidden to the Palais Rose, the Casa Rosada, which was the seat of government, to present our credentials. Well, there was such rioting that the only people who got there in time were President Allende of Chile – later murdered – the brother of President Castro of Cuba, and myself. The crowds were such that none of the other delegates got there for about four hours. So, in the circumstances, President Campora had not much to do, and I had about an hour's audience with him.

In that audience he talked a lot about relations between the Argentine and Europe, the Argentine and the United States, and the Argentine and its neighbours. I suppose he spent five minutes on the Falklands. I must say I came away with the impression from this visit, as from the telegram I had read about President Perón's views, that, yes, this was a problem, like Gibraltar with Spain, but not to be taken too seriously. Certainly not as the pretext of a war.

It had been the foundation of advice to ministers that for Britain to 'go it alone' in the South Atlantic and Antarctica depended on a commensurately strong defence capability there; something of which the British economy was now incapable. It was among the reasons the Foreign Office had advised giving up the Falklands. Why then was it wrong to do so when, by **Julian Amery**'s own time as minister, the constraints of defence spending were being felt ever more acutely?

Had we given up the Falklands, which was advised by certain elements in the Foreign Office, we would have lost the card of entry into the Antarctic. I was pretty sure myself that Parliament would not have accepted that, and I was proved right. The government of the Argentine was a pretty obnoxious one in those days. But there was also the strong feeling on the Conservative benches that the Antarctic could be important, that we would be foolish to throw away that card of entry.

Now unfortunately, here I failed as a minister, because I did not succeed, although I tried very hard, to get Lord Shackleton's view accepted that we must have an airport built. Had we had that airport built, there would have been no invasion. I'm sure of this. But the Treasury had objections to the finance and so on, and it proved to be the determinant. Also, perhaps I relaxed a little bit after my trip to the Argentine.

I always thought that whatever quarrel we might have with the Argentine could have been resolved by bringing the Argentine and Chile, who was always our friend, together into a joint operation to develop the Antarctic with whatever other countries in the Antarctic Treaty wished to join in. It was very interesting when the fighting came.[3] The Chilean ambassador was in my house every two or three days saying for God's sake don't give up! The Chileans were scared stiff what would happen if the Argentinians got control of the Falklands.

I saw no reason to drop the sovereignty issue. If it pleased the Argentinians to run up a flag over their consulate, or something of that sort, no objection. It would remain sovereign British territory, whether we shared the facilities, the real assets of the Falklands, with anybody who wanted to join with us in the exploitation of the wealth of the barren Antarctic continent.

3 That is, in 1982.

The Treasury victories in Amery's time confirmed the original Foreign Office analysis. British reluctance to pay the cost of sustaining the status quo over the Falklands was symbolized in the failure to build the airfield. The decision foreclosed an element of deterrence to Argentine ambitions for the future. In addition, by 1974 the 'hearts and minds' approach embodied in the Communications Agreements was slowly degenerating. The Agreements had been the only solid result to emerge after more than a decade of British and Argentine diplomacy. Now, Argentina was coming to view them as little more than decaying platitudes. **Henry Hankey** was the superintending under-secretary at the Foreign Office during this period, in the early 1970s.

Looking back on it I can see that what happened was inevitable. The Argentines are a temperamental, Latin people, and their armed forces, particularly the Navy, were very sceptical, I think, about the prospects of any real progress being made towards getting control of the Islands like this. They thought it was just a cunning device on our part to save time and fob things off.

Is there no merit in their suspicion this might have been so?

No. Our aim was really a double one. It was to take the heat out of the situation and to provide something which could be a lasting settlement. Nobody was going to mind if, in twenty years' time, the Islanders came along and said, 'Look, we're very happy, and the Argentines want us to hook up with them, we've been thinking about it and we would like to join.' Why should we have minded? We had already stated that we did not mind letting the Islands go on strategic and other grounds.

How do we leave your period at the Foreign Office, as it ends in 1974, in terms of dispute over the Falklands?

We leave it with the hope which is already dying, that the Communications Agreement will bring some kind of fruit. But we are appalled by the deterioration of the position in the Argentine itself, and the uneasy realization, to be borne out strongly in the coming years, that the Islanders must thank their stars that they were never hooked up with a society which had become so brutal. A society which proved its total inability, at that time, to produce any kind of protection with democratic rights comparable to those they enjoy now. The collapse of the idea was total, and we must by then have started foreseeing that, if things did not recover, the idea would be as dead as a doornail, even before the war which killed it forever.

By 1974, six years after the complete breakdown of 1968, once more Britain and Argentina had reached impasse. In the interim, Argentina had been back to the United Nations and emerged armed with yet another resolution, calling this time for '*accelerated* progress' in resolving the Falklands dispute. To meet this pressure Julian Amery had approved exploring the chances of joint sovereignty, or condominium. It was a measure of growing desperation that this was put forward at all. Buried in the long institutional memory of the Foreign Office was the history of untidy failures of the 'condominium' idea, as in the Anglo-Egyptian Sudan. For one thing it was regarded as a legal nightmare. In practice it recalled what an American secretary of state, Dean Acheson, had said about equal partnership, that he 'had been a partner in a law firm all his life and had never seen an equal partner yet'. The move to discuss sovereignty, in this diluted form, with Argentina overlapped the return to power of a Labour Government in 1974, with **James Callaghan** as foreign secretary.

> The Argentine Foreign Minister, Vignes, told our ambassador that President Perón, Isabel Perón, had considered this matter, and had decided, first, that *before* any condominium talks, Argentina's sovereignty must be recognized by the United Kingdom; secondly, that talks could then take place with a view to integrating gradually the Islanders into Argentina. This prior recognition of sovereignty, prior to *any* discussion, was unacceptable, obviously, to me. I minuted accordingly on the telegram, on the day on which it arrived, the 21st of June 1974. Three weeks later, on the 15th of July 1974, I instructed that talks should be suspended on the condominium proposal. This provoked dissent both from the governor, Toby Lewis, who was a New Zealander incidentally, and who therefore had some particular ideas about these matters, and Sir Donald Hopson, who was our ambassador. Hopson sent a telegram saying that suspension would prejudice the security of the Islands.
>
> Well, that was pretty serious, so we had some further discussion. It then became clear, what had been likely before but not *absolutely* clear, that the Islanders would not join the talks. The Executive Council[4] had been told earlier, by Toby Lewis, that the talks were to be held. They had raised no objection, but said that they did not wish to consult the Islanders at that time. As time went by, what Vignes, the Argentine foreign minister, was saying, got out. People in the Islands began to know about the tough attitude. Then the Islanders hardened *their* position, and said they would not join.
>
> Well, that made up my mind. I took the view that talks would be counterproductive without Islanders, and that to try to dispose of

4 That is, the Executive Council on the Falkland Islands.

them without any discussion with them was the worst form of imperialism. So I minuted, 'Leave this poisoned chalice alone!'

On 14th August 1974 our ambassador was instructed to tell Vignes, despite the ambassador, Hopson's fears about the situation, that HMG could not proceed.

That effectively ended the talks on condominium.

James Callaghan's 'no' to condominium, the attempt to turn the flank of the central issue by sharing sovereignty with Argentina, meant, effectively, that Argentina's overriding demand in any negotiation had once more been withdrawn from the agenda. This happened at a time when there was a heightened sense in Whitehall of increasing military risk. Ministers and officials prayed their cup might pass in the Falklands. In what one might call the dynamics of deadlock with Argentina over the Falklands, there was now a new element. Power had passed from the old dictator, Perón, to his widow Isabelita, who was young and politically inexperienced. The head of the Latin American desk from 1973 was **Hugh Carless**.

We had the constant nightmare in those days in the mid-1970s that we might find ourselves fighting a colonial war. We imagined that the colonial war would most likely be fought in Belize as a result of some Guatemalan aggression or guerrilla activity. The general thrust of our policy was still to concentrate on the rule of 'two plus four', as we called it. That was to do what we could to try and solve the two post-colonial problems in our relations with Latin America, the Falklands and Belize, and to concentrate our other efforts on improving relations with the four larger countries of Latin America, Mexico, Venezuela, Brazil and Argentina.

When we looked at Argentina we realized that the political situation was extremely fragile and shaky. There was every indication that the Peronista government would not last very long. That fact naturally inhibited any desire to enter into serious negotiations with the Argentine Government at that juncture.

The not unnatural wish to 'wait and see', in dealings with Argentina over the Falklands, came at the same time that other events in Latin America suddenly rekindled ideological enthusiasms of a fundamental nature which touched politics everywhere. A new climate was created in British domestic political attitudes, of which the Foreign Office advisers such as Carless now had to take account.

The overthrow of President Salvador Allende, and the coming to power of General Pinochet and his military government in Chile, had enormous repercussions right through the western world. I can remember how, in the early days of the Labour Government in 1974, deputation after deputation used to call on the foreign secretary, Jim Callaghan; delegations from the TUC, from the NEC, from the Parliamentary Labour Party, all demanding vigorously that the government should cut links with Chile, and that the government should restrain the delivery of certain warships for Chile which were either under construction, or modernization, in British shipyards. This political struggle over the warships for Chile continued for the better part of eighteen months. The Government and the Foreign Secretary stood on the principle that existing contracts for the delivery of defence equipment should be honoured.

How did the Pinochet issue directly affect official views of what might be possible over the Falkland Islands and with Argentina?

It was doubtless a gradual process. I believe there was a considerable alienation of intellectual opinion, and opinion on the left of centre here in Britain, against anything to do with Latin America. This came out later in several well-known incidents.

One was the British attitude to the state visit of President Geisel of Brazil, an invitation given some eighteen months earlier. Three or four months before his visit, one hundred and twenty members of the Parliamentary Labour Party put down a resolution against the visit to Britain of 'the Brazilian military Dictator', as they regarded him. In fact the Brazilian government at that time, although military, was relatively mild. Two members of the Cabinet stated publicly that they would have nothing to do with the visit. Wilson having resigned unexpectedly in March 1976, Callaghan as prime minister and acting foreign secretary had to carry the great burden of the visit – unpopular in Parliament, in the Party, and criticized in the press – on his own shoulders. I can remember him saying to me, half in jest, 'Well, Hugh, unless we win one large contract out of this visit you had better look for a new job!' In the end we did win two huge contracts for British industry in Brazil, both worth over one hundred million pounds.

Now, I don't believe our commercial success or failure in the rest of Latin America had anything to do with the Falklands. It certainly had some effect in Argentina. More important was the perception of the Labour Government that there was a military dictatorship first in Chile, then in Argentina, and there was a general drawing away, a disinclination to be connected with Latin America. We made a very considerable effort in Venezuela in the golden 1970s when the petro-dollars were pouring in through the door. That did not come to fruition until perhaps 1980 and 1982 when we were on the point of winning a very large contract for aircraft.

But Britain as a major manufacturer of armaments had several big arms contracts in prospect in Latin American countries, as with Venezuela and Argentina, in the 1970s. What penalties did we pay in the long run because of the sustained commitment over the Falkland Islands? Take the British Aerospace contract for the Hawk aircraft in Venezuela?

That contract, which was a very important one for British Aerospace, was on the point of signature when Argentina attacked the Falkland Islands. It was then suspended by the Venezuelan Government. It was worth two hundred million pounds and it would have put British Aerospace back on the map in Latin America.

Traditionally almost all Latin American navies had close connections with our Royal Navy. These connections went back to the wars of independence in the 1820s and they had been very well sustained for the following one hundred and fifty years. As a consequence Latin American navies, until perhaps ten or fifteen years ago, looked to British shipyards to build them the same kind of frigates, destroyers and aircraft carriers the yards were producing for the Royal Navy. During the 1970s these links undoubtedly lessened because of political circumstances. One of them, undoubtedly, was the critical view taken of the Pinochet government.

Another occurred in Argentina, when the Argentine military came to power in 1976. The Argentine Navy immediately seized the opportunity to go shopping. The specifications they laid down very much favoured the Type 23 frigate, then being built in British yards. Negotiations began between Vospers and the Argentine navy, but although they continued in 1977 they began to lose momentum. In 1978, Blohm and Voss of Hamburg filched this very important contract – it was said to be worth a billion dollars – from under the nose of Vospers. The Argentine Government may have perceived that the British Government were not particularly enthusiastic about the sale of frigates to Argentina, who might use them against the Falkland Islands.

There may have been a simpler explanation. I remember that the Argentine admiral who was in charge of these negotiations for the purchase of frigates, once said to a friend of mine, after a couple of whiskies together, 'You British could have had this contract months ago, but you never came up with the money.' He meant the money for the Argentine Navy's widows' and orphans' benevolent fund. That would have been about ten per cent of the final contract price, which was the going rate for very large contracts of this kind in Argentina at the time.

Historically arms sales are a method of winning political influence. Given the role subsequently played by the Argentine Navy as the principal driving force in the ambition to retake the Falklands, did Britain, by its arms sales policy in the 70s coupled with its commitment to the Falklands, lose the chance of establishing that influence?

Yes, I believe you are right. In the Argentine case, had we won this very important contract, which would have taken ten to fifteen years to execute, we would have been locked into a major industrial relationship with Argentina. Both parties would have found it very difficult to withdraw. Whether such a relationship would have prevented the Argentines attacking the Falklands in 1982 none of us can judge, but it seems more likely to me that they would have hesitated longer before they did so.

This 'drawing away' from Latin America by Britain, as Carless has it, following Allende's overthrow, was a development which, when it came down to the Falklands question, assisted a *de facto* alliance of opposites in British politics – the Conservative right and the Labour left. By 1975, James Callaghan having called a halt to the talks about sovereignty expressed in terms of condominium the previous year, Britain was entering a period of increasing tension with Argentina. The Foreign Office, where are reposed the inglorious arts of peace, produced yet another British initiative.

Meanwhile, the inconvincible population of the Falkland Islands who had just said 'no' to joint sovereignty, and their champions in Parliament, were organized as one of the most successful and influential lobbies in modern British politics, one that was deeply suspicious of the diplomats. Down to the lion's den at Westminster went a Foreign Office Daniel, in the shape of the former head of the Latin American desk in the sixties, and now Hankey's successor as the superintending under-secretary, **Robin Edmonds**.

I took my courage in both hands fairly early on as under-secretary. By God, it needed it too! I went to the House of Commons to meet various members of 'the lobby' in a room somewhere there. I say it took courage, because the atmosphere reminded me, most of all, of a really very difficult morning in the Soviet Foreign Ministry. I had not very long been back from Moscow at the time. However, what broke the clouds – and only one thing did, because the suspicion was so great already then – was when I, very diffidently as I remember, said 'Is there anything to be said for having a look at Anglo-Argentine *economic* cooperation?' I think I would call it the lowest common multiple, the LCM. I think one has to remember first of all the 'macroeconomic' atmosphere of the time. It was absolutely in the wake of the OPEC oil crisis, the great energy crisis. Therefore oil reserves anywhere in the world, not necessarily proven but just suspected, ceased to be 'marginal' overnight. There was quite a positive view of the sedimentary basin around the islands.

Equally, there was a 'micro' side to it all, which explains why my raising the subject at that little meeting at the House of Commons did strike a chord. By this time there was real concern about the social and economic decline of the Falklands. The population was down, I think, to eighteen hundred and going further down. Therefore anything one could do which was actually going to improve the economic and social lot of the Islanders was something to be taken very seriously. It was perfectly clear that if there was going to be oil exploration it could only be done if there was some measure of agreement; under some kind of sovereignty umbrella between the Argentine and British governments. Clearly, no oil company would spend a single dollar looking for anything in an environment as hostile as that around the Falklands, unless they had a reasonable certainty that there was not going to be a tremendous intergovernmental row about the outcome.

Overall, the climate was propitious for looking at the *economic* aspect. It was something which had never been done before and it was a generally shared view that it ought to be done.

The distinct whiff of oil which hung in the south-west Atlantic air by the mid 1970s revived in Whitehall the ancient faith that Britain, in the end, is always saved by the sea. It caused a certain recasting of the view that the Falklands commitment represented only burden rather than opportunity. By 1975 the OPEC crisis of the previous year, with its quadrupling of the price of oil, had overthrown many, if not all, previous assumptions. It was in this context and for the eyes of the Prime Minister, Harold Wilson, that the foreign secretary, **James Callaghan**, had written in 1975 a seventeen-page memorandum, unusual in its length and detail, concerning the Falklands.

The purpose of the paper was to say what policy should we now adopt, and what should we claim as regards the oil deposits on the continental shelf and, in the light of our decisions, what fresh instructions ought we to send to our ambassador in Buenos Aires.

In the immediate aftermath of the OPEC crisis of 1974, were you looking at the possibilities in the south-west Atlantic through different eyes?

Certainly, through the eyes of the OPEC problem and also as a means of securing cooperation with Argentina, because Professor Griffiths of Birmingham University had recently produced a report suggesting that there was a possibility of oil deposits being there. So obviously one tried to kill as many birds as possible with one stone.

So if, in the 1960s, it had been the broad intention of British policy to come to some agreement with Argentina on the sovereignty issue, and to make that paramount in the interests of our wider relationships with Latin America, would you say that by 1974 we were considering at least the possibilities of re-engagement *in the south-west Atlantic, staying on rather than getting out, largely born of the OPEC crisis?*

I think that would be putting too rational an explanation on our thinking. I would not say that we were thinking as far ahead as that. But it seemed as though this was a very fortunate conjuncture of events. There was a need for oil; Argentina would have as much need for oil as we would have, and Professor Griffiths's report had appeared. My mind was turning to economic cooperation, and this indeed was what I recommended to the Prime Minister in this memorandum. It seemed, therefore, the obvious way forward.

In this May 1975 memorandum to the prime minister, Harold Wilson, Callaghan had warned of the Argentine impatience for substantial negotiations, but, as well, that 'the Argentine government was now so unstable that it was questionable whether a negotiated settlement would stand the test of time.' Callaghan reported also the hints being dropped by 'the moderate foreign minister, Vignes' in Buenos Aires that, if Britain was not prepared to negotiate, 'the only other option open to the Argentine government was resort to force.'

Warning also that the balance of power was beginning to change between Britain and Argentina, with the Argentine Navy training and equipping to European standards, the British foreign secretary added this sobering assessment for the prime minister, in 1975, seven years before the Falklands War.

I recapitulated to him that on the 14th April, a month earlier, our new ambassador, paying his first call on the Argentine foreign minister, had said as follows, 'If the situation were to be further exacerbated by Argentine threats of armed conflict, pressure would mount on Her Majesty's Government to demonstrate their determination to defend the Islands. The Argentine Government must clearly understand that an attack on the Islands would meet with a military response. At the same time Her Majesty's Government wished to avoid any confrontation with Argentina. The only alternative to confrontation was negotiation and they stood ready to examine any proposal which the Argentine Government might now wish to put forward.'

I warned the prime minister at the time, in the light of the proposals that the Argentines were making, that we must assume that the Argentine Navy had prepared a contingency plan for an invasion. We would need to reinforce the thirty-three Royal Marines who were the only force that was standing at the time in the Islands. I said further to the prime minister, 'If we receive no warning of an invasion and we are obliged to liberate the Islands from an Argentine occupation, our political task at the United Nations, and in Washington, and in Latin America, would be formidable. The Secretary of State for Defence should therefore advise on the practical aspects of defending the Islands. The worst outcome both domestically and internationally would be to attempt to defend or liberate the Islands and fail. We must not do so.' I think that was the extent of the warning, except I said that the course that I was proposing was an imperfect way to keep the path open, but it seemed to be the best.

The dangers represented in this assessment, in a situation of political deadlock, were to carry Callaghan down an inclined plane towards resuming talks about sovereignty, to which he had put an end when Britain withdrew from them in August 1974.

With hindsight the dangers spelt out by the foreign secretary might seem sufficient to make one wonder why it took Britain so long to return to the central issue with Argentina. 'Leave this poisoned chalice alone', Callaghan had said. By general report, the treatment which Parliament had handed out to Michael Stewart in the previous Labour Government had entered few minds more deeply than James Callaghan's.

The foreign secretary's wariness of the possibly lethal political price to be paid in Britain for any move to change the status quo in the Falklands is well remembered by one of the junior Foreign Office ministers with responsibility for the Falklands who came and went, as in a revolving door, down the years. This was **Ted Rowlands**, MP for Merthyr Tydfil. He stayed longer, and more enthusiastically and whole-heartedly, than others, and he was also a close political confidant of James Callaghan. When Callaghan became foreign secretary, Rowlands went with him to the Foreign Office as minister of state.

First of all it was a great surprise to go to the Foreign Office. To be honest I had little or no experience. Indeed, when the prime minister summoned me, and he said, 'I want you to go across with Jim Callaghan to be in the Foreign Office', I said, 'The Foreign Office?

Where is it?' I had been pulled out of an essentially very domestic political background, building houses in Wales, to enter this whole new world. Jim Callaghan was very clear about my role. I was there at his behest, and he wanted me to watch 'the dots on the map', as he called them. He said that big issues of foreign policy very rarely bring governments down, but there are 'dots on the map' that create enormous embarrassments, if not bring governments down. I was going to be the minister for those dots on the map, for all those problems that might arise, and he would hold me personally responsible if any of them did cause us major embarrassment.

I quickly found out just how many dots there were. I was responsible, during the whole four and a half years, for the relationship between Belize and Guatemala – we nearly went to war *twice* in four and a half years – and, of course, for the Falkland Islands.

As a 'dot on the map' was there any particular quality about the Falkland Islands, as Callaghan saw it, when he gave you the job?

Oh yes, most certainly. There was the fact that if you read the history of ministerial involvement over the Falklands in particular, it had one recurring pattern. On the whole it blew up, and sometimes blew down ministers! He wanted me to be 'hawk like'. Those were his terms. To make sure that he himself would be personally briefed on any shifts or movements: that was his remit when I was made minister for the dots on the map.

The constant proximity of Parliament was the real force which determined how ministers acted. A nation with a long habit of Parliamentary discussion gave short shift to any discussion involving the transfer of sovereignty. Successive governments and ministers did not bring it up in the House of Commons because they did not wish to repeat Lord Stewart's withering experience. This, in turn, meant that an exhaustive explanation of the problem was never really tackled. What governed the approach as foreign secretary, and later prime minister, of that House of Commons man of long and wide experience, **James Callaghan**?

Throughout the whole of the period that I had anything to do with this my assessment was that, provided the Argentines believed that we were willing to keep discussing these matters, and to find various formulae which would enable them to satisfy their public opinion, then the issue would not come to a head. It was insoluble. There was *no* solution that could satisfy both sides. Therefore the first task must be to convince them that we were trying to find ways of accommodating them, without surrendering our vital interest in the matter of sovereignty to which the Islanders were opposed.

Now my opinion on that, which was a political hunch, was re-inforced certainly by the JIC[5] reports. They always took the view that, provided the Argentine governments were convinced that we were negotiating seriously, they would not then attack the Islands. This was my view too.

So, not in any attempt to dodge the issue, but to try to create conditions in which the Argentine government could feel satisfied, it was this that led me to propose the Shackleton Commission.

The Labour peer Lord Shackleton was the son of the Antarctic explorer and, therefore, the bearer of a great name from the heroic age of British endeavour in the Antarctic in the early years of this century.

'Is there anything to be said for economic cooperation with Argentina?', Robin Edmonds had asked of the Falklands lobby in the meeting room of the House of Commons, believing 'the climate to be propitious'. Given the conjuncture of the possibility of oil around the Falklands and the decline in both the numbers and material circumstances of the Islanders, that meeting had proved to be the genesis of the Shackleton Commission, a survey in the first instance embodying an intention to develop resources in and around the Falkland Islands. After an equivocal response to begin with, Argentina elected to see the proposal of Lord Shackleton's commission as a head-on challenge. This was hardly what the foreign secretary, **James Callaghan**, had in mind.

> The purpose was to explore the possibilities of economic development in the Falkland Islands, and in the south-west Atlantic, in a way in which we could engage the cooperation of the Argentine government. For example, with the difficulties over the continental shelf around the Islands it would have been difficult, if not impossible, for us to have done oil exploration or indeed oil production there without their cooperation. As there was a disputed continental shelf, to which both sides could legitimately have some claim, it seemed to me a reasonable proposition that we should engage the Argentines in this. There were also, at the time, large claims made about the possibility of krill development and exploitation. There again, it seemed to me that, rather than have a quarrel over fishing rights in disputed waters that were outside the Islands, we might cooperate with them in that way.

5 Joint Intelligence Committee.

Now the original response by Senor Vignes was positive. He thought it was a good idea. But my recollection is that it went back to President Perón, and the idea was then scuppered. So, what had seemed to be a very fruitful means of keeping the Argentines engaged, and recognizing some of their legitimate interests in the waters around the Falklands, disappeared. The Argentine government raised a lot of difficulty about the Shackleton expedition, as you know.

How did the sovereignty question fit into your thinking about the Shackleton survey?

These were *alternatives* to discussions on sovereignty. My intention, and I can claim that it succeeded in many ways, was not to divert *all* attention from the sovereignty issue but to engage them on matters where some progress could be made and, in those circumstances, ease the sovereignty issue.

What instructions did you give to ministers and officials in this respect? How were the Islanders themselves to be encouraged to view the Shackleton survey?

Encouraged to view it positively. Although I'm bound to say that because of some of the ill-advised propaganda from Argentina at the time, the Islanders' attitude, which I had been told when I first came to the Foreign Office was not totally opposed to further cooperation, hardened. I think the Argentine government handled the thing very badly in the sense that by their outright statements about their claims the rather shy Falkland Islanders turned away and said, 'No, not for us.'

Was it also your hope at the time of the commissioning of the Shackleton survey that this opportunity should be taken to ease the Islanders themselves into a closer relationship with Argentina?

I wouldn't use the word 'ease' about it. The Islands' economy, unless they had a tremendous infusion of capital from this country, which they were not likely to have – indeed, would not have *now* if it had not been for the war – was getting worse steadily. There did not seem to be a real future there. I think this is why Toby Lewis, the governor, as a New Zealander, held the view that we should make this encouragement to them to try to see their future lying in close cooperation with Argentina. So I would not use the word 'ease' about it. I think it was a very proper development. What I did say, in my concluding words to the prime minister, was that 'there was a great deal of prejudice about this issue, and we should attempt in the Islands, as well as in Parliament, to secure an informed approach.'

The Foreign Office conceived the Shackleton survey in terms of 'sentence first, verdict afterwards'. Lord Shackleton's report was intended to deliver Britain from the growing sense of menace in the Falklands dilemma by making its recommendations conditional on concessions from the Islanders about cooperating with Argentina.

Shackleton, however, produced a vision of improvements on the Falklands, and a harvest from the encircling seas, which appeared to hold out the promise of a more splendid isolation. Did the Shackleton Commission therefore return a verdict which accorded with the realities? The Foreign Office minister of state at the time was **Ted Rowlands**.

I think, truthfully, no. Not in the way which was expected. It identified an enormous range of opportunities. But clearly, rather like I did when I went out in February 1977, Eddie Shackleton lost his heart there also. A lot of the report was about the tremendous opportunities and enormous potential for development; and that, basically, all this could be done by the Falkland Islanders, and with the Falkland Islanders. Whereas *our* particular appreciation of the Shackleton Report, or any other developments of this kind, was that it would be just frankly physically, politically, militarily impossible to adopt. It was a grand scale concept of development without any form of negotiated settlement on the other issues.

I think Eddie Shackleton identified these resources and this tremendous potential, but was politically and diplomatically and militarily unrealistic in believing how much could be delivered without some sort of arrangement with Argentina. One other problem was that the report, by this time, had become a cause of conflict in itself. The combination of these factors made it very difficult to utilize what had been the original intention – of using an economic mission to promote a permanent solution to the dispute.

My personal critique of the Shackleton Report was that it actually misunderstood what the Islanders really wanted. The Islanders did not really *want*, I believe, the massive scale developments that were being proposed by Shackleton. They were much more interested in what I called in the House of Commons the 'doorstep hopes'. Eddie Shackleton underestimated, and did not actually develop, what I thought were a number of very sensible things we should be doing. Unfortunately, therefore, he did not give me the reinforcement to go and get more modest sums of money which we *could* deliver to the Islanders.

The Shackleton Commission, launched as an overarching concept, fell to the ground. For Argentina's part, because it embodied the British refusal to negotiate except on issues of economic cooperation, it was to be strenuously opposed. The fragile government of Senora Perón was about to give way to the military juntas of the seventies and eighties. Its position against the armed forces, particularly the Argentine Navy which wanted stronger action, was weakened.

Lord Shackleton's economic survey provided Argentina with the occasion for a demonstration that those hints of force, of which James Callaghan had warned Harold Wilson in 1975, were no longer to be shrugged off in Whitehall as ritualistic flourishes. The Foreign Office under-secretary supervising Latin American policy at the time of the Communications Agreements and the Shackleton Survey was **Robin Edmonds**. What efforts had been made to get Argentine approval of Lord Shackleton's mission?

That is very much in point. I'm afraid that this is one of the many examples in history of two initiatives taken by a government that were intended to be complementary turning out to be contradictory. That was not the intention at all. The *other* initiative, which preceded the idea of an economic survey of the islands, was in July 1975 when we proposed, with Cabinet approval, to the Argentines that there should be discussions of joint Anglo-Argentine development of the south-west Atlantic. Very soon *after* that, in the autumn, the invitation went from the Foreign Secretary to Eddie Shackleton to undertake his survey.

We really did, I promise, believe that these were two completely compatible things. I'm afraid the Argentines proved us wrong. They adopted an attitude towards the whole Shackleton exercise, long before his *report*, from the word go, of complete hostility. So violent was their reaction that I can recall – it was February of the following year, by which time Eddie Shackleton and his team were out there – that I came back from some tedious lunch, to the Foreign and Commonwealth Office, and was walking down the corridor when the Falkland Islands desk officer rushed up to me and said, 'They've shot Shackleton!'

For a split second I actually thought that he meant they'd shot Eddie Shackleton. Of course it was in fact the RRS *Shackleton*, the research vessel named after his father, on which an Argentine destroyer had just opened fire. Indeed, it was a rather hectic afternoon.

The fact is they took the dimmest possible view, to put it mildly, of the whole Shackleton enterprise, and I really don't know what might have happened if Senora Perón's 'crazy gang' – because you can't describe them as anything else – had remained in power. In a way we were saved by the gong, the removal of the crazy gang. Her chief minister and principal adviser was an astrologer. He had access to all the Peronista trades union funds and got away with millions. I don't believe he has ever been found. It was a Gilbertian situation.

The military Junta which succeeded Senora Perón offered the chance, it was thought, of negotiations with an at least stable Argentine government. None the less, the day the Red Ensign was fired on by an Argentine destroyer was the day Lord Shackleton's Commission – yet another initiative by British diplomacy to outflank the sovereignty issue – began to founder in 'the jolly-rogered sea' around the Falklands. The incident was reminiscent of the Earl of Kildare's celebrated reply to King Henry the Seventh, when asked whether he had burned down Cashel Cathedral: 'I did, but I thought that the archbishop was inside.' It seems that Argentina had thought Lord Shackleton was a passenger in the ship that bore his name. Such an event had long been forecast as a possible preliminary to Argentina's turning to military action to fulfil its ambition over the Falkland Islands.

Armed with maps to allay Argentine suspicions that the ship *Shackleton* had not been prospecting for oil, Ted Rowlands was dispatched to New York to meet the Argentine foreign minister. Rowlands, under instructions to make it plain that Britain would defend the Islands if it had to, was also told to ask Argentina what proposals *it* had in mind now about the central dispute over sovereignty.

This signalled Britain's return, in 1976, to the original path of negotiations with Argentina in the 1960s. Argentina, therefore, had successfully made its point. The British position was, euphemistically, expressed in what **Ted Rowlands** agrees was an awesome mouthful as an offer to 'explore the nature of a future hypothetical constitutional relationship'.

We had no very clear goal. That was quite evident. We had to feel our way on all these arguments. What those words meant – now that you remind me about them, and how lovely and wonderfully convoluted they are – was, again, an attempt to signal that, in some way, we could incorporate discussions on the sovereignty issue. We realized that we could not get *any* discussions going unless we made this initial step.

Gradually, in 1977, I was probably the author of an attempt to actually *divide* 'sovereignty' and split it up as between resources and people. We did not want to return to 'condominium' ideas which Jim had rejected, and which Julian Amery had mooted. We had not, at that stage, focused in any clear sense on any concept of 'leaseback', as such. So it was an endeavour to say to the Argentines, 'Look, we are willing to *incorporate*, in any discussions and negotiations, ideas about sovereignty issues which will arise, but not to put sovereignty on the table for debate, or for negotiation.'

It was a change of direction. Following the complete breakdown of British policy at the end of the 1960s many innovative ideas, and some hallucinations, had been swept out to sea. British diplomacy had clambered into one raft after another. Under the three-fold compulsion of denuded treasuries, and increasing pressure from Argentina and from the United Nations, Britain had been driven from 'sovereignty withdrawn', to 'sovereignty shared', to 'sovereignty restored' to the agenda for negotiation.

By the end of 1975, Sisyphus in Whitehall was about to push the 'sovereignty' boulder uphill once more. It is these next five years which all but set the long-maturing mould from which the Falklands war emerged.

3

Profoundly Disturbing Statements

In Argentina the last half of the decade of the 1970s, which takes us to the threshold of the Falklands war, was the time of the 'disappearances'. This sanguinary suppression of political unrest aroused international attention and interest in human rights in Argentina. At the same time, the advent of the military Junta had generated a swirl of nationalist feeling.

In Britain troubles came in battalions. By the autumn of 1976 there was a major economic crisis. High inflation and the threatened collapse of sterling compelled ministers to borrow from the International Monetary Fund: all of which was writing on the wall for British defence policy, exacting a reappraisal of the cost of the far call in the Falklands.

The mid-way point of the decade was overlapped by the birth, and eventual death, of the main point of departure for British policy concerning the Falklands, the report of the Shackleton Commission. The nonconformist strain in Labour thinking had easily translated into an avuncular and improving idealism affecting colonial policy in many parts of the world. By means of the Shackleton economic survey, the Foreign Office's baffling preserve in the South Atlantic was to be given some sort of order. The near derelict colony on the Falklands was seen as 'property in need of development'. This materialist approach, which sought to circumvent the passions over sovereignty, the central issue, had been greeted by Argentina with unreserved hostility. Buenos Aires saw in the maintenance of a degree of British influence and supervision only the continuation of the old order.

This period also saw a change at the top in Britain. Harold Wilson stepped down in 1976 and **James Callaghan** became the new prime minister. Callaghan, as foreign secretary, had established the Shackleton Commission.

The follow-up action was disappointing, and the Argentine government were, clearly, going to show very little cooperation. I suppose it is true to say that the whole thing grew harder during the next twelve months, in 1976 and 1977. I saw very little prospect of an improvement. My aim, therefore, was to keep the pot simmering without allowing it to boil over.

In March 1976 you undertook a major review of policy, and it poses this question, I think. What was it, essentially, which dictated the movement we made in our policy from 1974, when there is not much doing, to once again declaring our willingness, by 1977, to make sovereignty an issue for negotiation?

I suppose the answer must be that when one door closed you sought to open another one. As the economic prospects diminished, then it seemed sensible to discuss other possibilities – subject to all the safeguards that the Islanders wanted with Argentina.

So, I sent a message to Argentina on the 20th March 1976, proposing a fresh dialogue on all aspects of the dispute including, and here I quote, 'the nature of a future hypothetical constitutional relationship'. But that was because there was no other alternative. 'Leaseback' was not mentioned, I may say, at any time to the Argentines, even though I was prepared to consider it.

Why not mention it?

Because I think it would have been giving away a card too soon. The Argentines themselves proposed a leaseback and they suggested within a period of time, of eight years. Well, that was so foolish that it did not seem worth bothering with. I had in mind, and I wrote at the time, a period of *seventy* years, which would give the chance for the economies to grow and all the other necessary things involved.

I must say, and here I will confess to a certain amount of dissembling, that I knew the Argentines would not agree to any prospect of seventy years at all. But on the other hand, it did give us a very much better stance in the United Nations and with world opinion.

If it *had* come to that, that we had to make that particular proposition – because every year we faced this debate in the United Nations, in which they obviously sided with Argentina and against us – I was, therefore, preparing the ground for us to have something to stand on, pretty firmly, when we got there.

The mid-1970s sees the genesis of what later came to be seen as the most elegant solution of all, 'leaseback'. Leaseback combined two principles; British administration, which is what the islanders wanted, and the notional concession of Argentine sovereignty. Originally, as James Callaghan confirms, it had been a proposal from the Argentine foreign minister, Vignes. But although the transfer of sovereignty, combined with leaseback, had come to be regarded in London as the most realistic solution, it made little headway. 'Unwilling to give away a card too soon', in Callaghan's words, the British Government delayed. Argentina concluded the British were simply prevaricating, and the next two years consisted of the interplay between negotiation and the threat of military confrontation.

It fell to an intellectual heavyweight in the Labour Government, Anthony Crosland, Callaghan's successor as foreign secretary, to give the Shackleton Report its quietus and then to grapple with its failure as policy. As Crosland became foreign secretary in 1976, his minister of state was **Ted Rowlands**.

> Crosland came in, saw this, looked at it and said, 'If we can't carry on, we can't drift.' But I don't think 'drift' is a fair description. If you are searching for a solution to an almost insoluble problem, sometimes, if not 'drift', you've got to feel your way. But he came very straight-forwardly, and adamantly, to the conclusion that Shackleton was impossible to implement *without a political solution*. His was a very clear, incisive approach. He was very remarkable. He read volumin-ously and he used to challenge all presumptions. He virtually concluded, obviously with inputs from all of us, that this was to be the way forward: that you utilized what you could of Shackleton, that you put it in the context of improving political relations, and that sovereignty would *have* to come up. It would be far better to negotiate right across the board, *on South Georgia and the whole area*, because what you had to search for was a permanent solution, and not addressing oneself to another temporary situation. That was his great contribution. It led to terms of reference for the most substantive negotiation that had occurred for about two years.

A significant new fact had accompanied this development of British policy. Argentina had decided that military gestures were a necessary, and effective, means of getting Britain to make progress with negotia-tions. In February 1976, Argentina had indicated its displeasure with the Shackleton Commission survey by firing on and afterwards blockading the research vessel *Shackleton* in Port Stanley; whereupon Britain did modify its negotiating position. None the less, Crosland took his time, 'stooping to finish the game' as it were, somewhat to the alarm of his advisers, like the head of the Latin American desk, **Hugh Carless**.

> He was a fascinating foreign secretary, with his powerful intellect, and his forbidding manner, which I think was capable of silencing any backbencher in his tracks. At first he dismayed us, on the Latin American front, by refusing to take any papers on the Falkland

Islands for his first six months in office. But he gave a good explanation of this. He said, 'I know there's a problem there. We will have to do something about it, but meanwhile there are several other more important problems which I have to think through.'

Odd, though, that he should refuse to take papers for six months at a time when there was a progressive deterioration in our relations with Argentina, with military incidents in support of the Argentine ambition for the first time?

Refusing to take papers was shorthand for saying that he did not feel he was in a position to concentrate his intellectual energy on this problem for his first few months in office. He was not in a position to put himself out until the autumn of 1976 when he had cleared away a number of other issues. One was the 'Cod War'.[1] He was the MP for Grimsby,[2] you remember. He came to the conclusion, quite rapidly, that the Cod War was not in the British national interest and he stopped the Cod War.

When he was ready to take papers on the Falklands we compiled a dossier for him – a book with maps and statistics and every kind of information that you could want. He took this dossier away, and for one weekend, perhaps two or even three weekends. I don't know whether you've read that remarkable book by his wife Susan about his method of work? One can imagine him in his study in Notting Hill, then pacing up and down the lawn smoking one of his cheroots.

He worked through this problem. I think his concept was that first there *was* a problem, and it needed solving. The way to do it was by negotiating a series of agreements with the Argentines over a period which would have lasted perhaps several years. These agreements would have begun on the outer edges of the problem. One agreement would have been, and it almost came about, on scientific cooperation in the Falkland Islands dependencies. Another agreement might have been about fishing. You remember that, at that time, Argentina had called for a tender inviting foreign fishing fleets to fish in the southwest Atlantic. Another agreement might have been, in due course, about surveys for oil, or joint exploration for oil.

Did 'beginning with the outer edges of the problem' mean making concessions in the Falkland Island dependencies[3] in order to protect our position on the Falkland Islands?

It might have done. The view taken by Crosland, I think, and certainly by Ted Rowlands, was that what the British Government were most concerned about was people and not territory.

1 With Iceland, over territorial fishing limits.
2 Crosland's constituency was a major deep sea fishing port.
3 Including South Georgia, South Orkney, and the South Shetland Islands.

But he worked through the problem. He had a large meeting in the Foreign Office, perhaps two or three meetings. At the end of the last meeting he said, 'Well, you know, I'm beginning to see a way through. The first thing that I'll do is to make a Parliamentary statement.'

He made this Parliamentary statement on the 2nd of February 1977. In it he dealt with the Shackleton Report. He ended the statement by saying that he was going to send a minister to consult the Islanders, and to obtain their views. That minister was his minister of state, Ted Rowlands, who a fortnight later travelled out first to Buenos Aires, where he had meetings with the Argentine foreign minister, and then he went on to the Falkland Islands, where he got on extremely well with the Islanders. I think that he was by far the most successful British minister to have visited the Islands.

I went with him on that journey. The day we landed in Port Stanley, the first news given to us was that of the death of Tony Crosland.

Had Crosland lived, I believe it may have been that history would have been a little different.

An untimely death?

It was a most unfortunate death, particularly in this context.

Before his death Anthony Crosland had pronounced a final verdict on the Shackleton Report. He told the House of Commons in February 1977 that the Government was not prepared to accept its more costly recommendations; notably enlarging the airport and lengthening its runway. Both these proposals obviously had defence implications, and contained the seeds of future misadventure. 'Fortress Falklands', rejected by Crosland, would be summoned into existence only after the war of 1982, and then at prodigious cost – two billion pounds.

At the time of Crosland's death in 1977, the minister of state, **Ted Rowlands**, was out in Port Stanley with senior Foreign Office officials on Crosland's instructions 'to consult the Islanders and obtain their views'.

Perhaps it's the Welshman in me, but I don't think that until I went to the Islands I really understood what the argument was about. I'd read all about them, I'd read minutes from the Office, I had no criticism of official advice. The official advice was good, rational. It reviewed the relative balances of our requirements and interests. But it did not ever convey to me, until I went myself, the flavour of the place and what, therefore, the argument was.

And when I went to the Islands I found not Islanders seven thousand miles remote from their homeland, the United Kingdom: I found incredible *internal* isolation. I met people in Goose Green, and San Carlos, who had never been to Port Stanley in their lives! People who lived in this entirely isolated yet, you know, basically contented and just family society. They just did not want to be disturbed. They didn't want to push the boat out. They didn't want to go to war with Argentina. They just wanted to be left alone. And I think – this perhaps is a bit more controversial, and they would reject it if they hear it – I think we were fighting for their right to *decline*, not for the right to *develop*. That's what shook me. That's what changed my perception of the Shackleton Report and all the rest of it. It was their right and desire to be themselves. I think it was probably as a Welsh-man rather than a Foreign Office minister that I identified with it. They would not have minded, I think, Argentina developing resources but they did not want them strutting around the Island. That was a major interference with their style of life. It had a profound effect on my views about leaseback; it gives you the right to strut about and put up flags.

I came back convinced that it was a perfectly legitimate and, in my opinion, important right of British foreign policy to defend the rights of a minority. And when people said to me, 'But they're only eighteen hundred people', I would answer 'If they're only eighteen hundred people will you sacrifice three thousand people? What is the level of population that is required before you decide to fight for a principle? Is it ten thousand? Is it fifty thousand?'

During the debates within the Labour Party about the war and since, I have always been a supporter of the view that we had to fight in 1982, and for that reason.

That attitude derived – you might think I got all sentimental and mushy about it – from that visit in February 1977. I came back convinced that while I believed I could carry the Islanders with me, if we could get a workable solution and something the Argentines would agree to, I was also convinced that we could not actually over-rule the Islanders.

Having gone to see life in the faraway Falklands for himself, Row-lands's feelings surely came close to those subtle underlying deter-minants of British democracy which Edmund Burke defined as the first principle of public affections, devotion to 'the little platoon', the small minority. One can readily imagine that James Callaghan's hesitation in promoting the Hong Kong solution, or leaseback, at this stage, because, as he said, 'it would have been giving away a card too early', was also because he had to take account of the strength of such sentiments.

Anthony Crosland's 'way through' Britain's steadily narrowing options in the Falklands was being acted out, in practice, by **Ted Rowlands**.

In 1968 we had tried to bounce them into a solution and that had not worked. I realised that, in 1977, if I was going to come up with a solution I would have to go back to those Islands and stand at those same farm gates, and in those wool sheds, and try to convince a profoundly conservative, with a small 'c', community that some changes had to take place.

What led to the type of negotiations that followed was that I felt we could *divide* the concept of sovereignty. We should try to persuade them that there was sovereignty over people, and sovereignty over resources. This was quite a novel idea. It was called the 'mixed approach'. My critics said it was the 'mixed-up approach'. But it was called the 'mixed approach', and it interested and intrigued the Argentines who were all basically nineteenth-century international lawyers at heart, you know – at least those who were outside the military. The concept to them was intriguing. In a sense we were reversing what was traditionally seen as the British, 'perfidious Albion's', role. We were being accused of being economic imperialists in the area. We were accused of hanging on to these Islands, not because we really liked the eighteen hundred Islanders, but because there was oil there. Because there was krill. Because there was fishing. Because there were all these resources. The Islanders were our 'front'. This was the standard charge against us at the United Nations and in the whole of the Americas. Even our best friends believed this. And I said, 'Well, why don't we turn it around, and actually *give away* all that we apparently are supposed to be clinging to in return for the maintenance of sovereignty over the *people*?'

So, therefore, came this concept of dividing sovereignty over the resources and the inhabitants. The case then, automatically, was the uninhabited Islands, where you cannot make the same case. I was prepared to go that far, to actually make this division, in order to maintain the existing sovereign right, the position of the Falkland Islanders on the *inhabited* Falkland Islands.

So the strategy now was to make concessions in the dependencies, the outlying uninhabited Islands, in order to maintain some sort of position on the Falklands themselves?

Yes. Because, you see, we were turning Shackleton round the other way. I was turning Shackleton on its head. Instead of saying, 'We're going to develop all these resources, jointly', we were almost saying,

'Well, we can make joint efforts, but *you* basically can develop the resources. What we want are the ten cents of every resource for the Islanders.' We could have financed a lot of doorstep developments from just a percentage of the action. We did not then, ourselves, have to get into the action. One of the most incredible things I found about the concept of 'joint ventures' was that I could not persuade anyone here to go and do anything. When Victor Matthews and Cunards came to me and said, 'We would like to go in with the Argentines on the pilot fishing project', which could have led to the building of an Argentine fishing fleet in collaboration with ourselves, I could not find any government department willing to put up the million pounds we were looking for, or anyone willing to support an imaginative proposal of that kind. Gradually, I came to the conclusion that we did not have the capacity to do these joint developments. So why not make a virtue of necessity and turn it around as we did. Then we could go to the United Nations and to everyone else and say, 'We are *not* economic imperialists. We are not hanging on to these things. We are clinging to the rights of the people.'

Was resettlement of the Islanders ever seriously considered?

It was always the sort of 'bottom' option. I was a bitter opponent of compensation. I could see a younger generation taking the compensation and going and that left us with an even bigger problem. Then you would have a reduced and ageing population who did *not* want to go off to New Zealand at the age of sixty. Did you then sacrifice them? All that would have happened is what happened to my own Welsh valley and the valley community I represented. A whole generation upped and went. They left another generation behind to pick up the pieces. So I was a bitter opponent of compensation. I thought it was a cynical approach to people and to life and to society.

The Shackleton Report had been a last rally of paternalistic enthusiasm by Britain. 'Turning it on its head' was the adoption of a more worldly view. People and resources had been seen in terms of closest partnership, as between the rider and the horse. Rider and horse were now about to part company, for a sufficient but undisclosed reason.

At the end of 1976, Argentina once more resorted to direct military pressure, this time by occupying sovereign British territory in one of the Falkland Islands dependencies. This was the remote desolate island of Southern Thule in the South Sandwich group, 1,300 miles from Port Stanley, uninhabited and not much favoured even by the penguins. This Argentine presence was not revealed to the House of Commons for

another eighteen months. Rowlands agrees that Crosland's strategy was
not to make a stand in the dependencies, and that the British concern
now had become 'people' rather than 'territory'.

Hugh Carless was the head of the Latin American desk, and
Crosland's principal adviser, when the late foreign secretary had
adopted the strategy of working at these 'outer edges' of the Falklands
dilemma.

The Argentine research station, one of those Antarctic-type huts, was
evidently landed and erected on Southern Thule in the autumn of
1976. It was discovered by chance by a helicopter from HMS
Endurance which flew over this small and otherwise uninhabited island
in December 1976. Our response immediately was to protest to the
Argentine Government in order to reserve and preserve British
sovereignty. I can remember that, as soon as the photographs taken by
Endurance reached London, I summoned the Argentine chargé
d'affaires and demanded an explanation. We instructed our ambassador to protest, and a month later when Ted Rowlands was on his
way to the Falklands via Buenos Aires he again protested against this
violation of sovereignty to the foreign minister, then Admiral Guzzetti.
Guzzetti said to Rowlands, 'These Argentine scientists are only going
to be there for a short summer season.' We accepted that explanation
at the time. We accepted it because we were at the beginning of the
Crosland concept of long-term negotiation with the Argentines. We
were really faced with a decision to remove the Argentines by force,
which would have required a couple of frigates and risked a conflict
with the Argentine Navy, or to leave them there for the time being.

*With hindsight, are we right to see that event not just as a prod to get Britain to
negotiate seriously but rehearsing what in fact they ultimately did? That is, had
they been evicted by us with force from Southern Thule, their plan we know now
was to have taken South Georgia?*

Yes. With hindsight we see this as clear evidence of Argentine
imperialism in the south-west Atlantic and a long-term plan to
nobble all these British dependencies. Our concern at that time, in
1976, was for the Islanders and their future, rather than for the
dependencies. And one form of negotiation which did take place over
the next year or so was an attempt to reach agreement over scientific
cooperation. That is, the establishment of scientific research stations
by Argentina in the dependencies. This was a way, if you like, of
wrapping up the Argentine occupation of Southern Thule. It gave
them a card, certainly. On the other hand it helped us in doing what
we were constantly attempting to do, which was to play for time. To

play for time in the hope that events would arrange themselves in such a conjunction that some kind of a solution would emerge.

In other words, it was a recognition that major negotiations were required to keep Argentina in play at this time, and if necessary we would make concessions in these outlying Islands in order to do that? It's a holding operation?

Yes, it was a holding operation, and I think you've defined the drift quite neatly.

The occupation of Southern Thule was deliberately suggestive; a demonstration by the Argentine Navy of Argentina's rival claims to sovereignty over the Falkland Islands, and throughout sub-Antarctica, and a disturbing statement of future intent. The long-drawn-out minuet of diplomacy, which had been in progress for more than ten years, had now to be danced to this discordant new tune. Once again, as with the incident at the beginning of 1976 involving the research ship *Shackleton*, confronted by direct action Britain modified its position, when **Ted Rowlands** conducted his next round of talks.

I knew I had to get this, that they would evacuate Southern Thule, once the negotiations got going. They did, but of course they reneged on that arrangement in the autumn of 1977.

The British Government took no steps to make public Argentina's presence on Southern Thule. That did not become known to the House of Commons and therefore public opinion for another two years. Why was it decided to keep it dark?

Because then we would have to make our minds up as to what we did. It was because then it would become such an issue in itself, it would have scuppered the whole of the negotiating process which we were painfully and painstakingly building up. Was this worth while? Was this issue big enough to do that? We agonized over it considerably. But if we had made a public song and dance about it, we would then have had to decide whether to break off the whole negotiating process. We decided that negotiation was more important.

British intelligence reports in 1977 were forbidding. Ministers were told that if negotiations broke down 'there was a high risk that Argentina would resort to force including direct military action.' Invasion of the Falkland Islands was thought to be 'unlikely but not to be discounted'.[4] How was that risk brought home to Whitehall?

Hugh Carless, an adviser of importance, had been translated from his post as head of the Latin American department in the Foreign Office

4 Franks Report (HMSO 1983), para. 63.

by this time, and was reporting as minister, and chargé d'affaires, from the vantage point of Buenos Aires.

The years 1977 and, particularly, 1978 were a period of extremely high political tension in Argentina. The year culminated with Argentina being on the point, not of attacking the Falklands, but of attacking Chile. Nineteen-seventy-eight in particular was the 'year of the Beagle', the Beagle Channel dispute over three islands right at the bottom of Tierra del Fuego. An international panel sat, under the auspices of the British Crown, which the Argentine and Chilean governments had agreed to and had asked for arbitration over these three islands, Picton, Lennox and Nueva. It was known as the Queen's Award, although we British really had nothing to do with the arbitration, and it awarded all these three islands to Chile. This gave Chile control over the passage from the Atlantic to the Pacific above Cape Horn – an inland passage. They allowed Chile to dominate the Argentine naval base of Ushaia, the most southerly town in the world.

How consistent with British policy imperatives of negotiating a settlement to our dispute with Argentina over the Falklands is that arbitration decision over the Beagle Channel dispute, reached under British auspices, which makes a decision in favour of Chile, Argentina's opponent and with whom she is close to war?

Well, Argentina after mulling over the arbitration award which went against her then declared it null and void. They then began to apply great pressure to Chile, partly through mobilization, partly through expelling some of the large number of Chileans living in Patagonia, in Southern Argentina, and by demanding three out of the eight tiny islands called the Cape Horn group, which traditionally belonged to Chile. Because the Beagle Arbitration gave Chile a seaward frontier southwards pointing down to the Antarctic where Chile and Argentina have conflicting claims. So the award gave great advantage to Chile in maritime terms.

Exactly. But how consistent was that with our ambition to find a solution to the Falklands dispute? Were we not involved in two antithetical propositions? We were seen by Argentina to be party to a decision which goes against her fundamental interests in the dispute over the Beagle Channel when we are trying also to negotiate over the Falklands.

Well, Argentina was certainly on the point of attacking Chile and that situation doubtless gave rise to our unease here in London and was a precedent for the future. If Argentina, in this highly nationalistic, expansionist mood was ready to attack a Latin neighbour might they not, in due course, when a favourable moment comes, attack Britain in the Falkland Islands? We did seem, by chance, to be a party to the

Beagle arbitration decision. But it was due to an historical chance. Well-informed Argentines understood that it was historical chance because the British Crown had become involved in these frontier arbitrations between Argentina and Chile as long ago as 1902. Those arbitration awards had worked, very successfully. The man in the street, in Argentina, doubtless believed that the British had loaded the dice against Argentina.

What did we understand at this time were Argentina's foreign policy priorities? Where did the Falklands rank, before the Beagle Channel arbitration and after it?

In Argentina people concerned with foreign affairs believed that Argentina really had only three neighbours. One was Brazil, huge and dynamic, to the north. The other was Chile, small and tough, on the other side of the Andes mountains. The third neighbour, difficult to believe sitting here in London, was Britain. In the late 1970s Argentina had disputes with all three. First with Chile, and the Beagle was number one priority in 1977 and 1978, perhaps 1979. Secondly with Brazil, over the allocation of resources of the Parana river where Brazil, on their side of the river, had built an enormous hydroelectric dam. The third problem was the Falklands. In the period 1977–9 I would have said the Beagle was first priority, the Parana river number two and the Falklands number three.

Would you agree, with hindsight, it seems highly likely that we may have misjudged the importance Argentina gave to the Beagle and that, frustrated as they were by the outcome of their dispute with Chile over that, they were going to elevate the Falklands from number three to number one?

Perhaps so. Certainly they were able to settle their differences with Brazil when the new Brazilian president came to office. He was, I think, the first Brazilian president for fifty years to visit Argentina. That was a significant moment in 1979, a moment I think when the Argentine military begin to feel more comfortable with the Brazilian military.

They could turn south rather than north?

Perhaps so.

Hugh Carless summarizes the charged context in which the British became aware at the turn of the year in 1976/7 of the Argentine presence on Southern Thule, sovereign British territory. The Franks Report maintains that Argentina expected British reaction to the occupation of Southern Thule to be stronger than it was. The controlling thought in James Callaghan's mind was his political hunch,

reinforced by intelligence reports, that 'provided Argentine governments were convinced Britain was negotiating seriously', Argentina
would not then attack the Falklands.

The Labour Government's 1974 Defence Review had continued the
trend previously established of a phased run-down of commitments
outside the defence of Europe by NATO. It included a decision to take
the symbolic 'tripwire' in the south-west Atlantic, HMS *Endurance*, out
of service. But that decision was deferred, for one more deployment of
the ship, following the incident in which RRS *Shackleton* was fired on in
1976.

By the end of 1977, the situation with Argentina had deteriorated to
the extent that, with negotiations making little or no progress, Rowlands
was given cover, in case of breakdown in his next round of talks, by the
dispatch to the waters round the Falklands of a nuclear submarine and,
a thousand miles away, two frigates. Unlike the case in 1982, there was a
threat perceived in 1977, and a response made, although this response
was not revealed.

Anthony Crosland's replacement as foreign secretary, David Owen,
had presented a paper to the Cabinet in July 1977, which said that the
Islands were 'militarily indefensible except by a major, costly and
unacceptable diversion of current resources'. As the Argentine position
was hardening towards the end of the 1970s, what, as the prime minister,
James Callaghan, saw it, would deter Argentina from a military
fulfilment of its ambition?

The certainty that we would not allow that to triumph, as indeed
happened in 1982. That was it. Provided our resolution was clear, it
did not much matter what was the size of the force we had there – it
was rather like the tripwire. It didn't much matter, provided our
determination was clear. What happened with Mrs Thatcher's
government was that our determination was *not* clear.

*But why should the Argentine Government and officials at the time not see an
ambiguity in Britain's defence position abroad, when successive defence reviews
from the 1960s onwards are reducing our commitment to perform outside the
NATO area?*

For the very simple reason that it was made clear from April 1975,
when the first indication came 'that they would have no alternative',
that they could not do this without us defending the Islands. That we
would not permit them to take sovereignty away. That was the
guarantee, and we could do it. We *had* the force to do it. And when
they used to tell me that we had not got ships, I used to ask them
where they were. One of the consequences was that I had a fortnightly

map of the world, from the Admiralty, showing the disposition of all ships. I knew where they were, and I was determined that we should defend these Islands. And we did.

What, therefore, was the essence of deterrence for you? Was deterrence as you saw it, the dispatch of submarines and frigates to deter their landing, or was it our ability to retake the Islands in the face of Argentine occupation?

No, no. We would have had very great difficulty in retaking them. No, the essence of deterrence was to be prepared, in the event of any talks that we were embarked upon at any particular time breaking down, to be in a position to defend them. That was why I sent that small force when the talks started in November 1977.

Lord Carrington came to a different conclusion when that issue was put to him in 1982. The line he took was that if Argentina did not know about the dispatch of the force in 1977, how could it have deterred? What would be your own response to that?

They knew what *our* attitude was in 1977. They did *not* know what the Conservative attitude was in 1982 nearly so clearly. They had taken the decision to withdraw the ship, HMS *Endurance*, from there. There were other actions they took; for example, denying the Falkland Islanders certain rights of citizenship under a citizenship bill that was going through the House of Commons. That led the Argentine to a conclusion they never reached when *I* was prime minister. But they did when Mrs Thatcher was.

When it came to the Falklands, one of those 'dots on the map' of whose potential for danger he had warned when appointing Ted Rowlands, the prime minister had taken a close interest. James Callaghan may be said to have observed in this one of William Blake's injunctions: 'Labour well the minute particulars, attend to the little ones . . .'.

It might be thought also, in retrospect, that he was fortunate in a sense that Margaret Thatcher was not. 'Deterrence' in the south-west Atlantic was melting away in successive British defence reviews. By 1978 the aircraft carrier *Ark Royal*, which the chiefs of staff had advised would be required if ever the Islands had to be *recovered*, had completed her last commission. When the Falklands war broke out in 1982 she had been two years in the scrap yard. The question of what comprised deterrence, whether it was the ability to prevent a determined landing, or being able to repossess the Islands after an occupation – in former times it had been both – was becoming crucial by the mid-1970s. It is even more so to an understanding of the events which followed in the wake of the major defence review, conducted by Mrs Thatcher's government, in 1981.

There is no doubt that Argentina was moving more boldly as it took stock of the outcome of British defence reviews. While it could not be said the emperor had nothing on at all, he was seen as less likely to have a convincing wardrobe for the South Atlantic. But the stark alternative to a successful negotiated settlement was 'Fortress Falklands'. The chiefs of staff had put that alternative up on the wall to ministers by the mid-1970s. James Callaghan had given **Ted Rowlands** the task of avoiding this while reserving Britain's position on sovereignty, and yet making it plain also that Britain would defend the Islands.

Jim Callaghan was adamant about that, right throughout the period. In the end, if we had to, we would have to be prepared to fight. So that the contingency plan, of February 1976, on retaking the Islands, was not just paper planning, it was real. It was meant to show the enormous difficulty and to demonstrate, quite rightly, that the position to avoid was, what later was called, a 'Fortress Falklands' policy. Nevertheless it was never rejected. It was there for us to consider as the last of all last resorts.

On the other hand the two great defence reviews, in the 1960s Denis Healey's review,[5] *and in 1974, had increasingly diminished our ability to fulfil Mr Callaghan's last-ditch commitment?*

Oh yes, and Jim Callaghan was one of the men who drew attention to that. First of all there was the symbolic role of HMS *Endurance*, which had been proposed to be scrapped. As a result of the February 1976 incident,[6] *Endurance* was reprieved. We knew that that was only a symbolic gesture. It was, nevertheless, quite an important one. We now know from the Franks Report that the issue of the HMS *Endurance* was in fact seen as a symbolic thing by the Argentines.

Rather more important, of course, was *Ark Royal*. It's not an admission, it's just a plain fact. If we had had that type of aircraft carrier, 1982 would have been a rather easier exercise. Easier also than the contingency arrangements that we had devised in February of 1976. What I'm saying is, and it's quite an important matter of emphasis, that ministers drew one very simple conclusion. It ended up as 'Rowlands's remit' – almost at all cost to avoid a breakdown in the negotiations.

Even though leaseback, the 'Hong Kong solution', was by now believed to offer the best way forward, in the words of paragraph 67 of the Franks

5 Denis Healey's review in 1966, announcing phasing out of Britain's aircraft carriers and withdrawal from Aden by 1968.
6 That is, the Argentine destroyer firing on and blockading RRS *Shackleton*.

Report, 'Mr Rowlands was able to avoid proposing it.' Ministers drew back. The 1979 election was in the offing. At the same time it is clear that the Argentine military occupation of Southern Thule had done much to make the Labour Government appreciate the nature of its dilemma and the need for a new initiative.

What that did do is lead, in the autumn of 1977, to yet again a major reappraisal of how far we should go. Here there were genuine discussions and divisions – not divisions, but debate, within the Government and between officials, ministers and Cabinet ministers, for about two and a half months on how far we wanted to go.

Officials drew the conclusion that we now had to really make a leap forward and do what, subsequently, they persuaded Nicholas Ridley to do in 1980[7] in Mrs Thatcher's government. I watched the Nicholas Ridley expedition[8] with interest, because it was what they wanted me to do in October/November 1977, and we could not agree. I, initially, and very reluctantly, as a result of the evidence that was put on to my desk almost weekly, came to the conclusion that we probably had to embark upon some sort of a major new twist to the whole of the negotiating process.

Leaseback?

Yes, leaseback. But not only leaseback, it was not just leaseback. First of all, David Owen, the Foreign Secretary, rejected the first major official paper on leaseback and the tactics. I'd reluctantly gone along with it. I put it up. It's the longest minute I ever wrote on the whole show, looking back on it. In it I agonized and said that my worry was, and remained so right throughout, that I could not deliver the Islanders. I could see how I could do a deal on leaseback with the Argentines. I'd really begun to wonder whether I could deliver the Islanders, because this 'freehold' concept meant that flags would go up, and 'they' would strut around. That, almost more than anything else, was the most offensive thing for the Islanders. So I found great difficulty believing you could *deliver* the leaseback arrangement, and therefore was a very, very queasy and reluctant supporter of it.

On the other hand we should be in no doubt that leaseback as a proposal, a transfer of sovereignty, combined with some form of leaseback, is up and running as an idea in the last years of the Labour Government in the 1970s?

It was up and running inside the Government. Yes. The position of the Foreign Office officials in November/December '77 was that

7 That is, formally recommend 'leaseback' to the House of Commons.
8 Ridley's visit to the Falklands in July 1979.

leaseback was the only way to unlock the thing. Ministers did not go that far, and were not willing to go that far, unless compelled to do so.

That's an interesting moment, clearly. Franks tells us that at the end of 1977, the words used are you were 'able to avoid proposing it'. But you were prepared to?

I was given the remit to do so.

Thus, Britain managed successfully to 'play out time' in the last two years of James Callaghan's government. Given the divisive nature of the Falklands problem in domestic politics, patience had been put first in statecraft, before vision and the will to apply it.

In May 1979, the Conservatives came to power, led by Margaret Thatcher. The new prime minister spoke of 'nation' and put it first and foremost. When it came to the European future envisaged by her predecessor as Conservative leader, Edward Heath, she had little difficulty in restraining her enthusiasms. The Foreign Office was *not* her favourite department. Over many years, it had been advocating what it saw as a prudent withdrawal from an imperial postscript of barren islands in the South Atlantic. In general terms, and over Europe in particular, Margaret Thatcher felt it had protected British interests with insufficient vigour. The next in a long line of ministers to be presented with the dossier on the Falklands was Nicholas Ridley, and the new foreign secretary was Lord Carrington.

The potential for military confrontation clearly existed. But it is also true that down the years, unless and until they sprang from the shadows in the South Atlantic during crises, the Falklands sank to astonishingly low levels of interest.

In 1979, three years before the Falklands war, what considerations were active concerning the Falklands in Mrs Thatcher's government as the Conservatives returned to power? The permanent under-secretary of the Foreign Office and head of the Diplomatic Service from 1975 until 1982 was **Sir Michael Palliser**.

The first thing that one has to say is that, when a new Conservative government came into office, the Falklands was not very high on its list of priorities. That's not a criticism, that was perfectly understandable.

Lord Carrington was to say, subsequently, that it was Number 249 in his priorities! Now, allowing for the hyperbole of that, was it?

Well, he said that and I don't think that is incorrect. There were two, or perhaps three, main foreign policy priorities at that time. One was simply the development of the European Community. The other was the broader East–West relationship, Nato and the Warsaw Pact, and how we combined being fully within the European Community with being fully a member of Nato – that general context of questions which is always high on any foreign secretary's list of priorities. The other was Rhodesia. I think the Falklands was quite a long way down the line, and I believe it was right that it should be.

With what hopes, with what expectations, did the Foreign Office believe, with the Conservatives back in power, that the time had come to really try and settle the issue this time?

I think the poor Foreign Office has always had to accept a relatively low level of hope and expectation; because it has never been very easy to persuade ministers and Cabinets to pay much attention, either to Argentina, or to the Falklands. And if one thinks of what the Falklands represented in absolute terms – I mean, a small village in terms of size, and if one also thinks of the general sort of attitude towards Argentina which is prevalent in this country – it is perhaps not that surprising, but it is frustrating for the people in the Foreign Office who have to deal with Latin America and with the post-colonial problems and the relationship between the two.

But what was the essence of your advice that the time had *come to try again, given the hostile reception Michael Stewart and Lord Chalfont had had earlier, in the sixties?*

Well, first of all, that was some time back. Secondly, as always, there was a new junior minister, minister of state,[9] in the Foreign Office responsible for the problem. I think stage one in the process had been to persuade *him* – and I don't say that was difficult, it wasn't – that this was, probably, one of the most difficult and one of the most important problems within his area and responsibilities to that part of the world. To encourage him, when he could, to go out there and see for himself. Explaining to him what had happened in the past; outlining to him the ideas for settlement, including leaseback, which was not the only one. Explaining to him some of the difficulties we had had in the past about negotiating.

How successful had Lord Carrington been in getting the prime minister herself to concentrate on the Falkland Islands issue?

I think one has to say only moderately. I would say not just the prime minister, but more the Cabinet, or the Cabinet committee concerned,[10] where I think there was, again, a perfectly understandable

9 Nicholas Ridley.

10 The Defence and Overseas policy committee or 'OD', the standing committee of the Cabinet for discussing and deciding foreign policy and defence issues, chaired by the Prime Minister, includes the foreign and defence secretaries and the chancellor.

reluctance to seem to be negotiating away a British possession. And, as always, a feeling that perhaps this was not as significant a problem as the Foreign Office seemed to think it was.

We had of course negotiated away, over the years, a great many British possessions. What was the special quality about this one, at this time, with this government?

I suppose the more you've negotiated away, the more difficult each subsequent one becomes to negotiate. That's perhaps paradoxical, but I think politically that's probably the case.

Would you agree that Mrs Thatcher comes to power with an unspoken slogan, 'no more retreats' — neither on the domestic front against the trade unions nor in foreign policy issues? She stood for an end to retreat. Is that a psychological factor of importance when one comes to an issue like this?

I'm not sure how far the national mood was 'no more retreat'. That may be so. But I think it's more that we were dealing in the case of Argentina with what struck a lot of people in this country, both in politics and elsewhere, as a rather unattractive military regime. I think it was more – it comes back to the point of priorities. There is a limit, I think, to the number of problems that any government wants to have on its plate in a big way at any time.

The government had major problems in Europe with our European partners over the budget contribution and so on, which after all took a number of years to resolve. Then the government had an absolutely major problem with Rhodesia. I'm talking now of foreign policy problems. Also, although, at that stage, it wasn't perceived perhaps quite so clearly, there was no doubt that before too long there would have to be a negotiation over Hong Kong.

So, I think it was understandable, if regrettable, that the government felt, as I'm sure they did feel, 'Oh, let's not have more problems on our plate over the Falklands, surely that can be *managed*. We don't want the Falklands lobby adding to all the rest of the difficulties.'

So we have Sir Michael Palliser's word for it that Lord Carrington and the Foreign Office were 'only moderately successful' in engaging the prime minister's attention for the Falklands. Margaret Thatcher was insistent the question should not be brought before the Cabinet for decision until the supposedly much more charged and emotional Rhodesian negotiation was out of the way.

Throughout 1979 and 1980 Lord Carrington carried through a settlement in Rhodesia, the most unyielding of the issues from the colonial era, against the instincts of a formidable array of Conservative backbenchers; many of whom were Mrs Thatcher's closest supporters. The inherently divisive nature of the Rhodesian negotiations is one reason why Lord Carrington held back over the Falklands. The more trivial issue was simply relegated. It was only against the background of a serious risk of conflict if there were no progress in negotiations that he eventually won support in the Cabinet to attempt the 'Hong Kong solution', or leaseback.

However, it is clear that he did so without any lively anticipation of Nicholas Ridley's success. One of those present when the Cabinet approved the attempt to promote leaseback was the defence secretary, **Francis Pym**, now Lord Pym.

A number of prime ministers did not think the effort of trying to solve this 'problem' was worth while, because of the political difficulty of achieving it. To give Mrs Thatcher and Lord Carrington their due, they took a different view. They proposed that we *should* make a new attempt to see if we could not find some way of stabilizing a position which had worried foreign secretaries for decades, and certainly the Foreign Office, and quite rightly, because of the inherent danger of the problem. I think it's highly commendable that Mrs Thatcher and Lord Carrington decided to have a go at doing this.

We know what transpired when Nicholas Ridley came back. He simply proposed that he was going to have *discussions* with Argentina and with the Islanders, or rather continue the discussions which he had begun, to see what could be arranged. I think there was no voice in the House of Commons that expressed any sympathy for what he was trying to do from any party. That really did seem to knock the initiative on the head.

I think it was a very, very great tragedy. Because what has happened as a result of the Falklands war is that the problem and the difficulty remains precisely the same, but infinitely more difficult to solve. That's the position we're in today.

Can you recall what hopes the Cabinet entertained, when it took that decision in 1979, that its recommendations would have a different reception from the one handed out, ten years or so earlier, to the Labour Government's ministers, Michael Stewart and Alun Chalfont?

The Cabinet view was that the initiative was well worth taking; that it was likely to be difficult in the House of Commons, but that it was absolutely right to try. I endorse that completely.

What preparation there was within the Party, and within Parliament, for what Ridley was going to say I do not know. My impression from reading Hansard is that what he had to say took everybody absolutely by surprise, and when you come forward and make a surprise announcement in the House of Commons you do, almost always, land up with a flea in your ear. They do react rather like that. Whereas if there had been a considerable amount of preparation beforehand, the outcome, and the exchanges, might have been different. It may be that the chief whip and Nicholas Ridley himself may have tried to prepare the ground a bit. The impression is that they did not. The result was that the House of Commons turned down all idea of trying to do anything except maintain the status quo.

So I think it was a blow. Whether it could have been avoided by better preparation inside Parliament is a question which I couldn't answer, wouldn't know.

But it's one that you're eminently fitted to speak upon as a former chief whip and leader of the House? Here is an issue upon which former ministers and previous governments have been impaled by hostile back-bench opinion. That only makes it more remarkable that more care was not taken, to use this word subsequently used in the Franks Report, to 'educate the House of Commons, and public opinion'.

Yes, well, I'm bound to agree with that. It certainly would be my view that if that were the proposal coming forward it would have been possible to do a much greater degree of preparation – that is my clear impression – which might have led to a different result. It was new to people. Just like the first time joining the European Community came before the Commons. Everybody resisted it. But, no, when they *think* about it and talk about it they come round to it. Exactly the same applied in a big change like that as to the Falkland Islands. But in retrospect the House of Commons has to accept responsibility for an instant reaction which, on more careful consideration, might have been different.

No one came to Mr Ridley's rescue as he made that announcement in the House of Commons, as Lord Carrington subsequently lamented. But that does leave one speculating on the degree, or nature, of support that there was for it in the Cabinet?

Yes. I do not think it was an issue that the Cabinet regarded as of overwhelming importance, and obviously it was not. It is the kind of issue where a Cabinet would leave the thinking, and the preparation, to the ministers concerned, in this case the Foreign Office ministers and the prime minister, rather than become involved themselves.

The Government accepted the defeat of leaseback in Parliament, without accepting that this had consequences for negotiations, or for the predictable, and often forecast, response from Argentina.

The development of crisis, and eventually war, with Argentina is inseparable from the intense debate which began at this time about

British defence policy. It concerned the whole future direction of Britain as a nation state. Cuts were being demanded in defence spending which bore most heavily on the surface Fleet. Francis Pym, who was reluctant to make those cuts, was moved by the prime minister from his position as defence secretary in 1981. Pym's eventual replacement as defence secretary was **Sir John Nott**. As far as he was concerned, even though old bulwarks of the Navy were due to melt away in the contemplated defence review, implications for the Falklands barely intruded early in Mrs Thatcher's first term.

I did not attend the first collective discussion of it in Cabinet Committee, chaired by Mrs Thatcher, but I remember attending the second. I recall that there was a determination to press forward with the sovereignty negotiations on the basis of a long leaseback, but there was concern whether this could ever be pushed through the House of Commons. I was in favour of this move but I was sceptical about whether we could get away with it. There was deep opposition among a very tenacious group of the Tory party against any such idea. And, indeed, it failed.

Was it an issue which lent itself to manipulation by a few?

Yes. It was not an issue involving great national interest, but there were some very dedicated people who made it one of the key areas of interest for them. The Falkland Islanders had many very close friends. There were what I would call the 'global strategists'. I've never been able to understand the global strategists' views of the importance of the South Atlantic, frankly. I'm puzzled still by it, although I understand the importance of the South African question.

Then there were people who genuinely felt warmly for the Falkland Islanders and their ancestry, and the difficulty of their lives. There were people who were deeply attached to exploration, to 'Scott of the Antarctic', naturalists. It was an amalgam of a group of people, I think very admirable people – not just Tory 'backwoodsmen'.

But what were the imperatives as you saw it about the Falklands, and the need to settle it, given the risks that the Government would face predictably in the House of Commons?

I'm the wrong person to ask because, although I always had strong views on aspects of foreign policy, I was not and I am not by nature someone who's ever shown a particular interest in the subject. Therefore I attended meetings on the Falkland Islands as I attended meetings on a thousand other issues. But the Falkland Islands did not interest me; therefore I'm the wrong person to ask. It was never my

responsibility initially in Trade[11] and it had no relevance. When I
went to Defence[12] we had a platoon of Royal Marines there and, OK,
looking back on it I *should* have shown greater interest in their welfare
and equipment, but I did not.

I don't think I would have really spent a lot of time mugging up my
brief on matters surrounding the Falklands. I did not consider it to be
of any importance in my life.

Those last words of Sir John Nott echo almost exactly what Michael
Stewart, Labour's foreign secretary, had said of his time and the
Falklands dilemma in 1968. The Islands remained an adamant colonial
anachronism of loyalty, steadfastly preferring the rule of London.

On 2 December 1980, the minister of state, Nicholas Ridley, freshly
returned from Port Stanley – where he had found the majority of
Islanders opposed to it – put the 'Hong Kong' solution of leaseback
before Parliament as one of the possible bases for a settlement. There
was an immediate and conspicuous revolution of the Commons. The
minister was blown away by the guns of the Falkland Islands lobby. The
House united against what Julian Amery called 'a profoundly disturbing
statement'. One witness of this unnerving spectacle was soon to be
Ridley's successor as minister of state in the Foreign Office responsible
for the Falkland Islands, **Richard Luce**.

I can only say I happened to be sitting in the Chamber when Nicholas
Ridley was making this statement about leaseback. I have never seen
such a mauling, of any of my colleagues, in all my life. Nicholas
Ridley, who had shown great courage in putting this forward, was
looking pretty white by the end of it, poor chap. He had had a very
rough ride indeed. Now, that rough ride was not just from the
Conservative side; it was from the Labour side; it was from the
Liberals. It was absolutely united in its violent sense of opposition to
the idea of leaseback.

The insubordination of the House of Commons, with its tendency to
kick a man when he is up, was an even more punishing repetition of the
demoralizing defeat of the Foreign Office ministers, Michael Stewart
and Lord Chalfont, in the Labour Government in 1968. The case of the
Falkland Islands refuted the general truth that history does not repeat
itself. Infirm of policy, the Government faltered. It lost sight of the
burgeoning difficulties in the South Atlantic.

11 Sir John Nott was minister for trade 1979–81.
12 1981.

With the defeat of leaseback, the last of diplomacy's creative options, innovation was finally exhausted. It was left to the Foreign Office to try and square the circle, but armed now only with ineffectual good intentions. The Foreign Office could negotiate, it seemed, with almost everyone except the vigilant body of opinion in its own Parliament.

4

A Totally Uncompromising Lobby

Every dog, it is said, is allowed one bite. The Falkland Islands lobby, however, was a watchdog that bit all the time. In consequence, over the years, successive governments approached it reluctantly and with extreme caution. Twice, Foreign Office ministers responsible for the Falklands had come to deliver notice to Parliament that the national interest, and that of the eighteen hundred Islanders, required a political solution in which sovereignty eventually would be transferred to Argentina. They were chased back down this recommended path, forced always in the end to leap for safety behind the nullifying assurances that the wishes of the Islanders came first.

Ministers entered into these encounters, as Lord Chalfont has described for us his own experience in 1968, 'quite unprepared for the degree of passionate opposition'; they 'emerged white and shaken', like Nicholas Ridley after the mauling he received when he stood up to propose leaseback to the House of Commons in 1980. One of the most persistent and effective pressure groups in modern British politics was subsequently described by a former head of the Foreign Office, Lord Greenhill, as a 'totally uncompromising lobby'.

Its spearhead was the Falkland Islands Committee, formed in the 1960s to defend the interests of the Falkland Islands Company, the absentee landlord which largely controlled the Islands' farms and therefore their economy. This was at the time when under George Brown, and later Michael Stewart, as foreign secretary, negotiations were in progress with Argentina over the future sovereignty of the Falklands. The Committee's prime mover was a Lincolns Inn barrister, who was also a former Foreign Office diplomat who had served in Buenos Aires, **William Hunter Christie**.

In a preface to what became a standard work on Antarctic politics written by Hunter Christie shortly after the Second World War, Sir Reginald Leeper of the Foreign Office said, 'It was his task to master the past history of the Falkland Islands', and added, 'It is important to know why there should be any dispute about regions where no human settlements can be imagined in any foreseeable future.'

That's why I wrote the book. First of all in an attempt to anticipate the confrontation which, at that time, I saw as inevitable because there had already been confrontation over the dependencies when we were otherwise engaged during the war of 1939–45.

I have always regarded those regions as economically extremely important. I have also regarded them as politically important. Primarily it is the balance of power between Argentina and Chile, which for more than a century Britain maintained by having the Falkland Islands and keeping on good terms with both countries, and which we saw degenerate into something very nearly war between Chile and Argentina in 1980 and '81. It has always been an explosive part of the world. Finally, I wrote the book because I felt that they had been very neglected by the British people. People, on the whole, were ignorant about the Antarctic sector and the Falkland Islands and none of them had any idea – and few of them have now – of the colossal potential and economic importance of those areas. We are seeing something of it in the development of fisheries.

And it is going to be a very brave government that gives away what may be the largest remaining unexploited oilfield in the world. That was the kind of thing that I wished to get across to people.

Is that enough in itself to explain the situation which led to the formation of the Falkland Islands Committee in London in the 1960s?

Do you want its earliest roots? I attended a meeting of the Court of the Worshipful Company of Clockmakers, of which I was then a member, and, at the end of lunch, another member of the Court came up to me. He was a senior officer, serving at that time in the Admiralty, Captain Pennefather, Royal Navy and a member of the Committee still. And he said, 'Bill, George Brown's gone mad! He wants to sell the Falkland Islands to Argentina. I can't do anything about it. *You* have to do something about it!'

And so I came back and thought what to do. I knew the Chairman of the Falkland Islands Company, Patrick Ainsley, who was a solicitor in New Square, and I went round to see him, and I told him what I'd been told. He said, 'Well, it's astonishing. I'm just looking at a cable from my manager in Port Stanley saying more or less what you've said to me, and I haven't any idea at all what to do.' And I said, 'Well, we must get a committee together, and we must resist this. *You* can't do it, because everybody will say it's the Falkland Islands Company trying to defend its own property, and the capitalists and so on. We must have an all-party committee, and we must run a political campaign and get this into the open, and use the press.' And he said, 'Right ho.' And the next thing I heard, a few days later, was asking me to attend a meeting at the then offices of the Falkland Islands Company, at 97 Piccadilly. At that meeting Peter Scott was present. I was there. There were the directors of the Falkland Islands Company.

Peter Scott, the son of Scott of the Antarctic?

Yes, and we all gave our ideas. Peter agreed with me that that was the course to take, and emphasized that it had to be all-party, and we got a promise from the Falkland Islands Company that they would pay our expenses. We got Labour members of Parliament to join, we got Conservative and we got Liberal members. And we set to work.

The Falkland Islands lobby was an alchemy of politics drawn largely from the right of the Conservative Party, but extending also to Fabian socialists, who saw in the evolving Commonwealth a secular agency for good. The lobby was linked to great names which stirred the memory, like the last of the great imperial adventurers, Scott of the Antarctic, an Agamemnon dead on the ice, and a reminder of the moral quality in the British contribution to the Antarctic – unprofitable, but magnificent.

The House of Commons is flesh and blood, with its full share of great and petty aspirations. Combined with lobbying for a commercial commitment to the Islands was a political view that the Falklands were legally a part of the British community around the world; something to be defended. When Britain's secret diplomacy over the Islands' future became known in 1968, an indispensable condition for a pressure group to flourish was fulfilled. Among those present at its creation was a passionate traditionalist on the Conservative back benches, **Sir Bernard Braine**.

Many of us were concerned about the attitude of the Foreign and Commonwealth Office which seemed ambivalent on the issue. Indeed the impression given to us was that the Falklands were an obstacle to the improvement of relations. We might sell more arms, for example, to the dictatorships of Latin America if only we could get 'the Malvinas' out of the way. So, whereas Parliament as a whole was concerned about safeguarding the interests of these little people, British like ourselves, the Foreign Office was taking the larger view.

The real story is quite disgraceful. There is a perceptive passage in Joe Haines's book, Harold Wilson's press secretary, which shows very clearly how decision makers viewed the matter at the time. This is what he wrote. I have it here. 'If it were possible to compress the FCO's ideal world into a single concept I suppose it would look something like a Common Market peopled entirely by crusading anti-Communist Bedouin. If I lived in Gibraltar, or the Falkland Islands, I would not sleep at night for worrying about it. Because, so far as policy is concerned, those territories are peripheral.'[1]

It made no difference to you, from the outset in the 1960s, that this was indeed a very small minority, a handful of people?

No, not at all. The important thing is that the Falkland Islanders had been there up to six generations, they had peacefully settled in the Falkland Islands, and by what *right* did a fascist dictatorship, next door, demand that sovereignty over them should be transferred!

My recollection is that we were kept in the dark. Not only we, but the British people and Parliament, were kept in the dark about what was happening. We first learnt about the way things were drifting in 1968 when Falkland Islanders themselves addressed an open letter to members of Parliament of all parties saying, 'Do you know what's happening? We are going to be handed over to the Argentine. We don't *want* to be handed over to the Argentine. We're British. Can you do something about it?'

Well, no doubt other members of Parliament received the same letter, dated the 27th February, and it was from the unofficial members of the Falkland Islands Executive Council. 'Are you aware', the letter ran, 'that negotiations are now proceeding between the British and Argentine governments which may result at any moment in the handing over of the Falkland Islands to the Argentine? Take note, that the inhabitants of the Islands have never yet been *consulted* regarding their future. They do not want to become Argentines. They are as British as you are and mostly of English and Scottish ancestry, even to the sixth generation. Five out of six were born in the Islands. Many elderly people have never been elsewhere. There is no racial problem, no unemployment, no poverty, and we are not in debt. Are you aware that the people of these Islands do not wish to submit to a foreign language, law, customs and culture? Because for one hundred and thirty five years they have happily pursued their own peaceful way of life, a very British way of life. Lord Caradon[2] said to the general assembly of the United Nations in 1965, "the people of this territory are not to be betrayed or bartered. Their wishes and their

1 Joe Haines, *The Politics of Power* (Cape, 1977).
2 Permanent UK representative to UN, 1964–70.

interests are paramount, and we should do our duty in protecting them." British ministers have said the same until 1967, since when there has been silence. Question. Is our tiny community to be used as a pawn in power politics? Do you not feel ashamed that this wicked thing may suddenly be foisted on us? What can you do to prevent it? What *are* you doing? We need your help.'

Well, all I can tell you is that I, and the other recipients of the letter, did everything we could to prevent it. I might say in passing that this plea is on notepaper headed with the arms of the Falkland Islands colony, beneath which is the motto, 'Desire the Right.'

This bugle call from the far South Atlantic set the wild echoes flying. The true substance of the Falkland Islands lobby was always in Westminster and Whitehall, rather than Port Stanley. Its active supporters in Parliament were a relative, but significant, few. One does not look in the ranks of the lobby for those prepared to abandon former imperial commitments with apathy or resignation.

Their responses had their roots in tradition. Although the chiefs of staff advised succeeding British governments that the Falkland Islands no longer possessed strategic importance, the past, for champions of the Falklands, was not dead. To them it was, in the widest sense, a usable past, and it was a framework for the authority of a Conservative of intellectual conviction, like **Sir John Biggs-Davison**.

I had always been aware of the importance of the Falkland Islands to Britain. There were two decisive naval actions, in two world wars, fought in those waters and the strategic importance of the Falklands was clear. If there were to be another war, then Panama might well be put out of action, and the route around the Horn would be most important. It was therefore vital that the Falkland Islands should be in reliable hands. That is one argument, the strategic argument.

Then there is the argument that this is British sovereign territory. It is inhabited by a population that is certainly more British than the population of London. There is no reason therefore why those people should not be allowed to live their lives in peace, and it was the duty of any British government to defend that right.

One is very struck, though, by the fierceness of your denunciation in the Parliamentary debates in 1968 – 'A solution of shame and ignominy', you said, in talking of Lord Chalfont's proposals: 'Disastrous diplomacy'. You go on to lament the inability of the House of Commons to bring Chalfont to the Bar of the House, as of course he was in the House of Lords, and 'impeachment of him' was not open to you.

Well, I think that sounds rather good! I was younger then, and perhaps I was more lurid in my language. But I don't think I'm more extreme in my language than the language which is now applied to the Government[3] by those on the other side who would like to, even now, just surrender the Falklands.

But in those years the cardinal objective of British foreign policy was to pave the way for the new realities after empire. That pointed to the European Community. What resonance did the Falklands have for you, therefore, in that context?

Well, I myself made a proposal which I hoped would be conciliatory towards Argentina. I have always looked on Argentina as a country with which Britain has had close relations. There are many people of British stock in Argentina and they have always looked to this country for inspiration in many fields. Indeed, if Argentina had been part of the British Empire and part of what was now the British Commonwealth then this question might have been resolved in a better way. And that end was not impossible – that Argentina *could* have become part of the British Empire. That, of course, is all over.

But in 1968 I put forward my proposal that the Argentine flag should fly in the Falklands with other allied flags and that the Falklands might become the headquarters, and the base, of a South Atlantic Treaty Organization. We have Nato, but there are many dangers to the West in those areas which are not covered by Nato, and it has long been an idea that there should be a southern hemisphere defence organization stretching from Australia through Southern Africa to South America.

So with the Foreign Office advising ministers, down the years, that something must be done about the status of the Falklands, you saw it as in the portrait you paint in your book, Tory Lives, *of Viscount Falkland – that same Falkland who gave his name to what was then Falkland's Island? You wrote of 'his wise maxim' concerning the episcopacy, 'When it is not necessary to change, it is* necessary *not to change.'*

I think that is a very good Tory maxim. Yes. I think the Foreign Office was wrong. Indeed they have been proved wrong.

How far were you influenced by possibilities like those which Leo Amery had articulated as Secretary of State for the Colonies in the 1920s, when he talked of Britain's need to develop her role in opening up and controlling the development of the Antarctic?

Leo Amery is a statesman who has had a great influence on my own thinking. He was extraordinarily far-seeing. He saw, as Joseph

3 The Thatcher government.

Chamberlain[4] had seen before him, that Britain had already begun to decline and that the industrial decline of the British had really set in before the nineteenth century was out. He thought it was necessary for Britain to organize itself within a larger grouping. For Chamberlain it was the Empire. Leo Amery much preferred the term 'Commonwealth', and *he* saw that you could not hold together a group of completely sovereign states unless you had an economic structure. That is why he was an enthusiast for Commonwealth preference. Then, after the Second World War, he joined this enthusiasm for Commonwealth, and for a Commonwealth preferential area, with the idea of a United Europe.

Amery was one of those who thought out something very remarkable. It was called the Strasbourg Plan. It was accepted by the whole of the Consultative Assembly of the Council of Europe and then pigeon-holed by the ministers. It would have married the European and Commonwealth interests. It would have provided a first preference, in Britain, for the British Commonwealth, and a first preference, in France, for French Union territories. Then there would have been a secondary level of preference for the other European powers.

This extraordinarily imaginative idea was, unfortunately, shelved. I believe it was shelved because of the dominant concept in the Foreign Office that nothing should be done to offend the United States. The United States, frankly, did not *want* Britain to be very powerful. It had successfully undermined the British Empire's economic system. Nor, I believe, did it want Western Europe to be too powerful either.

We are closer, aren't we, to an understanding of why you felt that membership of the European Community did not imply retreat from older commitments overseas? What is the relevance of the Falklands today to the British position in the world?

It fits into the very nature of the British nation. It is an offshoot of the British nation. Not a polyglot community as London is today. It is perhaps the most *British* part of the British nation. To betray that is to betray the nation itself. It would have, I believe, a very bad and a very profound effect on our moral standing in the world.

Support for the 'Kelpers' in the Falklands was not only loyal defence of a small minority, but a flag of convenience which draped a view of Britain itself as a nation state, where and what it stood for, in the moral solemnity of self-determination. That support was overlaid by the

4 Colonial Secretary in Salisbury's Conservative Government, 1895.

knowledge that it had been British energies and enterprise which had done more to open up the entire Antarctic region than any other power. The opinion that Antarctica might turn out to be a frozen Eldorado was sustained by another influential Conservative who was the holder of a great name in matters of empire, Leo Amery's son, **Julian Amery**.

To begin with, I have always been interested in the Falklands. My father, when he was at the Colonial Office after World War I, took the view that the Antarctic continent could be the repository of great wealth, and he staked out claims for Britain which remain to this day. Some were overlapped with Chilean and Argentinian claims. But there may be untold wealth under the ice-cap and, when technology is advanced, there may be many things there that could be important to us.

There is also the importance, strategically, of the passage around Cape Horn, supposing the Panama Canal was blocked. This could be important to us; and not only to us in Britain, but to the whole western world.

Your father, I think, also took the view that our contribution to the task of building up a European union, which he had in mind, would depend on our remaining an imperial power. Is there something of that in these views of yours concerning the South Atlantic, and the opportunities that it offers Britain?

I think it is obvious enough that Europe is, after all, a rocky peninsula of the Euro-Asian continent. We've never had, in all our history of many hundreds of years, the resources to develop Europe as it should be developed; which is why the Spanish and Portuguese, French, Dutch, British went overseas to find the resources they needed to make Europe what it has become. And, therefore, this might be perhaps the last barrel in the gun which would provide new resources for Europe.

But Leo Amery's vision was founded on this notion of a Britannic commonwealth. There was not much left of that, in substance, when you became a minister of state at the Foreign Office in 1972?

But you must remember that my father was a vice-president of the European Movement precisely because he thought that the development of Europe depended on cooperation with the Commonwealth. When I was an under-secretary for the Colonies[5] there was quite a lot left of the old British imperial system. By the time I went to the Foreign Office most of that had gone.

5 1958–60.

That is why one wonders where the validity of your father's ideas lies in the world you inherit as a minister in 1972. Why are sub-Antarctica and Antarctica relevant to the building up of a European union?

We were present in the Falklands and South Georgia. The islands are the natural approach to the Antarctic continent. If the wealth of the Antarctic continent were to be developed, we were in a position not only to take part in that development but to offer others, like the Argentine, Chile, the United States – or other European countries – facilities by sea, or by air, to develop this wealth.

It seemed to me always absurd that we should surrender this asset when we could join in it, and get others to join with us in it. When you think of it, if people are to invest capital they want security. I doubt whether many international or multinational companies would have had much sense of security in Argentine or Chilean firms. They might have had in something that was British based.

The belief that Britain should make a commitment to the fruits of its exploration in the Antarctic region found strong echoes in 'Fabian imperialism' and Labour policy. It was exemplified, in the 1970s, by the survey of resources in and around the Falklands, the Shackleton Report. Lord Shackleton, a Labour peer, was the son of the explorer. His father's epic open-boat journey to South Georgia, following the loss of the Antarctic expedition ship *Endurance* during the First World War, was the climax of the day and age of the explorers. As a parade of the classical virtues, it ranked with Scott. The name of Shackleton's ship was passed down to its naval successors. Following the Second World War the ice-patrol ship HMS *Endurance* became the symbol of the British interest in, and commitment to defend, the Falkland Islands. The imperial urge in general might be over, but the feeling that the British were bred to great things was not dismissible. Whether sitting in Labour Cabinets, or on the back benches, **Lord Shackleton** himself could hardly help but serve as an at times reproachful reminder of the heroic age of British endeavour in the Antarctic.

I was in Cabinet when George Brown first raised the future of the Falklands, and I remember, I made a brief intervention in which I said, 'Are we talking about the Falklands? What about South Georgia?' And there was a sort of hush, because nobody had heard of South Georgia. I remember Harold Wilson saying, 'Does anybody live there?' And I said, 'Not regularly, although *my father is buried there*', and that was that.

In those days I did not have any very strong views regarding the Falklands. I was not tremendously committed to the Antarctic.

Having had a famous Antarctic explorer as a father I had rather deliberately kept away from the Antarctic. I mean it was . . . I did find it moving to go to his grave, but I belonged to a generation before the war when, at Oxford and Cambridge, we were debunkers. We didn't believe a great deal in carrying the British flag.

My father wished to carry the Union Jack to the South Pole and subsequently lay it at my mother's feet. That was not our generation's motivation. But, going to South Georgia and seeing his grave, and seeing that incredibly beautiful island, I did find it moving. I may disappoint people by not being *more* moved by it. People who were there – my secretary was there – thought that it liberated me from my inhibitions over my father. Perhaps it did a bit. There is no doubt it was the most astonishing achievement. You've only got to look at South Georgia, and look at those mountains, to wonder how three men could have crossed it without any equipment late in the year.[6] I tried to fly over his route when I was down there in a helicopter, and we couldn't get over those mountains because the weather was down. If my father, and it was later in the year, encountered that weather, he would never have got across. It was a great achievement. I had a hero for a father.

The 'explorers' were another element within the lobby of support for the Falklands. They joined there the 'old imperialists' and the 'global strategists'. In addition to those Conservatives who simply wished to 'conserve', by resisting or deferring all choices of which the nation was suspicious, were those who felt that loyalty to the Falkland Islanders was loyalty to the ancient polity and homogeneity of Britain itself.

At the time the Falklands diplomacy was first under way in the 1960s, the question of Ulster had once more surfaced at the heart of domestic politics. Like the Falklanders, the people of Ulster demanded separation from their nearest neighbour, and a loyal union with Britain. Any precedents established in transferring sovereignty over a small British minority abroad had resonance, therefore, closer to home. This concern about possible precedents for the way other British minorities might come to be viewed, like the loyalist population of Ulster, enlisted in **Sir John Biggs-Davison** a natural upholder of the Falkland Islanders' cause.

Of course, the Ulstermen have made a comparison between their position and that of the Falkland Islanders, and they have placed the

6 In September 1915, *Endurance* was crushed in pack ice and sank. Five months later Shackleton and his men took to the boats, landing April 1916 on Elephant Island. From there with six men he sailed 800 miles in an open boat to South Georgia.

Foreign Office in the dock as an agency which has been trying to get rid both of the Falkland Islands and of Northern Ireland. And there is a certain truth in this. It seems to me that Argentina was almost encouraged to invade the Falklands. It is another unnecessary war. Winston Churchill called the Second World War 'the unnecessary war'; perhaps both world wars were unnecessary; perhaps both came about because of uncertainty about the resolve of the British. Certainly, General Galtieri would not have attacked if he had *known* what the response would be. To this extent, there are elements in the Foreign Office who certainly were guilty of virtually encouraging the Argentines to invade.

Now, in Northern Ireland, I can remember once talking to a Foreign Office official concerned about the Ulster question and he said, 'Oh, of course we in the Foreign Office are neutral about the Union.' Now, he spoke only for himself, and I do not think he is in that position any more, but that was their manner of thinking. It arises, I think, not so much from a sort of Enoch Powell 'conspiracy', as a desire for the removal of questions which embarrass relations.

But was it this preoccupation of yours with 'separateness' that led you on to champion the Islanders? Like the ancient heroes of Ulster that you have written about, you saw perhaps, in the Falklands issue, what they upheld in Ulster? That their fight was a separatist, *not a nationalist, fight?*

The stand of the Falkland Islanders was not separatist. It was a desire to remain part of the community to which they belong – the national community of the British! They are my fellow subjects and I think any Briton worthy of the name would support his fellow subjects when they are confronted with unjust annexation.

But separate in the sense of their refusal to accept 'Home Rule' ever since it was proposed by Gladstone, and to remain separate from the Republic?

Coming to the Ulstermen, yes, they did refuse to accept Dublin government. I think they were right. In *theory*, Home Rule constitutions which were proposed were not destructive of the United Kingdom itself. I would say that it was clearly seen by Carson that it would not stop there. Just as he saw that the Dominion status conferred upon the Irish Free State would not stop there either. And these predictions were perfectly correct.

But that, to me, is the connection made in your mind at the outset in the 1960s when Britain is preparing to cede sovereignty over the Falklands. The Falkland Islanders were not demanding 'nation', they were simply demanding not to be incorporated, and that clearly had overtones for someone with your own active concerns for nation, I suggest?

In Ulster, there is clearly an element of 'separateness' in the national consciousness. Of course there is. You are different from other people. I think it takes a patriot to appreciate the patriotism of other countries. But *the nation* is a reality. I do not believe that the nation is some sort of transient phenomenon due to be sucked into wider and wider international organizations. I do not believe in world government. I think that world government is the doctrine of world conquerors. I think that the glory of human civilization is the diversity of nations. That does imply 'separateness'. But it also implies understanding, and regard for separateness.

But it would also explain your violent antipathy, as witness your enthusiasm for impeachment of Lord Chalfont, to a solution which proposed to incorporate this 'separateness' of the Islanders in union with Argentina and in what the Foreign Office saw as the wider, and the larger, British interest?

Well, it would not be in the British national interest to hand these Islands over to an undependable power. We know that we have, at the moment, a democratic government in Argentina. We have had democratic governments there before, and they have fallen to military dictatorship. I believe it is necessary to the security of the Western Alliance that the Falkland Islands remain in dependable British hands. So, *that* is the British interest.

What I want to emphasize is that while resolute for British sovereignty, and the rights of British people in the Falkland Islands, I was always proposing that we go into some grouping with Argentina which would include the Falkland Islands and would enable Argentina to play some part – with us – in the security and development of the South Atlantic and, indeed, Antarctica.

The feeling that the British interest in Latin America and Antarctica had been only feebly upheld makes an early appearance in, and was a theme of, the book written in 1949 by **William Hunter Christie**, the organizer of the Falkland Islands Committee.

In *The Antarctic Problem*, Hunter Christie had set out the political background to the disputed claims involving Argentina, Britain and Chile. He sought to address the reason why there should be any argument over a frozen continent where the largest living animal was 'a wingless gnat, five eighths of an inch long'. Dr Nicanor Costa Méndez, the Argentine foreign minister, wryly acknowledged the role played by this former British diplomat in the frustration of Argentine ambitions, and referred to him as 'another devilish lawyer'.

Hunter Christie's success as a lobbyist was to mobilize and publicize what were, at times, unvarnished sentiments for the proposition that it was inconceivable any land inhabited by British peoples could willingly be surrendered to the domination of a foreign power.

> People who have made their homes somewhere ought to be able to run their own affairs. To some extent, therefore, the book was defensive. It was defending the right of the people in the Falkland Islands to decide their own future for themselves. That is what has always motivated everybody who's helped them, at this end, in the United Kingdom Falkland Islands Committee. If they decided they wanted to become Argentines, fine. It was just Britain's bad luck if she lost all these resources. But, as far as I was concerned, I wanted to get the record straight, get the facts out, show what it was that Argentina and Chile were saying about the Antarctic territories, as well as putting our own case.
>
> Decolonization has got nothing whatever to do with ceding territory to other countries. Nothing at all. It is the right of the people who inhabit the country to decide their own future for themselves. I feel very strongly about that, and I always have done.
>
> I'd like to instance a Labour member of Parliament, Stan Newens, who said in a Foreign Affairs Labour Party Committee that he'd spent his whole life working for the freeing of the subject peoples of the British Empire, and he wasn't going to hand the last two thousand over to a bunch of . . . er . . . he used a word which today would not be very popular, and I won't repeat it.

To a bunch of what?

> I think he said, 'dagos'. He was a left-wing Labour member of Parliament, and he took the view that he wasn't going to see his life's work finished by simply handing over a colonial people against their will. It did not matter whether they were black, white or khaki. He felt just as strongly about white people in the Falkland Islands as he felt about black people in Africa.

It is not the normal function of back-bench MPs to originate policy, but they can frustrate the adoption of policies they dislike. The rise of 'party' has diminished their chances of independence, and the ability of the House of Commons to check the executive is limited today by the growth of power and complexity in Whitehall.

In this sense the Falklands provided a good issue from the outset. Unlike the major spending departments of government in Britain, the Foreign Office is not down at the House of Commons every day. It was at a considerable disadvantage, particularly in the early years of the Falklands dispute, before the innovation of Select Committees and therefore a Foreign Affairs Select Committee, in explaining to the political parties what the dangers were, and why it felt a settlement had got to be reached. The consistent advice of the chiefs of staff that the Islands were indefensible, and that there were immeasurably greater British interests, sustained the Foreign Office in taking a larger view. **Sir Bernard Braine**, however, saw only a little people.

I am a Parliamentarian, and to me Parliament is supreme. Ministers are answerable to Parliament. Of course they take advice from highly professional advisers who tend to weigh up the facts and so on. But at the end of the day, just as the civil servants are responsible to the ministers, so the ministers are responsible to Parliament. And my complaint is that in this context, I'm not saying that this extends to other fields, but in this context, successive governments have been weak and ineffective because they did not heed the voice of Parliament. The voice of Parliament on this has been consistent right the way through, whether we had a Labour government in office, or a Conservative government. The majority of members have always been suspicious of attempts to railroad a small British community into a country which was at all times unstable, and which for most of the period that we've been talking about has been under the control of a vicious dictatorship.

Right the way through this sorry saga, covering a period of almost twenty years, government has been reluctant to place its cards on the table with the House of Commons. And the reason for all this? It knew perfectly well that a democratic Parliament would not agree, and certainly not agree easily, to any transfer of a democratic community, however small, to a dictatorship. It was not on! Those who were responsible for our affairs ought to have had the wit to see that from the very beginning. They did not.

At a time when Britain had less and less room to manoeuvre for a negotiated settlement, Argentina's political instability, the 'dirty war' and the 'disappearances' of the 1970s, gave a more obvious plausibility to the champions of the Falklands. If, as has been said, imperialism added to politics new passions, the residual issue of the Falkland Islands excited them no less in a leading back-bencher like Sir Bernard Braine.

Successive British governments failed in their duty. It was only Parliament, at the end of the day, that saved the Falklands, prior to the Argentine invasion. And of course I think the historians will come to recognize that it was this combination of ineptitude and in-difference to the wishes of the Falkland Islanders, and moral blindness throughout, which has characterized British policy, which led directly to the Argentine invasion.

The Falklands were a nuisance. Ministers were engaged in great schemes in Europe and big developments in the Middle East and the Falklands was a pin-prick of an issue.

Whoever was responsible, whether it was civil servants or ministers not paying sufficient attention to the views of Parliament, we should not have encouraged Argentina, by acquiescing in negotiations, to believe that there would be any transfer of sovereignty *unless the Falkland Islanders wanted it*. They did not want it. That is still their position today.

Secondly, after the military take-over in Argentina in 1976, it was palpably wrong, morally wrong, to negotiate with a regime guilty of murdering large numbers of its own people. Incidentally, people of twenty-nine other nationalities were among the 'disappeared ones'. They included British subjects. It was I who discovered that there were three British subjects who disappeared during this period, when British ministers were negotiating the question of sovereignty.

If President Giscard d'Estaing could protest about what was happening to French subjects, if the Swedes could protest against what happened to a Swedish girl who had been murdered by these thugs – what was the British government doing about it? They were negotiating a possible transfer of sovereignty!

The future does not lie, in my opinion, in capitulating to the demands of a country which is only very slowly learning how to govern itself. We have a solemn duty to the Falkland Islanders, and in so doing to protect our own dignity and self-respect.

Lord Greenhill, who was permanent under-secretary of the Foreign Office and responsible overall for the period of the late sixties and early seventies in British policy, said in the House of Lords, looking back on this, as you will no doubt remember, that ministers and their advisers in the Foreign Office were faced in the House of Commons with what he called 'a totally uncompromising lobby'. He clearly numbered you almost foremost in that constituency.

So were the appeasers faced in the House of Commons in the 1930s. When you are up against evil there is no room for compromise. Through the greater part of the period we've been talking about, we've not been dealing with a government like that of France, or the Federal Republic of Germany, or Canada, or Australia. We were dealing with a government that was actually killing its own people. It was torturing people. During that period bodies were being washed up. Some of them decapitated, with their feet in concrete, were being dredged up from the La Plata river. The gallant Argentine Navy during this period was gouging out the eyes of dissident priests. It was murdering lawyers, former Parliamentarians, journalists. It wasn't bothering about nationalities. People of twenty-nine other nationalities were destroyed by these monsters. To say that we could have negotiated with these people at any time is totally out of the question.

The British people are those who alone, in '39, took the decision to go to war with Germany over Poland against, incidentally, not merely Nazi Germany. Remember that Poland was carved up as a result of a conspiracy between Nazi Germany and the Soviet Union. For a whole year after the fall of France, it was the British people who stood alone against the might of Nazi Germany. We are not a people easily put down. To me, our rulers during this time, certainly those responsible for this aspect, fell below the level of history. They forgot that appeasement of dictators, in the end, leads to ruin.

If the loss of material power by Britain, following the Second World War, had given the nation an opportunity to become wiser and more contemplative, to elevate, as it were, the calibre of the national mind, for some the unwillingness to suffer this last retreat from empire arose out of that kind of reflection and introspection.

William Hunter Christie, organizer of the Falkland Islands Committee, recalls a conversation.

I do agree with Lord Shackleton, who said to me about ten years ago, 'You know, the Falkland Islands could be the making of Britain', and he did not mean the financial making of Britain. What he meant was the *moral* making of Britain. This was long before it all came to a head.

I'm bound to say that I always regarded it in another way. If the Falkland Islands had been an overseas department of France, you can't see the French behaving like we behaved. They would have held on to the Falkland Islands whatever happened, and had a very good moral case for doing so.

In other words, General de Gaulle's solution to the French dilemma after the Second World War was one that you applauded? France took stock of its changed situation in the world and somehow managed to retain its relationship with its empire in a way that Britain did not?

No, I think Britain's done rather well actually. I think that the Commonwealth was a good idea and I'm rather in favour of it.

I don't like seeing the minnows chucked out into a pond full of pike, that's all.

And how is one to understand 'the moral making of Britain' reposed in this issue of the Falkland Islands?

I think in two ways, probably. I share Lord Shackleton's view here. One, actually to make something out of a place with enormous potential – that's why we started the South Atlantic Fisheries Committee, which is the origin of all the fishing that's going on out there. We made the world aware that the seas there were valuable. Whether that was wise or not I don't know. But, it was that. It was trying to get the *pioneer* instinct going in a country which has great opportunities, unattractive though it may seem to some.

The other thing is, not being pushed around. A lot of us in Britain felt that we were always being pushed around. We were sinking all the time. We were becoming first a second-rate power, and then a third-rate power, and rapidly on our way to becoming a fourth-rate power.

It had not proved possible to resist Harold Macmillan's 'winds of change' in the larger arenas of the Commonwealth, like Rhodesia, which perhaps is not the least among the reasons why emotion and sentiment became so concentrated on the Falklands issue. The Falklands, with its all-British population, was unique. Conservatives who placed the Falklands question in the grand sweep of global activity preferred, like Edmund Burke, the prescriptive rights of the British to the prefabricated rights of man. They did so on the basis that history is made by God and man, and not by false laws of historical determinism. Liberal, or Marxist, views they felt had conditioned a general acceptance, or half acceptance, of guilt and condemnation of the great European colonial achievement. In the opinion of **Sir John Biggs-Davison** there had been, in consequence, a loss of heart and of confidence which, as in the case of Rhodesia, had opened a flank to the foe.

It was a tragedy that the British government did not decide to sustain the Smith/Muzorewa, black/white coalition that had the authority of a massive vote amongst the people of Rhodesia. But that multiracial government was betrayed. It could have succeeded because supposing we *had* recognized it as the sovereign government of Rhodesia then sanctions would have lapsed. They would have been able to rearm themselves. The Front Line States were in virtual collapse and a better independent Zimbabwe could have come about than that which we have now, which is bitterly divided between the Shona and the Matabele.

Will the historians be justified in seeing these antipathies within the party aroused over Rhodesia as, in effect, crippling Lord Carrington as an effective foreign secretary when it came to the issue of the Falkland Islands?

On Rhodesia we would have sustained him, given the policy that I have outlined. I don't think myself that what happened in Rhodesia, what was happening in Rhodesia, necessarily deflected anything that was going on in relation to the Falkland Islands. Is there any evidence of that?

Well, the Franks Report makes it clear to us that the issue could not be taken, was not taken, to the Cabinet largely because Rhodesia was such a hot issue in the Party. It was felt to be unwise?

Yes, taken to the Cabinet in the sense of departing from the principle that British sovereignty was inviolate.

Well exactly. And crippling what Lord Carrington proposed to do?

One cannot say that was a particular disadvantage. In the end we *had* to defend, at great cost, the sovereignty of the Falkland Islands and we need never have had that unnecessary war.

May I quote to you what Lord Carrington said in the House of Lords debate on the Franks Report in January 1983? He says this. 'If I may say so, it seems to me that there are some in Parliament who actually seem to believe that there is something disreputable, or even treacherous, in trying to seek agreement with foreign governments. It's their view that to negotiate is a sign of weakness, even when the settlement of the problem is in the interests of both sides, and designed to prevent a situation arising which is detrimental to the political and economic interests of this country. They carry chauvinism and insularity to such a degree that one almost feels they disapprove of anyone from the Foreign Office talking to a foreigner. Negotiation is, it seems, feebleness and unpatriotic.'

Do you recognize that as a description of what you stood for?

Well there seems to be a certain uneasiness in the phrasing of that particular speech. I was in favour, and I am in favour, of negotiating with Argentina. I was in favour, and am still in favour, of trying to bring them in to a grouping which will cover the whole area, including the Falkland Islands. But it is necessary for strategic reasons, and it is necessary because that is the will of the people of the Falkland Islands, that British sovereignty should be maintained there. And if it's chauvinistic to say that we cannot betray our own citizens, then so be it.

In one of your writings about famous Conservatives you recall what Disraeli said. 'The Whigs', he said, 'appeal to the people. We appeal to the nation.' Now Lord Carrington comes, I think, from an old Whig family. Is there something of that in your mistrust of him, and what he was trying to do?

Yes, I would agree that he is probably more Whiggish than Tory, but I judge issues on their merits. I observed what he was doing in connection with Zimbabwe and I observed what the Foreign Office, under his control, was doing in the South Atlantic.

And?

And I opposed him. On both.

One more thing Disraeli said I would like you to reflect upon, and ask whether it might express the essence of the Falkland Islanders' rights as you saw them: 'The local sentiment in man is the strongest passion in his nature. This local sentiment is the parent of most of our virtues.'

Yes, I think that is so. It is wrong for people to wish to submerge that local sentiment. That is my quarrel with the internationalists. They seem to want to absorb nations which believe themselves to be a historic community, into a larger whole. They say 'the nation' is finished. They say 'the nation' is a cause of war. It is not. It is the frustration of legitimate national aspirations that has been the cause of war – not the nation itself. The Falkland Islanders are, and I view them as, part of the British nation.

As the British turned away from Queen Victoria's empire and made themselves once more a European nation, there remained those conservatives who looked on the colonial achievement, with its long history and bold exploits, as part of Britain itself, and therefore belonging to a great unity. They were joined in support of the Falklands by Fabian socialists. While they might sing 'The Red Flag' at party conferences, on the whole Fabians approached colonial affairs with positive intentions. A good colonial system had been looked upon as something which could usefully reform and educate. Because it offered an opportunity for a degree of benevolent British socialist supervision, such thinking came close to an imperial earnestness.

   Among those who ensured the failure of British diplomacy over the Falklands by the defeat of Nicholas Ridley's leaseback proposal in 1980, in what it has to be assumed was a calculated intervention, was an influential Fabian, Labour's shadow foreign secretary, **Peter Shore**.

I wanted to express strongly my opposition and my party's opposition to what we thought was a dangerous and unwelcome proposal. When it comes to 'calculation', you must always remember in Parliamentary affairs and events that the amount of time one gets to calculate is very small indeed, as with all government statements. I think I probably got the text of Mr Ridley's statement about twenty minutes before he actually delivered it. So, there was not obviously time for a vast amount of research for me to prepare my reply to him. Nevertheless I would have said, if I had had considerably more time, broadly what I did say at the time.

But as you got up in the House that afternoon, December 2nd 1980 – public men have private thoughts – and while speaking that day as shadow foreign secretary, how much of yourself was invested in that scathing denunciation of the government's proposal?[7]

It represented what I had to say, what I genuinely thought and felt about the issue. I could not imagine that a British government would abandon the people of the Falkland Islands to an unwanted solution that brought them under the rule of a foreign power.

Is it also a corollary of the European argument, and Britain's role in Europe, to which you were passionately opposed, that you see something bound up with the integrity of this nation in our attitude to the support for a tiny minority of Britishers on the other side of the world?

No, I don't think so. I think it proceeds from the rather different principles that they are British people, but secondly they have a right to choose for themselves the kind of government they want.

So you would differ from the right wing of the Conservative Party in that Mr Powell, for example (although not now in the Conservative Party), saw this as an issue of 'nation'. He saw the Falklands as representing the indivisibility of nation. If you gave way there you might give way in other parts of the British nation at home. Is that an argument you found persuasive?

I respect that argument. And I think that if, in fact, we had simply accepted the Argentinian occupation, we would have had trouble in a number of other parts of the world almost at once, and most certainly in Gibraltar.

I was thinking of even closer to home, let us say Ulster.

Perhaps in Ulster too.

Therefore the Falklands issue was 'code' for something else for a wider concern? It is code for Britain after empire and how it sees itself?

Yes, it certainly is a view of Britain as being a nation that will not abandon its own people, even if its power has been greatly reduced, and even if, of its own free will, in many areas it has withdrawn from the rule over other people. It's an entirely consistent position.

Diplomacy's failure, and in particular the reaction to the subsequent Argentine invasion, revealed the appeal the Falklands issue made to deep but hidden emotions in the complex personality of Britain.

It was said of Britain's humiliation over Suez, and Anthony Eden's downfall, that no one could understand it without taking into account

7 See pp. 97–8 for the Hansard record of Shore's response.

the growing unease that Britain's position in the world was being whittled down through lack of firm leadership. Margaret Thatcher looked over her shoulder at these latent and previously lethal sentiments for a Conservative leader, as British diplomacy over Rhodesia and the Falklands was being conducted by the foreign secretary, Lord Carrington. Sir John Biggs-Davison had been a member of the Suez Group in the Conservative Party, mortally opposed to Anthony Eden's withdrawal from the British base in the Suez Canal zone in the 1950s. So too was **Julian Amery** who, a generation later, was also opposed to Lord Carrington.

Lord Carrington is, in my experience, the supreme negotiator of my generation, absolutely brilliant at reaching agreement and smoothing over disagreement. I venture to say that he has no grasp of foreign policy as such. That is to say he is a supreme tactician and a bad strategist. He did not understand, I think, at all, the importance of the Falklands in relation to the Antarctic or to the south-west Atlantic. He did not want to find an agreement with the other people who claimed to have a stake in it, the Argentine and so on. He wanted to avoid any extra expenditure that might be involved in a more forward policy.

I have great regard and respect for him. We've been friends from school-days onwards. But just as what I've said applies to the south-west Atlantic, I think he made the same mistake in Rhodesia/ Zimbabwe. He wanted to get *agreement*. He did not see where it was going to lead and we now have, I think, a situation in Zimbabwe and Central Africa which is perilous, which could have been averted by a greater concentration on *strategy*, and rather less on diplomacy.

How should history judge this connection between these two issues, the outcome of the settlement in Rhodesia, and Britain's going to war over her position in the Falkland Islands?

It's very difficult to judge between diplomacy and foreign policy. Mr Neville Chamberlain had a triumph of diplomacy at Munich. It was a disaster for foreign policy. There was a great divide between the intellectual thinking in the Foreign Office, with Treasury considerations in mind, and the feeling of the House of Commons. The feeling of the House of Commons prevailed – fortunately.

But there's another dimension to this when you talk about instinct and the gut feeling of the House of Commons. What is the validity of that, given the duty with which the Foreign Office is charged, which is to map a secure, long-term future in the national interest?

Well, after Suez there was a great streak of defeatism which entered into the hearts and minds of the British civil service establishment, and which did *not* enter into the gut feeling of the representatives of the British people in the House of Commons.

How important an issue do you think that this has been in modern British political history? Is it a peripheral issue, a skirmish in a far distant place, or is it of greater importance?

No, it's a peripheral issue. But after the terrible psychological shock of our defeat – I would not use any other word – at Suez, it was an element of redemption. The Americans let us down, they betrayed us, at Suez. This time they stood by us. I had a very interesting letter from ex-President Nixon, who was vice-president at the time of Suez, in which he said that, looking back, he thought that the American action at Suez had been disastrous. It had led not just to the boost it gave to Colonel Nasser, but to the withdrawal of France and Britain from accepting responsibilities in the rest of the world. He added that he had talked to President Eisenhower, by then ex-President Eisenhower, who had agreed with him.

This time they did the right thing. There was a phase when the Americans wanted to take over the European empires, the British, French, Belgian and others. They managed to destroy them but they did not manage to take them over. They realized then how alone they were in the world after Vietnam and that without European support it was going to be a very difficult ride. Maybe they have understood this now and the Falklands was the first evidence of it.

Every action taken over the Falklands since the 1960s, by successive governments and their Foreign Office advisers, had been surrounded by this cloud of witnesses who made their contribution to the Falkland Islands lobby, and to a belief that the only way to preserve a tradition was to prolong it. What the lobby did not do was accommodate their future views and designs to what Adam Smith, in *The Wealth of Nations*, called, 'the real mediocrity of Britain's circumstances'.[8] They promoted sentiments which ultimately wrecked British diplomacy.

Britain, however, was not the only nation in play which had brought to its attitudes a conscious sense of national decline over recent decades. So, also, had Argentina.

Text of Peter Shore's response to Minister of State Ridley's proposals in House of Commons, Hansard 2 December 1980, Cols. 195–204:

Mr Peter Shore (Stepney and Poplar) This is a worrying statement. Will the Minister confirm that involved here are the rights and future of

8 (Clarendon Press 1976), vol. 2, p. 947.

1,800 people of British descent in a territory which was originally uninhabited – people who, above all, wish to preserve their present relationship with the United Kingdom? Will he reaffirm that there is no question of proceeding with any proposal contrary to the wishes of the Falkland islanders? Their wishes are surely not just 'guidance' to the British Government. Surely they must be of paramount importance? Has he made that absolutely clear to the Argentine Government?

Is not the Minister aware that proposals for a leasing arrangement represent a major weakening of our long-held position on sovereignty in the Falkland Islands, and that to make them in so specific and public a manner is likely only to harden Argentine policy and to undermine the confidence of the Falkland Islanders? Will he therefore make it clear that we shall uphold the rights of the Islanders to continue to make a genuinely free choice about their future, that we shall not abandon them and that, in spite of all the logistic difficulties, we shall continue to support and sustain them?

5

Argentine Attitudes

When the British Empire breathed its last at Suez in 1956 it was confirmed to world opinion that Britain had lost the imperial will, and the imperial inheritance remained to be contested. Argentina, with its venerable claim to the Falklands, and its ineradicable belief that there was an old wrong to be righted, had been among the first of the heirs to assemble. For Argentina there were no Falkland Islanders, only *colonists*, no matter that they had been there for five generations, and Britain in the Falklands was a relic of colonialism. Argentines entered the post-colonial world to be dazzled at intervals by the issue of the 'Malvinas'.

A venturesome stage comedian in Buenos Aires had portrayed the Argentine Caesar, General Juan Perón, as saying, 'Without my balcony I am nothing.' From that balcony in the 1950s, Perón had thrown a miraculous ideological blanket over Argentina, and he had stirred passionate emotions. Perón told the masses that politics was not for politicians in banquet halls, but for them, the people themselves, to accomplish in the streets. In the streets, outbursts of xenophobic and nationalist enthusiasm, slogans and banners, from time to time proclaimed, 'The Malvinas are ours.' Although Juan Perón never presented the Falklands to the British as a *critical* problem, he established a climate for a generation.

After 1956, because it was considered unwise to have all the British eggs in the now unreliable east-of-Suez basket, the Foreign Office had cast about afresh. After many years of indifference, Britain had set out deliberately to renovate the British interest in Latin America, and particularly in Argentina. The diplomacy which began in secret over the Falklands in the 1960s was seen as offering the distinct possibility that Argentina's ambition would be fulfilled. The Argentines felt that they had been encouraged at a meeting held in New York, in 1967, with the British foreign secretary, George Brown. George Brown 'left an impression' on his opposite number. This was **Dr Nicanor Costa Méndez**, who was to serve again as Argentina's foreign secretary when, fifteen years after this encounter, he returned to the post in the crucial months before the outbreak of the Falklands war.

I have an excellent memory of that talk with George Brown. He was a 'character' and very sharp and intelligent. Much to my surprise he was really interested in the issue, and I think that he was really willing to do something positive. I met him, for the first time, when Argentina was a member of the Security Council and there was a meeting, at foreign minister level, because of the 1967 war.[1] We took up similar positions, with both Brazil and Argentina very near Britain, as Britain was trying to maintain some sort of agreement between Arabs and Israelis. So, we made a very good friendship.

We had two long talks on Malvinas. First of all, Britain had not voted against Resolution 2065 of the UN.[2] So, when I asked George Brown for a meeting and he said 'yes', and we began to talk, I found a very able politician who *wanted* to talk and who had a good knowledge of the whole affair.

Now, he did not say, 'Yes, we will hand you the Islands', but he said, 'We can discuss this, we can see how this problem of a population can be solved', and he said 'We British are interested in two things: in keeping a good friendship with Argentina, and in having better communications and better trade with Argentina.' Remember, that this was in 1967, and Britain was out of the Common Market at that time. I think that Britain was genuinely interested in improving its trade with Argentina.

When it came to the Falklands, what was the actual point of agreement between those two things?

We had those two good talks with George Brown about the possibility of reaching an agreement that could have been on the basis of recognition of sovereignty by the British, and, in turn, acceptance of British authorities, for a certain amount of time, by Argentina. That was the basis of the whole thing. The Labour trend was towards decolonization.

George Brown was staunch Labour, in that sense, and I think he was committed to continue the work of Ernest Bevin in that direction. They had not accepted, but they had not *rejected*, Resolution 2065. But my predecessor had begun to talk with Michael Stewart,[3] so my

1 The Arab/Israeli war of 1967.
2 The UN General Assembly resolution of December 1965 calling on Britain and Argentina to negotiate the Falklands issue.
3 Foreign secretary January 1965–August 1966, and 1968–70.

meeting with George Brown was not entirely new and was not something completely different from what had been going on before.

What inferences were drawn by Argentina, in terms of policy making, from Stewart's visit in 1966, the first by a British foreign secretary, and the emphasis he gave to commercial relations?

We thought this could be a bargaining possibility. You may say trading 'Trade', for the *political* objectives of Argentina.

It was a personal reverse for Dr Costa Méndez when what appeared to be a shared objective over the Falklands with George Brown was put beyond reach by the hostile reaction of the House of Commons in 1968. It was also a lesson Costa Méndez would not forget as he watched Lord Carrington's similar incapacity in 1982.

The Argentines had been Britain's oldest friends in Latin America. The Republic's railways and its meat trade were largely the creation of British capital. By the turn of the century Argentina had been integrated into the international economy as Britain's best client. Then, after the Second World War, the pro-British political class in Buenos Aires had been largely driven from power. A fierce denunciation of 'foreign imperialism' had been the leitmotif of Perón's foreign policy. But there was still a considerable fund of Argentine good will for Britain in the 1960s.

The corollary of Britain's resurrected interest in Argentina had been the need to do something about the Falklands, which had affected relations for more than a century and a half. After the disappointment of 1968, therefore, everything was different. In addition, Argentina came to link its own national decline to that of Britain, with a belief that it had stuck to a relationship with Britain for too long. In the opinion of one Argentine foreign minister, Britain never fully understood the deeper feelings aroused. **Oscar Camilion** was Argentina's foreign minister in 1981 and held the post until three months before the invasion of the Falklands. For a time, therefore, he was Lord Carrington's counterpart.

It is a fact that the British never fully understood that the problem of the Islands was really very important in Argentina. Mainly because, after one hundred and fifty years of it, the Foreign Office in Britain believed that it was just a chronic diplomatic question that maybe, one day, could be dealt with. Also, at the beginning of the 1980s it was not easy to understand the deep frustration of Argentine society. Argentina was frustrated because of the failure of the military government; the armed forces were frustrated because of the stance adopted in dealing with Chile; it was frustrated also by the crucial problem for Argentina of foreign debt. The Argentine people were beginning to think their future was unforeseeable. Always, this was a country where to live was rather easy but, at the beginning of the eighties, life was beginning to be difficult. Maybe for that reason the old problem of the Islands, the old wound, began to hurt.

I was convinced, when I was foreign minister, that it was necessary to find a new way to deal with it because, for Argentina, the idea that the Malvinas could somehow remain 'the last colony' was something very difficult to swallow. For Argentina, the Islands meant a very important priority. It was not exactly the same for the United Kingdom. I received this impression when I had a rather long talk with Lord Carrington.[4] Among Argentines of my generation, it was accepted as a matter of fact that the Islands are a part of Argentine territory, always, and not as the subject of a campaign against the United Kingdom.

In those days, during the thirties, the relationships between both countries were really excellent. But it was a fact that the Malvinas were Argentina's. 'Malvinas were Argentina's', it was something that was beyond any kind of discussion. Why? I think just looking at the map, is the best way to understand the problem from the Argentine point of the view. Of course, the fact that the territory is four hundred miles offshore is not a self-evident title, but in the middle of this large sea-desert of the South, it is more understandable.

In any case, it is a fact that there was a gulf always between a country for which the Islands was really a question of her territory, of sovereignty, in some ways also of her *dignity*, and a country that, very understandably, considered the Islands were really a very marginal affair. It is, maybe, metaphysics. From the point of view of the British it was just a far away territory. It was not a problem of the *essence, of the being, of the state*, as it was for Argentina.

This contrast between 'a marginal British concern' and something which was seen by Argentina as 'the essence of the state' is a key explanation of the emotional Argentine attitude to the Falklands. The issue was massaged as an injury to 'national dignity' in Buenos Aires, while the Argentine complaint was hardly felt in London. That is, of course, Argentina's complaint. In this Argentine attitude were echoes of de Gaulle's 'a certain idea of France'. Argentina's, likewise, was no modest pride. The attempted conquest of the Islands in 1982 was seen as the nation's encounter with destiny.

Roberto Guyer is a former senior Argentine diplomat involved from the outset, in the 1960s, in the protracted manoeuvrings of the modern era with Britain over the Falklands.

4 In New York, in September 1981.

I think we finally got the feeling that you took us a little bit for granted. In the sixties there were the efforts to see if we could reach conversations on the vital issue, which is the question of sovereignty. Then this lapsed, and talks went on. We were always told, 'Well, there is not too great an interest in the Falkland Islands *per se*, but it is the Islanders. You', we were told, 'have to convince the Islanders.'

Thinking of it all now, in 1986, I think it was just a comfortable way out, instead of simply saying, 'We will not touch the issue. The Islanders will not acquiesce, and we will go on evading any solution of the problem.' The evasion was 'Let us *continue*. We have no interests really in those Islands. It's just a question of convincing the Islanders.'

But the constant repetition of national 'honour', and national 'dignity', as being at stake would seem to reflect some deep-seated themes in Argentine culture, which perhaps the British insufficiently understood. What do you think they were?

Well, it's logical for us. Being a young nation we had some points which we thought were very much attached to that. We are not the only ones. Look what the Germans did to get back Heligoland.[5] They exchanged it for a whole colony in Africa. I don't know if it was Cecil Rhodes or Rudyard Kipling who would say, 'You were changing a button for a whole suit', but the Germans felt very strongly about it. Heligoland was *German*, and we felt, going back in history, that the Malvinas were Argentina's, *are* Argentina's. So, for us it *is* a question of national honour and national dignity, yes.

The British always found it difficult to understand why you attached more importance to this issue than concentrating energies on the development of, let us say, the mineral wealth of Patagonia, rather than pursue claims to a territory which had been under British control for more than a century and a half.

One does not exclude the other. I do not see that there was ever an alternative, 'concentrate on Patagonia' or 'concentrate on the Malvinas'. Time, in itself, leads to no perfection of any title. This is from the legal point of view.

But from the political point of view, if the passing of time does not perfect a title it is difficult to imagine how a civilized world order can last. If every country with a claim as long as yours had recourse to force, the world would blow itself to pieces within a week.

Well, without entering into what happened in 1982, I say that we thought our claim was legitimate. It was so legitimate that *you*

5 The island in the North Sea, at the mouth of the Elbe, ceded by Britain to Germany in 1890 in return for concessions in East Africa.

continued discussing it. You did not take up Lord Palmerston's attitude, 'There is nothing to discuss!' If I might remind you, it was not the Argentinians who closed the doors to discussions. It was the British in their debate in the House of Commons of December 1980. If one reads Hansard one can really *feel* that the door has been closed.[6]

What is your response to what one Argentine political writer[7] has said since the Falklands war, that 'Argentina's history as an organized country has shown a repeated tendency to defy certain aspects of the international order. A refusal to align herself in two world wars; her refusal to accept the decision of the Arbitral Court over the Beagle Channel dispute in 1978; and the war of 1982'? Are these things not a long-term trend which is proving increasingly costly to Argentina?

Yes, we have had our costs. However – being neutral in two world wars as something akin to immorality? Switzerland was neutral. Sweden was neutral in World War II. Were the Irish immoral? I know Mr Churchill was not happy with Ireland. But people could not say that we did something morally wrong. As to the Arbitral Court, we thought it had acted *ultra vires* and that it had decided issues that had not been brought before it. I cannot fathom that in any way, shape or form we ever went against any of the tenets of the international civilized community. What that Argentine historian said might be *politically* arguable, but from a moral and legal point of view I see no validity.

But how far does the disposition to challenge great or greater powers stem from a deeply held feeling in Argentine culture about two aspects in particular: a feeling that Argentina has always lost territory and a feeling that Argentina was or should be a greater power?

We are not challenging greater powers, we simply wish to reaffirm our own individuality. Our relations with the UK have always been excellent.

Is that part of the problem?

I think it *is* a part of the problem. There is a strong case here of people who are very close to the British. We were always very close. My own wife is of Scottish descent. We were also a little bit hurt during the question of 1982. There were strong things said on both sides. I will not diminish the things we said of the UK at that time. But from your side, one sometimes felt transported to the time of Queen Elizabeth the First. The whole anti-Latin, anti-Catholic bias, the word 'dago',

6 The hostile reception given to Minister of State Nicholas Ridley's leaseback proposal.

7 Carlos Escude, *Buenos Aires Herald*, April 1986.

was thrown at us. Showing 'the lesser breeds' where they get off. This Third World, in Charles Dickens's words, 'must comply, like the deserving poor'!

That seems to me to confirm the suspicion that there are *these deep-seated frustrations in Argentina, that you had, for example, a foot in the 'Third World' and wished to be a great power. A sense of grievance – Argentina alone, embattled, taking on the world?*

No, not at all, that is utterly untrue. You may think that there is one big difference. It is that we are at different times of history. You have had one revolution. You have passed *your* time of intense nationalism. God knows you had it! I could go on about the war of Jenkins's Ear[8] and God knows how many other episodes.'

The name 'Malvinas' derives from French and is the Hispanic version of 'Malouines', the seal-hunters and fishermen from St Malo in Brittany, who went there in the early eighteenth century. By 1981, the Islands which the Spanish at the height of their Empire had not thought worth a name, were within a few months of being thought worth a war. This rapid evolution of the Falklands issue, late in 1981, as it went from being crucial for Argentina to being critical, took place almost a year after Nicholas Ridley's leaseback proposal was furiously attacked in the House of Commons.

In 1981 both sides were stuck in a classic impasse. For the British, the situation created by years of barren exchanges concerning sovereignty echoed Churchill's description of Britain's bed of nails in Ulster, as conveyed by the dreary prospect in Tyrone and Fermanagh, that 'The situation was desperate but never serious.'

The British detected some similarly baffled overtones in Argentine attitudes when, six months before the conflict, in the Autumn of 1981, Lord Carrington met the Argentine foreign minister, **Dr Oscar Camilion**.

It is a paradox, but Malvinas was never the immediate preoccupation of foreign ministers. I have the reputation of being one of the first foreign ministers in Argentina who began to study the problem of Malvinas, trying to find a new approach to the problem of sovereignty, for instance. Why did the foreign ministers never *study* Malvinas, on both sides? Because it was not a matter of *urgency*. For

8 An English merchant captain who, in 1731, allegedly lost an ear (some said it had been in the pillory) when boarded by a Spanish sloop. The popular clamour forced Walpole to consent to war against Spain.

instance, when I met Lord Carrington in 1981, the impression that I received was, first of all, that Lord Carrington had a very superficial grasp of the problem. That was really understandable, because Lord Carrington was a very busy, a very important foreign minister, and he had a lot of matters of higher priority – at least from his point of view. I said to the Argentine ambassador to Britain after the meeting that for Lord Carrington the Islands are the 214th priority – joking of course.

I got the impression, when I presented the problem of the Falklands, he was in some ways thinking 'Why is this fellow questioning, and with such a marginal problem, such a busy man as I?' And it *was* marginal. Even for Argentina, the question never received the level of attention that it really deserved. For that reason people never tried to find sophisticated approaches, and it needed sophisticated approaches.

Look, in the Franks Report, there is a paragraph summarizing a telegram sent by Ambassador Williams[9] after a conversation with me.[10] I say that, 'For serious and constructive negotiations it was necessary to tackle all the component parts of what was a complex issue.'[11] I was trying to suggest to your ambassador in Buenos Aires the possibility of exploring new ways to solve it; for example, the differing elements that composed the idea of sovereignty. Sovereignty is a formal concept, but it is also the sum of various things – rights and tasks and so on. There was also the possibility of analysing the different groups of islands in different ways; even in the case of the Malvinas group, to stress that there were almost deserted islands, islands with just a few shepherds, and islands with a community. I thought it might be possible to have different approaches.

Ambassador Williams reported to London, on this October 14th meeting, that 'Meaningful negotiations would have to be long and difficult.' That was taken by the Foreign Office as Argentine recognition that no early solution was obtainable. It was welcomed in the Foreign Office as showing reluctance on Argentina's part to move to confrontation. Is that an adequate reflection of what you were trying to convey?

Yes. I was trying to convey first of all that it was necessary to start meaningful negotiations, and it was necessary to find a new approach. In those days I was toying with something like a Hong Kong style approach – essentially the difference of functions. My idea was a bit

9 British ambassador to Argentina.
10 14 October 1981; Franks Report, para. 105.
11 Franks Report, para. 105.

intellectual, if you wish. It started from the old idea of sovereignty, the concept of sovereignty in the sixteenth and seventeenth centuries, by Bentham or Hobbes, that always distinguished between formal sovereignty and elements that really integrate the notion of sovereignty. For instance, defence, justice, taxes, education and so on – functions of the state. I meant the possibility of an approach to the problem starting with *functions* and then, only after that, the global problem of sovereignty. However, I insist that usually both sides considered the issue in a very superficial and elementary way. From the point of view of the British Government, the typical approach was self-determination for the Islanders. From the Argentine point of view, it was formal sovereignty.

Ambassador Anthony Williams's talk with Foreign Minister Camilion in October 1981, six months before the Argentine invasion, disclosed this different emphasis, therefore, compared to the historical Argentine position, which had always been that sovereignty was indivisible. The approach Camilion 'toyed with' was to winnow out the differences between real possession, expressed in the functions of actual dominion, from the disputed 'global' question of sovereignty. Camilion's constructive thoughts were felt to offer scope for 'protracted dialogue'.[12] How brief the vision was!

At this time, in retrospect, Lord Carrington underestimated his own importance as seen in Argentine eyes. The fact that he had raised expectations by his performance in reaching a settlement over a *really* divisive issue, Rhodesia, is attested by Camilion's successor just six months before the war broke out, **Dr Nicanor Costa Méndez**.

I had put great expectations in Lord Carrington's ability to deal with international disputes, and I had followed his attitudes and his policies in Rhodesia. There he made an excellent effort and a very successful effort to settle the problem. While I had not met him, I thought that he was the man that could deal with *this* affair.

How far were you aware that his success with that very problem, Rhodesia, was causing Lord Carrington difficulties over the Falklands within the Conservative party and the government?

Yes, of course I was aware of that. Otherwise I would be having champagne!

Lord Carrington decided not to take the lead but, instead, to ask Argentina for constructive proposals to resolve the dispute. For doing so

12 Franks Report, para. 105.

he was criticized by the Franks Inquiry, as thereby acknowledging that Britain was in a weak position, and thus passing the initiative to Argentina. If the Argentine diplomats always asked more of Lord Carrington than they did of themselves, it is clear that they expected much from him, for reasons amplified by **Oscar Camilion**.

> We considered, in the Chancery, that Mrs Thatcher's government had five problems to solve: Rhodesia, Belize, Hong Kong, Gibraltar and the Malvinas, in that order. Maybe we aspired to change the order a bit by giving Malvinas priority *vis-à-vis* Gibraltar, even though we believed that Gibraltar was perhaps a more difficult problem because of the size of its population[13] and, obviously, it is different in the defence priorities of the United Kingdom. We were extremely interested in the realistic approach of the Conservative Government to the Rhodesia problem. The solution of Rhodesia demonstrated that the British government meant business.

> *Therefore when Rhodesia was settled by Lord Carrington, you saw at once an opportunity to accelerate your diplomacy over the Falklands?*

> Maybe. Our concrete reaction was something very obvious. These kind of settlements are easier with Conservative governments. A typical example was Nixon with China. Also, we appreciated that Lord Carrington was no common foreign minister, he was a foreign minister with 'volume'. What's more, it was our appreciation that there was an *agenda* in the British Government, on all these outstanding problems.

Such disposition as there was in Argentina in 1981 to modify its historical 'all or nothing approach' on sovereignty was conceded in Camilion's analysis that Argentina needed a more sophisticated and flexible diplomacy. It suggests that leaseback, which addressed the central issue – sovereignty – might well have been accepted by Argentina, had Lord Carrington been prepared to force it through Cabinet and Commons at home. But, as the Franks Report discloses, 'The time was never considered to be ripe.' The adoption by Lord Carrington, albeit temporary, of the 'doctrine of unripe time' meant, from Argentina's point of view, protracted stalemate. This coincided with the appearance of new disparities in the balance of power between Britain and Argentina. The implications of Britain's far-reaching defence appraisal in 1981, it is clear, had a seductive significance for Buenos Aires, as **Nicanor Costa Méndez** explains.

13 Approximately 26,000, compared with the Falklands' 1,800.

I think that there were signs that the British government had to concentrate on other problems, mainly for economic reasons. There was one sign to which I really paid attention when I went back to the ministry. That sign was the Defence Debate of 1981, where the problems of security were really debated, and the heart of the problem was discussed. I detected that the policy of Britain was, first, to reduce the defence budget, and that Mrs Thatcher and her ministers were very adamant about that, and for the future, the Royal Navy was to be concentrated on the submarines, on the Trident, rather than the surface fleet. To that we paid attention.

And what did you conclude?

My conclusion was that it would be very difficult for Britain to maintain the Islands without our cooperation or collaboration. And that the Communications Agreement, and all that was connected with the Communications Agreement, was going to be of paramount importance. Also, that Chile was going to become more than a pawn in this chess game. But my first conclusion was that either Britain was losing interest in the zone or, because of the defence budget, Britain was compelled to leave the zone and pay less attention to the area. We thought these economic reasons would at least offset the power of the Falkland Islands lobby.

The belief that the Thatcher government, preoccupied with economic problems which, as they were going to reduce the role of the Royal Navy's surface fleet, made it less likely Britain would prove a determined opponent over the Falklands, now began to reshape the Argentine analysis. For its part, Argentina, in 1981, was experiencing its worst economic crisis of the century, with a rapid increase in social unrest. And who does not know that a foreign war has often put a stop to civil discords?

The Falklands crisis of 1982 approached with Britain having no policy other than to keep the negotiations going, while maintaining the status quo indefinitely. The role which these trends in British policy making performed, in encouraging Argentina to reunite domestic opinion on a wave of national enthusiasm, was reflected in new designs for forceful action.

In December 1981 new leaders emerged at the head of the military Junta: General Galtieri, the army commander-in-chief, and Admiral Jorge Anaya of the navy. If there was no progress in negotiations over the Falklands with Britain, what was it this new government, which had brought back Dr Nicanor Costa Méndez as foreign secretary, was threatening to do?

I can assure you, and I can show documents, that at that time my idea was to put on as much *diplomatic* pressure as possible during the year 1982. It did not occur to me, and I did not discuss the problem with General Galtieri or Almirante Anaya, before the Georgias,[14] of occupying the Islands. President Galtieri had told me that he had other plans, alternative plans, but he did not give me any instructions to make diplomatic moves, and he did not request my opinion on the possibility of invading or occupying the Islands. I did not discuss that possibility with the Junta before the 22nd and 23rd of March 1982, when the Georgia affair came up.

You are speaking only of your own ministry, the Ministry of Foreign Affairs?

The ministry that's in charge of political and of diplomatic affairs. So at the diplomatic and political level this had not been examined, analysed, or discussed or planned.

Surely we can agree at this distance, because a good deal has been published to the effect, that the Junta, if not you, had ordered a military alternative if negotiations failed?

The Junta had ordered a military alternative, as Britain had ordered military preparations too, as any country having diplomatic problems with another would order a military alternative or preparations. Of one thing I can assure you, from the *political and diplomatic* point of view there were no plans to support a military attitude.

So you are saying, for the benefit of future historians, that when this new government came to power in December 1981, as far as you were concerned, it was only updating contingency plans? It did not have a completely new blueprint in order to deal with the Falkland Islands issue?

Well, 'updating' or having new plans, there is more than a shade of difference between the two. Probably they were preparing new military plans. But, as you perhaps know, military plans for occupation of the Islands had been prepared many times in Argentina, and many years before the new government. So, the new government either updated the old plans or, and this is a second alternative, and I think the true one, it prepared *new* military plans.

But as far as I know, and I have discussed the problem at length, the Junta did not make the decision of occupying the Islands before the Georgia affair. Perhaps, of this I'm not sure, the Junta had in mind the possibility of a military demonstration, or even a military 'touch and go'. But this was discussed at a military level, and not at political level, and no political decision was made on this direction.

14 That is, before the affair of the 'scrap workers' on South Georgia.

But do you confirm that the only place where a military demonstration, or a military 'touch and go' as you call it, would have been credible in terms of demonstrating Argentina's seriousness of purpose, would have been on the Falkland Islands, at Port Stanley?

No doubt about that. What I am saying is this was a possibility, not a decision. That was just an alternative.

Whether Costa Méndez was being disingenuous in supposing the military leaders viewed this as an alternative, rather than an opportunity, awaits another judgement. At least, it seems, he was party to the knowledge that a 'touch and go' invasion of the Falklands was planned, if not decided. But the Foreign Ministry had little leverage over the Argentine Navy, the crucial element in the military government.

Events accelerated surrounding the last set of talks held between Britain and Argentina in New York in February 1982, and were followed by the affair of the 'Argentine scrap workers' on South Georgia. This was the immediate prelude to the Argentine invasion. At this time, an informed witness in the Argentine Navy, who was intimately involved and who did the planning and was the operational commander for the Argentine landing on the Falklands, 'Operation Rosario', was **Rear-Admiral Carlos Busser**. It would seem the Argentine Navy was not, this time, just 'dusting off' an old contingency but, indeed, drawing up a new blueprint. How were his orders to update the invasion plan for the Falklands in January 1982 interpreted by Admiral Busser?

The order was not to *update* the plan but to draft a plan from *scratch*. Argentina had made many plans in the past to recover the Malvinas, but the order we got was to make out a new plan. We started doing so in January 1982. The basic idea was to negotiate throughout 1982, but at the same time have a military plan, just in case the negotiations failed. In that case we would take the military option. But that would be only towards the end of 1982, or the beginning of 1983.

Was this completely new plan you began to draft in January worked out in the expectation that the talks with Britain in February 1982 would succeed or fail?

The military plan was to go side by side with diplomatic efforts. Argentina was hoping for diplomatic success, but we had long experience of negotiations which never achieved a solution, and so we drafted a military plan in case those negotiations failed.

But there is a difference of emphasis in January from all preceding years? There was a real probability of recourse to military action to solve the problem of the Falklands?

Yes. There were preparations in case the negotiations failed.

The difference, I think, is that the British acknowledge the likelihood of military action but cannot quite bring themselves to believe that it will happen, whereas by January or February 1982 you are expecting that will be necessary?

On 27th January 1982[15] Argentina proposed to Great Britain a round of negotiations that should take a year, and received no reply. It is a crucial moment. On 27th January 1982 we made our proposal, asking for a reply to be delivered to us before the negotiations began again at the UN in New York in February 1982. But we never got a reply. That was the detonator for the unilateral communiqué issued by Argentina after the New York talks. We were drawing up a military plan, but that does not mean that we had taken the decision to invade. As you know, in military terms, there is a huge difference between a plan and an order.

What therefore decided the timing of the 'execution' order?

It is a long story. On March 19th a group of Argentine scrap workers arrived on the Georgias to dismantle whaling stations on San Pedro island. It led to a misunderstanding and a misinterpretation by the British Government. Positions then toughened and this leads to the decision to recover the Malvinas and the Georgias.

The British came to the view that the presence of the scrap dealers on South Georgia was being used by the Argentine Navy as a front to establish a presence there. Captain Barker of HMS Endurance sent a signal saying there were indications of collusion between Senor Davidoff and the Argentine Navy.[16] Naval Headquarters in Buenos Aires had congratulated the Bahia Buen Suceso 'on a successful operation'.[17] Why should the British not have suspected collusion?

Captain Barker's message is rather curious. He sent it while he was sailing from the Malvinas to the Georgias on the 22nd March. He was carrying on board marines to remove the Argentine workers on the Georgias. Now, it must be said that the Argentine Navy transported Davidoff's men, on a navy cargo ship, because the navy for many years has run a short-haul service to develop and promote economic activities in the south. So when Davidoff was unsuccessful in getting *British* cooperation to take his men there, the Argentine Navy decided to go ahead because it was promoting activities in its own territory.

15 Argentina proposed the establishment of a permanent negotiating commission with a fixed agenda, to have a duration of one year, 'to peacefully, definitively and rapidly solve the dispute' (Franks Report, para. 126).

16 Senor Davidoff was an Argentine scrap merchant with a contract to dismantle the old whaling station on South Georgia.

17 Franks Report, para. 175. The *Bahia Buen Suceso* was an Argentine naval support vessel.

It must be said that Argentines consider that the Georgias are *theirs*, in the same way as the British say they are British territory. For the Argentine Navy, therefore, this task that had been asked of them was just promoting a service in Argentine territory.

The British version was that they were not just scrap workers, but included military personnel, and the Argentine flag had been raised.

Your question points to one of the most crucial episodes that led to the major misunderstanding which arose on March 19th. The British Antarctic Survey[18] itself had to change its story when, two days later, the British Government asked them to be more specific. They had *thought* that it was military personnel, because of the type of clothes people were wearing. In fact the ship *Bahia Buen Suceso* had *no* military personnel, they were all civilians. This trip of the scrap dealers was well known to the British Government. They knew who the workers were, what ship they were sailing in, and the date the ship sailed from Buenos Aires. All this was known officially to the British Government. Therefore it was not an Argentine 'presence' in the Georgias, but just a contract that had been signed in 1979, between a British and an Argentine firm, and with the knowledge of the Argentine and British parties.

The British response to the Argentine scientific station established on Southern Thule in 1976 was more or less to let it pass. At least it was an episode not made public for eighteen months. Should we suppose that when the British responded as they did over the presence of the scrap dealers in South Georgia, there, as was thought, in collusion with the Argentine navy, Argentina then decided negotiations were going to get nowhere?

The Thule episode was known to British intelligence in Buenos Aires but, for reasons I do not know, it was not disclosed to the British public. Nevertheless a British ship did sail to the area and ratified the presence of Argentina in Thule.

Concerning the Georgias the British knew that Davidoff had signed this contract and was going to send his workmen there. This time the reactions were different. Why is that so? My personal opinion is that when Davidoff had signed this contract in 1979, with a British firm, to dismantle the whaling station, the British then had the Antarctic Survey and the *Endurance* as a support and a continuous presence in the area. But when the workers go there in 1982, the situation has changed entirely. The British Antarctic Survey was going to leave the area, in 1982, and HMS *Endurance* would be out of

18 The British Antarctic Survey observed the *Bahia Buen Suceso* in Leith Harbour and a sizeable party of civilian and military personnel ashore (Franks Report, para. 169 ff.).

commission by the end of 1982. The prospect was that, in a matter of months, the Argentine workers in the Georgias would be there but *without a simultaneous British presence*.

That, in fact, would establish the Argentine as the only presence on South Georgia?

That is correct. That is what was going to happen, and that is precisely what the British did not *want* to happen.

But precisely what you *did?*

We did nothing. The workers just went there. This provoked a British reaction which started a whole new story. The threat, issued by the British, decided Argentina that it was not going to accept a withdrawal under threats. We decided to support our presence there, in view of what we considered was an ultimatum and an aggression. So another crucial date is March 23rd, when Britain sent its ultimatum. That determined our future conduct. Because we were aware that if the British did not *act* then, it was only because they did not feel they were *strong* enough. That is, if there was to be a confrontation, Great Britain was not sure to win at that time.

Now, on the 25th of March we get reports saying that there were British ships sailing towards the south. Argentina therefore had a very short period in which to act, and during that period Great Britain could *not* act. *After* that the position would be absolutely the opposite. The British *could* act, and Argentina would not be in any position to stop the scrap workers being removed from the Georgias. So we should consider the situation on the basis of the evaluation we made on the 23rd and 24th of March. According to press reports Great Britain had despatched a nuclear submarine. The Franks Report says it was on the 29th of March but our press was saying the 25th of March. It is only a difference of four days. What is certain, the ships were sailing south. Great Britain had said it was going to evict the workers from South Georgia, unless they were taken away by the Argentinians themselves. It was not possible for us to wait until the end of 1982, when the British presence in the area would have diminished. The problem was immediate. Very soon the workers would be evicted. Argentina just could not wait.

On the 23rd March when the British ultimatum was received we then thought we had some days ahead of us to carry out this operation. The Argentine government had set up a planning committee,[19] and it had been agreed that in no way would this operation[20] take

---

19 Rear-Admiral Busser was the naval member of this planning committee.
20 Operation Rosario, the Argentine invasion of the Falklands.

place before the 15th of May. Planning was being done slowly, therefore, and totally independent from negotiations about the crisis on
the Georgias. When the ultimatum came, the evidence was that when
the British ships arrived the workers would be violently removed
from South Georgia.

The Junta consulted the planning committee on the 24th of March
about the earliest day on which the operation could be mounted. The
reply was given on the 26th March. It said the Argentine forces could
be ready to sail on the 28th of March. This meant, in effect, the operation could be carried out on the 1st of April.

The overall situation, at the time, was set up in the following terms.
British forces are heading south. Either we continue negotiations,
which would not solve the problem but would give the British ships
time to arrive. Or we could send our claim to the UN Security Council,
but there the British had a veto and the prospect was dim. Third was the
military solution which would *force* Britain to negotiate. The basic idea
was to recover the islands with a small force, and leave a small force
there. As we did. Of all these alternatives, only the military option
offered the promise of a solution. All others would have meant humiliation for Argentina when the British ships arrived at South Georgia.

The dominant influence in these considerations which led to invasion was
the navy commander, and the navy member of the three-man leadership
of the military Junta, Admiral Jorge Anaya. Admiral Anaya was in detention in Buenos Aires when these interviews were being recorded and the
new government of President Alfonsin preferred that he should remain
inaccessible. There is important evidence at first hand of Anaya's controlling belief that a steady decline in British military capabilities made it
improbable Argentina would have to fight. It comes from the Supreme
Allied Commander Atlantic at the time, **Admiral Harry Train**, United
States Navy. Shortly after the Falklands conflict, Train personally
'debriefed' Admiral Anaya, for a classified American study of the war.

The evidence is what Anaya told me personally. However, he took it
back one previous decade, to 1956, by pointing out that in the Suez
crisis of 1956 the United States failed to support the United
Kingdom. You should add to that his perception of an eroding
national will, and an eroding maritime capability on the part of the
UK. He had a political and military situation where at best he could
hope for United States neutrality – he never did hope for United
States support – he hoped for United States neutrality, and he
thought that would occur. He thought also that Her Majesty's
Government lacked the national will to respond to military pressure.

In addition, he thought the Royal Navy lacked the capability to respond eight thousand miles from home.

What did Anaya say determined the timing of the Argentine invasion?

When the BBC announced, I believe it was March 17th, that HMS *Superb* had sailed from Gibraltar,[21] Anaya felt, as he told me, that this was his last opportunity to carry out his life's ambition to retake the Malvinas Islands for Argentina. He said, when this nuclear-powered submarine arrived on the scene, it would not be possible to execute the surface operations that would be required to place Argentine troops ashore at Port Stanley. The window of opportunity was limited by the steaming time it would take HMS *Superb* to get from Gibraltar to the vicinity of the Falklands.

His decision was based on a BBC broadcast?

Right. That was a 'war-starter', that is what Anaya describes as a 'war-starter'. That announcement turned out to be false. But based on that announcement he decided to execute a contingency plan. They had always had contingency plans to do this. He had just recently updated it. This contingency plan had called for an execution in the *summer* of 1982, not an early date like February, March or April. He decided to advance it because, if he did not, he would never be able to do it. He said that when HMS *Superb* arrived it would be just like back in the seventies[22] when the nuclear submarine was on the scene for a long time, and they never knew when it left. They did not know when it was safe to start operating with freedom in the vicinity of the Falklands again.

This was a question examined by the Franks Commission; whether the dispatch of a nuclear submarine in the crisis of 1977 did act as a deterrent. Lord Carrington asked his officials, 'Did they know about it?', and subsequently took the view that if the Argentines did not know about it, it could not have been a deterrent. What was Admiral Anaya's response to that?

Anaya obviously knew about it. He knew about the presence of the Royal Navy submarine in the vicinity of the Falklands in the 1970s because he referred to it.[23]

---

21 The BBC has no record of any such report on this day. The decision to sail the first British nuclear-powered submarine for the Falklands was taken on Monday 29 March (Franks Report, para. 331).

22 Action was taken by the Callaghan government in 1977, when two frigates and a nuclear-powered submarine were deployed to the area in order to 'buttress negotiations' (Franks Report, para. 327).

23 In contrast, Rear-Admiral Busser told me, 'We did not know. Argentina did not have the means to detect their presence and the Argentine attitude was not conditioned by the presence or absence of British ships.'

Anaya is unequivocal, is he, about this? They did *know in 1977 and therefore it was a deterrent?*

I cannot take it that next step forward but, since no invasion occurred, since the Argentines did nothing militarily, it was in effect a deterrent.

Why is a submarine, which is invisible, a deterrent? What did Anaya say about that?

Let me tell you what *I* think about that first. A submarine is a lousy peacetime naval-presence vehicle. It is *not* an effective way to influence events in favour of a nation in peacetime. But you must have submarines if you are a major maritime power. You must have submarines in order to possess that level of war-fighting capability that will deter war. If you do not have a clearly perceived ability to fight a maritime war, then you risk failing to deter war. Submarines are an essential part of your war-fighting capability. Therefore you must have them.

If you want to influence events, to prevent coercion, or to protect your interests then a submarine is *not* a good vehicle to send, for a number of reasons, not the least of which is that they are invisible. The best 'event-influencing' force in the history of the maritime world is the carrier task group. I mean a *real* carrier. Submarines? They scare people. People don't understand them. They don't see them. They don't know *how* they will relate to a series of events they have in mind. They can push you past the threshold of war, which is what happened in the case of the Falkland Islands, I am personally convinced – just as Anaya is – that *that* was the 'war-starter'.

That decided the actual timing, *not Argentina's intention.*

The timing and the decision. To understand the Argentines you have to accept that, for years, they have had on the shelf military plans to 'retake' – that is their term – 'retake' the Falkland Islands. The British would say 'seize'. From their perspective their plan was to 'retake' the Malvinas for Argentina. They have had active contingency plans to do that for years and years. They update them at their naval war college and in the naval staff. When Anaya assumed the mantle of chief of navy staff in Argentina, and was the navy member of the Junta, the first thing he did was update[24] the plan which *he himself had written* four or five years before.

When Anaya heard a news report, false as it proved, of the dispatch of a nuclear submarine, HMS Superb, *how do his actions after that conform to the idea that this was a determining factor for him?*

---

24 Cf. Rear-Admiral Busser, who says, 'The order was not to *update* the plan but to draft a plan from *scratch*' (see p. 111).

His order to Vice-Admiral Lombardo, to execute the plan, was given within two hours of the announcement on BBC. And at the time he told Vice-Admiral Lombardo to execute the plan, he said that he would give the execution date within a day or so, which he did. I believe that the decision on the execution date was determined in large measure by Lombardo's response as to how long it would take him to 'load on' and execute. We had an American officer, an exchange officer on one of their ships – on the *Belgrano*, as a matter of fact.

On the Belgrano *? Did he survive?*

They put him ashore, and sent him away. That little piece of information did not get picked up in the intelligence circuits.

British? Or American?

Neither British nor American.

What is Anaya's version of the South Georgia incident, the events which accompanied the landing by Argentine scrap dealers led by Mr Davidoff on South Georgia?

That the initial Davidoff venture, as conceived by Davidoff, was a bona fide business deal. Davidoff was a scrap dealer. He purchased three whaling stations to dismantle for scrap in the South Georgia islands. Being rather a careful man with his money he tried to get free transportation for that scrap. He asked the British if they would let him send his scrap home on HMS *Endurance* in the course of one of *Endurance*'s visits to South Georgia. He was turned down. He then asked the Argentine Navy if he could use one of their support ships, either the Antarctic support ship, or the Falklands support ship, to bring the scrap back. At that time the Argentine Navy recognized that there was a potential for establishing, in a clandestine way, the same type of presence in South Georgia that they had established in South Thule. They, therefore, developed a plan, called Operation Alpha, which called for inserting military people into Davidoff's party and leaving them behind when Davidoff left. If Operation Alpha were to be implemented it called for replacing some of Davidoff's people with trained commandos.

So, what started as an innocent scrap-dealing enterprise was taken over as a military operation by the Junta?

The plan was not executed. It was cancelled, approximately a month before Davidoff sailed, for reasons I did not fully understand.

I was going to say, why was it cancelled?

I do not have the rationale to share that with you. I can tell you that I have seen the documentary evidence that it *was* cancelled. And the Davidoff party consisted of forty bona fide workers.

It is tempting, more plausible perhaps, to see it as the exploitation of their experience on South Thule, when there had been no immediate British response, and this was another such probe. When it did not, on South Georgia, meet with the same response as Southern Thule, then they decide to make it a military operation?

It is tempting. But I am satisfied, as a historian, that they did not. But I can see where there is a basis for some scepticism. But I do not share it. I do not think the operation was executed.

What did Anaya give to you as the reasons for his fundamental misreading of all the signals? He misunderstands Mrs Thatcher, the United States does not exhibit 'benevolent neutrality'?

He believed that on the basis of the events of 1956, when the United States failed to support the UK in the Suez crisis, the United States would remain neutral in the case of conflict between Argentina and the United Kingdom. Added to this was the fact that in the year prior to the Falkland Islands conflict, there had been a long series of visits by high-level political and military authorities to Argentina, which indicated to him that there was a thawing of the rather cold relationships that had existed prior to that time, and that the United States' current government saw that there were definite mutual interests between the United States and Argentina that were of value to both countries.

How did he think, though, that having carried out the invasion, he could manage the crisis that he had promoted?

Anaya thought – and these are his words to me – that he was just 'giving a nudge to diplomacy', by landing five hundred troops in Port Stanley.

He certainly gave it a nudge!

He certainly gave it a nudge, right. Even weeks after the landing, the Argentine leadership believed that they were still under crisis management mode, whereas the UK believed they were at war, and correctly so. So we had one nation believing they were fighting a war, and another nation that thought they were 'crisis managing'. It was not until the *Belgrano* was sunk that the hard fact came home to the Argentines that they really *were* at war.

What did Anaya say he had supposed would be the British reactions to his 'nudge to diplomacy'?

He said, categorically, that he did not believe the British would respond militarily to the landing in Port Stanley. He went on to say that, if the British *did* react militarily, he at no time thought that he could prevail in a military conflict. It was perhaps for this reason that they kept themselves in the mind-set of 'crisis management'.

But that makes him sound irrational in the action he took.

Neither Anaya nor Galtieri were irrational. I believe they were the captives of the cultural background and their heritage – a heritage that had not involved fighting a war for a hundred years.

So it boils down to this: Anaya took the action he did because he did not believe he would have to fight?

Precisely correct.

Admiral Harry Train bears witness to Anaya's assumption that Britain would accept a *fait accompli* and that therefore he was only 'giving a nudge to diplomacy' by landing at Port Stanley. If so, it was with an uncommonly blunt instrument. The belief in the *coup de main*, the short, decisive war, is among the most ancient of human hallucinations.

If Admiral Jorge Anaya considered he was the surf at the edge of the wave of Argentina's advance to national dignity, history may feel he could be forgiven his illusions. At least the militarism so peremptorily summoned by Argentina was based on perceptions more widely shared. **Nicanor Costa Méndez** acknowledges that Suez had been analysed by the Argentine foreign office as an appropriate model for likely British and American responses to the resort to force over the Falklands.

Yes, it was analysed in two ways. One, as a USA intervention in order to prevent the extension of a war, and two, as a token of the end of a certain British foreign policy. To put it in Mr Healey's words, I think, 'From now on, Britain will be a European power and no longer a global power.' So it had no definite influence, but we paid attention to Suez, as we paid attention to the USA intervention in the Yom Kippur war.

But the important thing about Suez was the United States, and United Nations, both proved restraints on what Anthony Eden tried to do. It would seem that you expected much the same sort of thing to happen this time?

This is correct. Yes. We placed expectations in the United States' intervention as a mediator. Let me talk just a bit more about our expectations concerning Britain. I think that there were gross mis-perceptions. I think that Britain thought that we were moving exclusively for domestic reasons. And *we* thought that Britain would react only at international level, and for international reasons. But, much to our surprise, we realized, afterwards, that Britain was reacting mostly for domestic reasons.

What do you mean by that, 'for domestic reasons'?

I mean that the so called 'Thatcher factor' was a very important factor, and that Mrs Thatcher was very much interested in promoting her image.

But that is tantamount to saying that Britain, given the opportunity, deliberately sought the war. This did not convince the world at large, it convinced nobody in the United Nations, nor in the European Community. So how is one to understand you? The war was caused by your invasion of the Falkland Islands.

Yes, but the invasion of the Falklands, or the occupation of the Falklands, was caused by a long-time British attitude and, in my judgement, mismanagement of the Georgia crisis by the British government. Really, a gross exaggeration of the Georgia crisis.

The invasion which Rear-Admiral Anaya had planned, or conceived, as 'a nudge to diplomacy' was intended for the British summer of 1982, winter in the Antarctic. It was advanced to April 1982, the Argentines have maintained, because of the way Britain responded to the South Georgia crisis. Although Admiral Harry Train was told by Anaya that this plan was in fact never executed, today it is known, according to British intelligence sources, that the Argentine Navy recognized there was an opportunity of establishing, clandestinely, the same type of presence in South Georgia as they had previously established with impunity in 1976, on Southern Thule, in the South Sandwich Islands. The plan, Operation Alpha, called for inserting Argentine commandos into Davidoff's party, and leaving them behind when Davidoff left.

The overall context is vital. Three months before the conflict, events in the longer term must be judged as running all Argentina's way. The British defence review, the proposed withdrawal of the white ensign from the South Atlantic with the ice-patrol vessel HMS *Endurance*, a new Nationality Act which denied British citizenship to Falkland Islanders, the intended closing of the British Antarctic Survey, the only British presence on South Georgia; all these things suggested, as Costa Méndez put it, that 'either Britain was losing interest ... or ... was compelled to leave the zone'. However, at the last round of joint talks to be held before the conflict in February 1982, Britain had offered no advance on sovereignty. Tensions increased. In March, when Davidoff arrived in South Georgia there were ambiguities over landing procedures, and whether simple landing cards or passports were required. However, Davidoff had landed at Leith, on South Georgia, without passing go, as it were, by presenting himself for formalities at Grytviken. The Ministry of Defence in London sailed HMS *Endurance* with orders to arrest and remove the scrap dealers if they did not acknowledge

British authorities. This peremptory announcement was accompanied by what were seen as exaggerated responses in British newspapers.

Admiral Anaya had reached the limits of toleration. Argentina had huffed and puffed down the years, now it would act. Anaya seized the pretext to fulfil his 'life-long ambition' of restoring the Falklands to Argentina. This interplay between Britain's defence cuts and reaction to the scrap dealers' affair was invested by Argentina with great importance. In retrospect, it ensured that South Georgia became an Anglo-Argentine 'Sarajevo' in the Southern Ocean. **Dr Nicanor Costa Méndez**, George Brown's interlocutor in 1967 (when Britain had first stated formally to Argentina its willingness to cede sovereignty under certain conditions), had been brought back by the military junta in December 1981 and was now, therefore, Argentina's foreign minister for the second time.

When we were squabbling around the Georgias, I made a proposition in my negotiations with Lord Carrington through the ambassador and through the chargé d'affaires in London. I proposed that the Argentine workmen go to Grytviken to have their white cards stamped.

Why didn't they do so in the first place?

Why didn't they? Because there are many discussions about the *need* to have those white cards stamped. But anyhow, at that moment, that was our offer. The British reaction was through Governor Hunt,[25] who was the man behind this idea, to ask for passports with visas. This was unacceptable to Argentina and *had* been unacceptable for many, many years.

Are you saying that initial British and British press reaction to the arrival of Senor Davidoff's famous scrap-dealing party, of forty or so, was taken by you to represent failure of the British Government defence policies announced in 1981, and that you saw some retreat from those decisions and their significance?

Yes. Or, having to adopt positions that were going to create indefinite deadlock, stalemate.

Would it also be right to suggest that you, who had been foreign minister in the 1960s, saw all that happening again?

This is correct.

In other words, your experiences of the past came to influence your judgement strongly at a very important moment?

This is correct.

25 Governor of the Falkland Islands.

Why did you not follow the normal procedures of protest, as in the past? Why did you and the military leaders feel that you could no longer think this way over the Georgias incident?

Because of many reasons. Because, in the past, protest had had no effect whatsoever.

I don't know why I should think that nothing must be done by the Argentine Government, because anything done by the Argentine Government would irritate the Falklands lobby, and that, therefore we should stay at home and forget all about the Islands, even very pacific movements such as landing workmen who were going to dismantle a very old whaling factory.

But you strip that of its political significance, and I'm sure you don't mean to. If the British Antarctic Survey had been withdrawn, the Argentine scrap dealers would have been the only inhabitants on the Georgias; thus reaffirming, which was part of Argentina's policy, an Argentine presence throughout all the Islands, wherever possible.

In the first place, no one was sure, not even the British authorities, that the British Antarctic Survey *was* going to be dismantled. Frankly, we could not ask an Argentine citizen not to go there because we had suspicions that this would cause a reaction in the British people, or the lobby.

I would like to put this to you. You felt here in Buenos Aires, the Junta felt, that by increasing the level of threat to the United Kingdom, which included the military alternative of a touch and go landing on the Falklands to which you've referred, that would be the spur and justification the Conservative Government needed to negotiate with you?

What the Junta thought was that, as things stood, deadlock was unavoidable and that, in the light of past history, deadlock would be very long. On the other hand, intervention by the United States or by the Security Council could *avoid* a deadlock and, if not reach agreement, then at least activate talks. The other thing was, if Argentina accepted the British position concerning the Davidoff men, that would erode Argentina's position in the world, both legally and politically. The Government would lose credibility both domestically and internationally.

While Lord Carrington's gifts as a diplomatist included a widely acknowledged ability to charm the birds from the trees, in Argentine eyes it was his apparent immobilization over the Falklands issue which succeeded in scaring them into the air. Argentine frustration boiled over. By 1982 the sovereignty issue, twice brought to the negotiating table by Britain, had been twice effectively removed. Democracy, it is said, often changes its mind, because it seldom knows it, and so the charges of perfidy arise. What of Argentina, which was not a democracy? The former foreign minister, **Dr Oscar Camilion**, presented his own talks with Lord Carrington six months before the invasion as 'A most significant development in the Falklands negotiations, with the British agreeing for the first time that the present status of the islands cannot be maintained'.[26] Looking back, Camilion says of Argentina that, 'It had never really examined its mind over the Falklands.'

> Something that I learnt during my diplomatic life is that you always need to negotiate, that you should *never* interrupt a negotiation, and you must know your minimum goals. Look, this problem of the Islands, the Malvinas, *was* in fact negotiated after the invasion with the mediation of General Haig.
>
> I think that the real, critical problem for Argentina was that its *minimum* goals were never well determined in Buenos Aires. For that reason the negotiations failed. In those negotiations, with Haig, that started after the invasion, that was very clear, and it was very tragic for us.
>
> *The basis of any successful negotiation must always be that you must know your own position?*
>
> Of course, of course.

With what disastrous ingenuity, therefore, did Argentina choose the short cut which led to war.

Having come as far as the brink of the conflict in the South Atlantic as seen by Argentina, it is time to return to Britain as it, in turn, set out on this collision course in 1981.

---

26 Franks Report, para. 103.

6
A General Micawberism

In 1981, the year before the war, British policy over the Falklands was falling into the unhappy condition once described by Churchill as 'adamant for drift'. The House of Commons, in a furious all-party assault at the end of 1980, had rejected the proposal of the Foreign Office minister, Nicholas Ridley, to transfer sovereignty to Argentina and then lease the Islands back. Following almost seventeen years of negotiations with Argentina it became evident that Lord Carrington, the foreign secretary, no less than his predecessors, was hamstrung by 'the paramount wishes of the Islanders'.

The major defence review undertaken in 1981 set out Britain's future as a European nation and a regional power. This highlighted the ambiguities inherent in the commitment to defend the Falklands. A consequence of these developments was that Britain continued to remain indifferent at a time when, for domestic reasons, the Argentine Junta needed an achievement. In the summer of 1981, the Foreign Office officials were sufficiently alarmed to call ministers to a special meeting at Carlton Gardens. It was agreed that only leaseback stood any chance of solving the dispute.

In the autumn, some six months before the invasion, the diplomats pressed Lord Carrington to advance the priority of the Falklands issue by taking it to 'OD', the Defence Committee of the Cabinet, for a firm decision in favour of leaseback. Lord Carrington, one of the most popular and successful foreign secretaries for many years, had nodded, but said it was not possible. This meant that throughout the year before the war, government policy toward the Falklands was never discussed formally outside the Foreign Office. As events transpired, these were months which the locusts ate.

Of the three courses open to him, Lord Carrington decided to go on playing for time, neither breaking off negotiations nor promoting leaseback. This drew a protest in a dispatch to the Foreign Office from the British ambassador to Argentina, **Sir Anthony Williams**.

All the alternatives which confronted the British Government at that time were very unattractive. I think it is not surprising that there was great difficulty, because the third of those alternatives was 'Fortress Falklands'. That is really what it meant. If you say you are going to let the Argentines realize that negotiation is finished, and then make contingency plans, you had to start thinking seriously about defending the Falklands against forceful action.

In the absence of new policies, after Ridley's defeat in the House of Commons in 1980, it meant that we either had to come up with something new, or renew commitments we were on the way to abandoning?

Yes, I think the basic difficulty with a sovereignty dispute of this kind is that there are really only three solutions to it. Either 'I have it', or 'You have it', or 'We share it.' The essence of leaseback was that it was a fairly acceptable method of sharing.

It fudged the issue?

Yes. Clearly, a surrender of the Islands, which would have been politically totally unacceptable, was 'You have it.' If we could not do 'We share it', and we could not have '*You* have it', the other thing was '*I* have it.' In which case, of course, you had to defend it.

You gave to the modern history of British diplomacy over the Falklands a phrase which has stuck, and, I venture to say, is bound to stick. Towards the end of 1981 you protest strongly that Carrington's decision not to pursue a public education campaign was a decision 'to have no strategy at all beyond a general Micawberism'. What kind of warning was that intended to convey?

Well, in that letter I said Micawberism is not all that unusual in policy; the only thing is to try and conduct a policy of Micawberism as intelligently as possible. That meant looking to what the consequences would be. I was protesting, in fact, that the OD meeting had not taken place. This was where, I had understood from the Carlton Gardens meeting, we were proposing to get authority for meeting the Argentines again after the Falklands elections.[1] In practice we had nothing to meet them with afterwards. Consequently that was a question of buying time once again, while we thought what on earth we should do.

Is your reproach a more general one? How insistent were Lord Carrington's official advisers at this time that he not only should, but must, do something?

There was, of course, continuing 'in-house' discussion. The question, for instance, whether HMS *Endurance* should be allowed to

1 That is, the local elections to the Falkland Islands Legislative Council, completed 14 October 1981, which reflected a hardening of the Islanders' attitudes against negotiations on sovereignty.

carry on coming out during part of the year and being limited to the Falklands area; whether Grytviken on South Georgia should be closed down. All those things. The Foreign Office view was that now it was very important not to give signals to Argentina that we were losing interest in holding up *our* side of the business.

The problem of 'Fortress Falklands' was not in fact a Foreign Office problem. It was a Ministry of Defence problem, and particularly it was a Ministry of Defence *budget* problem. We were asked to operate this Argentina difficulty within certain parameters. One of those parameters was that, actually, we had no money to spend. Indeed, such money as we were spending was being cut down. The difficulty, and why in my view we needed to go to OD, was that we were saying, in these circumstances, that one alternative is to make concessions, the other alternative is to be tougher. But being tougher involves a re-examination of what you're prepared to spend. This is what really needed to be taken into account.

Lord Carrington had tackled Rhodesia, a very emotional issue in terms of domestic politics and a cause of division within the Conservative Party. What hopes were invested in Lord Carrington by the Argentines when it came to the future, and such 'very difficult problems'?

Two things happened in that autumn. Both of them were useful in our general ploy. One was the meeting between Lord Carrington and the Argentine foreign minister, Oscar Camilion, in New York at the General Assembly of the UN. They succeeded in establishing, first, a certain personal contact. But they also established, clearly, that this was a problem that had got to be dealt with, but in a rational and civilized way. That was what was really agreed between them.

The other thing is that when Camilion came back to Argentina he had a very long evening's discussion with me on how we should tackle this. He was really doing a 'thought-clearing' operation. His own suggestion was that we should try a 'methodology' for tackling it and that we should deal with all the complexities of Anglo-Argentine relations, particularly in relation to the Falklands. We should first try to catalogue them and then deal with them *seriatim*. All this, I must say, seemed to me, and I think it seemed in London, a good idea from our point of view. Not necessarily that it was terribly important in itself, but it was certainly a splendid way of making sure that time was filled; that time ran on, during which other things could be thought out and discussed.

Was it a 'given', still, that there was no diminution in the Argentine ambition? The transfer of sovereignty?

That has been true for seventeen years or one hundred and fifty years.

Camilion goes. The new government which takes power in Argentina in December 1981 has been dismissed as Fascist by many, and that perception is part of the adversarial politics of the House of Commons. It unites people on both sides of the House. To dismiss it as Fascist is to dismiss the possibility of joint understanding or accommodation; so how did you describe the character of that government?

Of course, it was not essentially different from its predecessors. 'Fascist' is a very general term. In a specific sense it was *not* Fascist, because it really had no ideological basis. It was a military government and a caretaker government. The military government which had been in power since 1975 had built in a process for changing the personnel. When the commanders-in-chief of the three services reached retirement age, their place in the Junta was taken by their successors. Consequently there was a normal succession.

It did not happen all the time. Indeed, when President Viola was pushed out there was a change in the presidency. He was, as it were, the fourth man. He could, simultaneously, be one of the three but could also be a fourth. In consequence there was not an enormous change in December. There certainly was not a change in ideology. There was a change in personality and there was also a change in the balance of power within this tribune government.

You reported that the Argentine Navy was playing a decisive role in the change of government in Argentina. What significance did that have for you at the time?

This significance: the Argentine Navy had been, traditionally, the most nationalistic of the three services on the subject of the Falklands, and indeed concerning Argentine nationalism in general. Twenty years ago, when there was an earlier military government, the navy were known as 'The Gorillas'; not *guerrillas*; 'gorillas', because they were so much more fierce than the others. It was also true that the commander-in-chief of the navy at that time, Admiral Anaya, was a strong nationalist of a rather anti-British stamp. Any increase in influence that he had was rather bad news for us.

What evidence existed that this new government meant to achieve success over the Falkland Islands in a much shorter time-scale than its predecessors?

The main evidence is the programme which the military government had set itself from the beginning in 1975 when it took over. They called it 'the process', '*Processor*'. They had always maintained that they would deal with three things: the question of internal subversion, the collapse of the economy, and the question of outstanding international quarrels with Chile, with Brazil and with ourselves. It was reckoned that when General Viola took over, in the spring of 1981, this was going to be the last chapter of the military. They felt they had solved the security problem and that they had the economic problem very much in hand. All that was needed was to solve the problems of the Beagle Channel and of the Falklands. They were making progress with the Pope,[2] and, therefore, all that was left was the Falklands. So they had got to this point on their agenda and they were really approaching their own time limit for when they had said that they would go back to barracks, having completed the tasks they had set themselves.

How do you believe you weighed the evidence at this time in your reports to Whitehall? You have emphasized the importance of the role being played by the Navy and 'that is not good news for us'. At the same time you point out in your annual review of 1981, sent home in January 1982, that the ministers in the new government which has taken over 'are a great improvement on their predecessors'.[3] What possibilities did you think your judgement of the new Junta supported concerning the Falklands?

When I said that, I was not primarily, I must confess, thinking of what it meant for us over the Falklands. I was talking about Argentina in general. It is true that whereas the minister for the economy of the Viola period was a modified disaster, his successor was a very much abler, indeed a very able man. This was true of various other ministers.

As far as the minister for foreign affairs was concerned, the one under Viola, Oscar Camilion, was actually rather a good minister. Dr Nicanor Costa Méndez, who succeeded him, was President of the Friends of Oxford University in Buenos Aires. He was a person who had very close relations with Chatham House.[4] He was a highly educated and highly civilized man. Altogether, he looked perhaps a rather better bet than Camilion, who was not someone who had had any particular contact with the United Kingdom.

Camilion, because he came from the 'outside', in many ways had to work his passage. One of the difficulties we always felt with Camilion was that *because* he was a little bit of an outsider in the government he had to work that little bit harder. Nicanor Costa Méndez looked as though he was someone quite familiar in Zion and would be able to play things reasonably. I believe that judgement, in itself, was right. The circumstances under which he came to perform, as far as we were concerned, clearly did not show that degree of greater civilization which I had hoped to see from him.

2 The papacy was a mediator in the arbitration over the Beagle Channel.
3 Franks Report, para. 122.
4 The Royal Institute for International Affairs.

It is unlikely, surely, that the Junta in December 1981 would have recruited Costa Méndez to the post had he been opposed to the sense of urgency over the Falklands with which they invested it? After all, he had been the one to whom George Brown in the 1960s had first communicated Britain's willingness to cede sovereignty to Argentina.

I don't think you could find an Argentine foreign minister who would *not* be sympathetic to the idea of solving the problem rapidly. But I do not think that the role of minister of foreign affairs in the military government of that time was a central role. It was a little bit like the Soviet system at the time when Gromyko was foreign minister, but nothing else. A very important man, but not at the centre of policy making. I think that was true of the Argentine political set-up throughout the military government. The Ministry of Foreign Affairs was an executant of policy, rather than a creator of policy of its own.

There were two reports home in January of 1982 which reviewed the year just passed, 1981: your own and that of Governor Hunt, the governor of the Falkland Islands. They reflect differing views about the possibility and the desirability of pursuing a negotiated settlement. How important were those differences in their influence in Whitehall?

I think that the interesting thing about them is that, of course, we were looking at different screens. I was looking at the Argentine screen, he at the Falklands screen. It is the *combination* of them which produces food for thought in Whitehall, one would have thought. What I was saying in my report was that 1981 had been a very wearing process and sensitivities on both sides had got considerably more acute during the year. Consequently the problem was more difficult. What *he* was saying in his report was that, as far as the Islanders were concerned, they did not much like the idea and had concluded, in the end, they did not want to be with the Argentines at all. Therefore, it was clear it was a collision course. There is not much conflict between Rex Hunt's report and mine. We were reporting on different things. But the two *together* made a fairly glum picture.

What was the function of the governor of the Falkland Islands? Was he part of British policy, which was to produce a negotiated settlement, or to represent the Islanders' views?

I think the role of the governor of the Falklands was a very difficult one. Earlier on, he had both to represent the British Government to the Falkland Islanders, and the Falkland Islanders to the British Government. This is an extremely difficult task. In so far as it is possible to do both at the same time, I think he did it very well. In practice, it was right for him to make the British Government aware of what the Islanders were thinking and, particularly, what his own Council was thinking.

Yet there is that recurring Foreign Office phrase revealed in the Franks Report. It was felt that the 'unguided thoughts' of the Islanders were very unlikely to lead them to accept British policy directions over the Falklands. The point I was really putting to you is that Hunt did not seem so much concerned, judging by his reports, to 'guide the thoughts' of the Islanders, as to reflect their view that the policy cannot be carried into effect because they are so totally opposed to it?

But, you see, the decision which had been taken by Lord Carrington was that we were not *supposed* to guide them. This term, 'educating opinion in the Falkland Islands', has always seemed to me a slightly offensive one. I think it is a short-hand term. What I said in my reports, which I still feel was the trouble with the Falkland Islanders, was this: the real alternatives which lay before them were never really put to them. The idea that they actually had a *choice* between 'doing nothing' and 'leaseback', or whatever it was going to be, was fallacious and deceptive. The difficulty was that the Falkland Islanders did not *realize* that there was no way in which they could carry on as they had in the 1960s and '70s, because things were going to change. As indeed they did.

But this is the uncertain trumpet in London? We never resolved this question, whether the thoughts of the Islanders were to be 'guided', and our policy fails because of it?

Not only I, but many others, have pointed out there was a transition from saying that the *interests* of the Islanders must be paramount to saying their '*wishes*' must be paramount. This happened, as far as I can see, almost in a fit of absence of mind. It just slid across. Rather like mention of the Falkland Islands dependencies. If you look back into history you'll find occasions when they are included and occasions when they are left out, apparently, simply, by carelessness in drafting.

From the very early stages I contested the idea, from Buenos Aires, that the *wishes* of the Islanders could possibly be a paramount consideration in British policy. The wishes of any part of the British public are not paramount and, in addition, this did not seem as if it would work. However, it certainly became the doctrine. Once it did, the great question was 'Who determines what those wishes are?' It became a very hot political potato, particularly after the House of Commons in December,[5] and, in practice, our terms of reference

5 That is, after the 'shouting down' of Nicholas Ridley's leaseback proposal in December 1980.

were 'the wishes of the people' as one could determine them. The wishes being, apparently, that nothing should change at all.

You say the real alternatives were never really put to the Islanders. But there is a letter written by Richard Luce, the minister of state following Ridley's departure, on 4th March 1982, concerning Governor Hunt's annual review. Hunt has pointed out that the new elections to the Falkland Islands Legislative Council have returned members who are unanimously opposed to leaseback. We are only a month or so away from the invasion. Luce confirms the pessimistic analysis by Hunt in his review and comments that 'given the Islander and Argentine attitudes we are now perilously near the inevitable move from dialogue to confrontation.'[6] This, we are told in Franks, was 'meant to serve as a warning to the Islanders of the consequence of a breakdown in negotiations'. Yet it does not seem that we really believed what we thought?

I think it's true that what comes out of London, at that time, is full of foreboding that things could go wrong quickly and badly. I was very glad to see that. It was what I had been feeling for some time. But I am not so confident about the extent to which that was conveyed to the Falkland Islanders. We are back into the 'pre-OD'[7] meeting stage. My long interview with Camilion the previous October, and then the talks in February, were all really buying time. The question is for what were we buying time? As far as I could see it was buying time for a meeting of OD.

Sir Anthony Williams had advocated telling Argentina frankly, if Britain was unable to move, that negotiations were pointless as long as the Islanders had the right of veto, and then facing the consequences. That meant 'Fortress Falklands'. But, this had been constantly rebuffed down the years by the Treasury, to whose oncoming tread all heels in White-hall and Westminster were, at this time, particularly sensitive. Britain was therefore pretending to negotiate in good faith while ruling out additional security for the Islands. It was trying to make strategic bricks without financial straw. With what degree of insistence did officials press ministers to review the policy? Because successive governments were unwilling to pay the cost of a 'Fortress Falklands' policy, the Foreign Office had maintained a fairly consistent pressure to settle the question. Historically, was there an 'in-house' view of this commitment held at the Ministry of Defence? The permanent under-secretary of the Ministry of Defence, for six years preceding the Falklands conflict, was **Sir Frank Cooper**.

6 Franks Report, para. 125.
7 The 'OD' is the Cabinet defence committee.

First of all, they always wanted to minimize the commitment. They were also keen to see it disappear, and they never really raised their hand against the idea of it disappearing. A few people, who were passionately interested in Antarctica, and making rather romantic sailings in South Atlantic waters, were well outside the mainstream of thinking. So, I think, the Ministry of Defence attitude was, 'Well, please don't bother us more than you must with this', and, quite frankly, 'May it go away!'

What was implicit for the Falklands commitment in those big strategic decisions made in the sixties and seventies over Simonstown, and later in the defence review of 1974?

I think they diminished the interest, never very large in the Ministry of Defence, in the Falkland Islands. Indeed, in *any other* rather 'out-of-the-way' part of the world. Quite clearly, the decision taken by the Labour Government of the sixties never to undertake an invasion in the shadow of hostile air-power was strong, and clearly felt, within the Ministry of Defence.

But after the formation of the OPEC cartel in 1974, and because the Falklands commands the entry into both oceans, did we retreat from those positions? What did the Ministry of Defence urge? Were you inclined to hedge our bets and delay the choice we had begun, at least, to make over the Falklands?

No. I think there were one or two small voices who occasionally argued for the strategic importance of the South Atlantic and the Falkland Islands. But with the passage of time, and the closer we became to Europe, the less those voices were heard, and the less they had any platform on which to speak. So, I think, *there was a gradual increase in the lack of interest*, if you could put it that way, over a twenty- or twenty-five-year period.

When it came to the possible exploitation of oil, or other resources in sub-Antarctica and Antarctica, what view did the Ministry of Defence take? On the basis of 'Whoever thought, as recently as twenty years ago, that the North Sea contained anything but fish?'

Quite frankly, I think they tended to take a very short-term view of what their current interests were. I do not think we are very good, as a nation, at taking long-term views. It is not part of the central political philosophy of this country. From time to time there were reports, of various kinds, that there might be vast quantities of oil under the Antarctic; that the seas were rich in fish and so on; but I don't think they affected the mainstream of thinking. The general tendency was, 'This remains to be proved', and, 'It is for others, not the Ministry of Defence, to establish the value, or otherwise, of resources of this kind.'

One notes the very negative reflections of the chiefs of staff, by the late 1970s, revealed to us in Franks, as the balance of power is changing against us in the area. In which case what was the essence of 'deterrence' against Argentina pursuing her ambitions by force if political means failed?

There was very little element of real deterrence. There were occasional visits by Her Majesty's ships, the ice-patrol vessel was there from time to time, and there were a few marines scattered around. Arguments used to go on as to how many there should be, more or less in single figures. Deterrence? I think it was seen as something that was going to be solved by negotiation and – let the Foreign Office get on with that, frankly.

Was the Ministry of Defence content that 'deterrence' should be conveyed by symbols rather than realities? Given that the commitment remained on the books until it was successfully negotiated?

Yes. The reason for that was quite straightforward. After the 1960s, nobody could conceivably have thought it was going to be a priority, for *any* of Her Majesty's Governments, that they would be asked to go back and retake the Falkland Islands, or mount a major deterrent on a permanent basis there, when it had no interest for defence as part of a national security policy.

Were we relying, in that case, on the good sense of Argentina in waiting until the Falklands fell into their laps after a negotiation?

I don't know if we were relying on the good sense of Argentina. I think one relied on the Foreign Office somehow finding a diplomatic solution. What became, progressively, more evident was that whatever solution they found, neither of the major political parties was able to get it past their own supporters, or the House of Commons as a whole.

What role was played, in our diplomacy, by arms sales to the Latin American continent in the 1970s?

Britain's defence industries export relationship with South America as a whole was patchy over a long period. We've got very close historical relationships with a number of South American countries, notably on the naval side. In the early seventies, there was certainly a very strong drive by the incoming Conservative Government, predicated on the basis that we ought to increase our arms sales, worldwide, whenever we could. South America, showing signs of becoming a much richer part of the world, was a prime target. Arising out of that came some of the sales of ships and aircraft in the seventies. Every time there was a question of something going to Argentina, everybody looked at it rather carefully. On the whole, this was seen as something likely to bring about a better relationship with the Argentine.

Quite a lot of care was exercised in the individual decisions. The general thrust of it was that this would tend to calm things, rather than aggravate them. It was seen as part of being 'more friendly'. On the whole you sell arms only to friendly countries. You don't sell them to those with whom you have major quarrels. There was a push, really, from both the Labour Government and the Conservative Government in favour of exporting more arms to South America.

Then you had the situation where the Americans more or less reversed their policy; having thrown the American blanket, as it were, over South America. Particularly during the Carter presidency, the Americans looked askance at selling any kind of arms. This was seen, I think, as an opportunity for the European countries.

Were there specific instances when Britain paid penalties, where the Falklands question was a barrier to commercial success in Latin America? There were the cases of the frigate contract with Argentina, and the sale of the Hawk aircraft to Venezuela, billion dollar contracts which came to nothing, it is said, because of Argentine and Venezuelan attitudes to Britain's shilly-shallying over the Falklands?

The major impact was delay, I think. It was impossible for the government of the day to make up its mind whether it should sell a particular piece of equipment to a particular country in South America. I think this was due not so much to the Falklands but to the overall political relationships we had with South American countries. Certainly, there was a period with the Argentine when arms sales were held up, quite specifically, because relations had gone sour, particularly in the middle seventies. So, it was an erratic policy, in the sense that you could be very near a deal and people would say, 'Hold it!', and then the 'hold' might go on for a year or two.

Is that to say that the difficulties we had in raising our commercial interest, and performance, in South America were due more to our inability to resolve the contradictions in our policy, rather than attitudes taken up by the South American states?

We have volatile relationships between Britain and South America. It goes up and down. It is not a smooth, continuing, relationship by normal diplomatic standards.

The Franks Report tells us that after the hurling back of Nicholas Ridley by the Commons for his mooting of leaseback in December 1980, officials were looking to ministers to review the outcome of contingency planning 'in the light of a potentially more aggressive posture by Argentina'. We are told also, 'In the event, government policy towards Argentina was never formally discussed outside the

Foreign Office after January 1981. Thereafter the time was never judged to be ripe.'[8] *How unusual was that in your long experience of Whitehall?*

First of all, the Falkland Islands is 'one off'. It is not part of the normal Whitehall or Westminster process. It is a small place, a small number of people, and it does not really generate much political interest. It is not, in its own right, a major political issue, unless it suddenly becomes a major political issue through the force of other circumstances.

I think, after Nicholas Ridley's unfortunate experience, officials did what they normally do on such occasions. They retreated to their tents and wondered what they should do next. They gabble between each other and try and see if they can pick up at least some of the pieces of the jug that has been dashed from their hands and lies in many pieces upon the floor. They certainly went through quite a considerable period when they were saying, 'Well, you know, ministers *ought* to address this as an *issue*.' Ministers were simply saying 'Look, we've just *been* through all this. Why are we being asked to do it again? Go away and see if you can find some different solution. You know *that* one will not work.'

And then, of course, there were quite considerable changes of ministerial personalities, and incumbents in the various key offices, at that time. So I think it does happen from time to time, but I do believe very strongly that the Falklands was *not* something by which you can judge the rest of Whitehall standards.

But 'in the light of a potentially more aggressive posture by Argentina', just how hard were officials pressing their ministers to take this issue back to the Cabinet?

I don't think they ever really persuaded ministers that this *was* a matter of the highest importance. I am not convinced myself that officials *did* regard it like that either. I much prefer to see it as saying, in effect, 'Well, here we are. We've tried over two years. We got Nicholas Ridley, "up to the post", and then everybody fell on him, and then he fell over!' So I see it as a much more natural thing, rather than the kind of process described in the cool prose of the Franks Report.

Lord Carrington was well known to you all at the Ministry of Defence, where he'd been navy minister, later defence secretary, in the years before he was foreign secretary. How large a departure from Carrington's own performance and history as a minister was the fact that, following that reverse for Ridley in December 1980, it was the last time the Falklands was discussed, outside the Foreign Office, until the Argentine invasion, fifteen months later, in April 1982?

8 Franks Report, para. 291.

It was odd, and I know a number of people who did feel it odd, at the time, that there was not a discussion amongst ministers. Various attempts were made to get ministers to discuss it. It was a mixture of circumstances, quite frankly, that failed to have it discussed.

Of course, it was curious, in some ways, that Carrington did not send a paper and say 'Look, I really must *insist* that this be discussed.' I think he took the view that it was not going to get any further forward by discussion with his ministerial colleagues and, indeed, it might make his task very much more difficult in trying to go ahead with the various negotiations. He may well have been right in that. I don't think I would seek to blame him in that context. It's quite possible. Certainly, if one had been talking about the Falklands in some kind of political context, or in relation to a political initiative, discussion might have actually been harmful rather than helpful.

I think the security side of it is a different matter. But it's interesting that the *security* card was never seriously played, because there was no intelligence, or any other belief, or any other signal, which led people to believe that there *would* be an invasion.

There were intelligence assessments however, in 1981,[9] which *did* predict that Britain's bluff might be called in the second half of 1982, leading, as it said, to the 'strong likelihood of military action'. But *invasion* was a very big word it seems, and not set in the dictionary of Whitehall, or Westminster's, thinking about the Falklands.

As Lord Carrington looked out of those famous windows in his office, before which, for example, Sir Edward Grey had stood, and spoken of 'the lamps going out all over Europe', what were his distractions?

Principally, there was the major preoccupation of the European policy. In both personality and policy, Margaret Thatcher marked a break with the more recent Conservative past. The prime minister did little to discourage the belief that she was incandescent over the unfairness of Britain's payments to the Community budget. She was determined to prosecute a major battle over this for national ends, and, in this and other important matters of foreign policy, to assuage popular feeling.

The head of the Diplomatic Service, Sir Michael Palliser, has told us that Lord Carrington was 'only moderately successful' in getting the prime minister to concentrate on the Falklands question. As the Franks Report disclosed,[10] the prime minister, herself, ruled that Cabinet discussion of the Falklands should be postponed until *after* a Rhodesian settlement. Rhodesia, for some fifteen years, had been among the most

9 Franks Report, para. 95.
10 Franks Report, para. 76.

emotional issues in British politics, and it was Mrs Thatcher's first big test in government. Lord Carrington had led the prime minister and Cabinet to the achievement of a settlement, following months of the most intensive negotiations in 1979 and the early part of 1980.

The unanticipated outcome, in the subsequent Rhodesian election, of an outright victory for Robert Mugabe which, at least when the Rhodesian diplomacy began, had been considered the least desirable result, had provoked a greater degree of hostility to Carrington within the Conservative Party. Particularly because it would have meant taking up the divisive issue of 'kith and kin' *twice in the same Parliament*, to what extent did the existence of such animosities inhibit the foreign secretary from pressing for action over the Falklands? The head of the Foreign Office at the time was **Sir Michael Palliser**.

I do not think he felt like that because he thought there was personal animosity to him. There was not personal animosity to him in the Cabinet. On the contrary, there was great admiration for him in the Cabinet. I think it was more that – and maybe this was a misjudgement he made: I understood *why* he did it, and I agreed with him, but as the Franks Report brings out, Mr Ridley and the officials in the Foreign Office, including myself, had hoped that it could be brought to the Cabinet, towards the end of 1981; at any rate to the Defence Committee of the Cabinet, which comes to the same thing. I think that for reasons which I personally understood, and was perfectly content with at the time, Lord Carrington just felt that the *timing* of that was wrong. That reflected not in the least hostility to him *in the Cabinet* – I really don't think that was there at all – but more a feeling that the only time when one would really get a British Cabinet to *focus* on the issue was at a time when it was manifestly going to cause real difficulty if they did not. And, in the early autumn of 1981, it was not clear that that was the case.

But it seems clear that Lord Carrington was pressed by all his advisers that the time had come to make a choice *after the failure of Ridley's leaseback proposal in the House of Commons. We either had to opt for Fortress Falklands, or public and Islander opinion had to be 'educated'. What do you recall of his responses?*

The instinct of senior officials, and I think this instinct is a healthy one, is that one should not try to 'go public' with a policy, try to inform people of what it is, or persuade them that it is the right policy, until there is a very firm government-approved policy. It was not so, in the case of the Falklands, at that stage.

Certainly, the conclusion we reached was that we should advise Lord Carrington that we *ought to try* to get the Cabinet to decide what it wanted, because time was getting short. He considered all that, and he concluded that, on the basis of where he had got to at that point with Argentina, it was not the right moment to go to his colleagues with what they would be liable to say were 'hypothetical questions'; and that, given the lack of interest in the problem elsewhere in the Cabinet, this was liable to result in a confused outcome.

Is it a matter of personal regret to you looking back, and as a convinced 'European' yourself, that you did not more powerfully insist to Lord Carrington, at this time, that 'something must be done'?

No, I don't think so. If you put yourself in the position that we were in at that time, this was essentially a matter of political judgement. I did not feel then, and I don't feel now, that his judgement was wrong. I think that if we had taken it to the Cabinet, or its Defence Committee, at that time, we would *not* have got a very firm conclusion out of it.

The senior officials, the minister Mr Ridley, and the ambassador in Buenos Aires, felt we *had* reached that point. But on the question of handling a Cabinet, you, actually, have to take the judgement of the Cabinet minister. It was our duty to point out to him, as we did, the nature of the problem as it seemed to us at the time. He did not dissent from *that* at all. But it was also his judgement, and I do not disagree, that the Cabinet would not face up to it at that point.

Lord Carrington's decision administered a powerful sedative to diplomacy and, as the ambassador in Buenos Aires, Sir Anthony Williams, objected, it left the Foreign Office waiting, like Mr Micawber, for something to turn up. It did. In the absence of a prospering negotiation, deterrence to *military* action by Argentina failed.

The genesis of the Falklands War must also be considered, therefore, against the background of the renewal, in Britain, of profound argument about future defence policy. Margaret Thatcher had brought to Conservative government a sea-change in economic doctrine, by installing the intellectual reign of 'monetarist' discipline. In 1981, she replaced her defence secretary, Francis Pym, with **Sir John Nott**. An economic hawk was now perched in the topmost branches of the Ministry of Defence. Many pretty chickens were marked for slaughter in one fell swoop, as the new secretary of state acted with speed and audacity.

It seemed to me that there wasn't really any great grasp of the long-term financial realities facing the country, in the Ministry of Defence. The trouble was that the expectations of the Ministry of Defence were greatly raised by the Tory election manifesto and by the aspirations, which we all shared, to meet the Nato '3 per cent' guide-lines.[11] In addition, and of course you've seen exactly the same thing happen in the early period of the Reagan presidency, an enthusiasm for defence turned into a very expensive and over-elaborate long-term programme. Things start going into the long-term programme which, frankly, are unlikely ever to be financed.

Francis Pym, through no fault of his own, ran into a particular problem in 1980. This was the slow-down in economic growth, and hence the multiplication of deliveries to the Ministry of Defence which their cash flow could not meet. Defence equipment was pouring into the Ministry of Defence and they had run out of money to pay for it. So, there came a crisis. It led to the moratorium on defence expenditure, and to all the dramas about how the *commitments* were to be clawed back to meet that moratorium. There was its impact on small businesses in the West Midlands, and on unemploy-ment. It became a very difficult issue.

Francis Pym found himself in a very difficult position, at a rather delicate moment. The prime minister felt that this was just bad management. She felt that, you know, someone like Derek Rayner[12] could come along, and put it all right by just sort of looking at it.

You could run Defence rather like running Marks and Spencer?

Or, you could run Defence like Michael Heseltine reorganized his headquarters staff in the Department of the Environment. All very naive and rather silly, but there was this view that a Rayner exercise would solve the problem; that the 'brass hats' were driving around in too many cars, and if you merged the bands and everybody ate in the same Naafi, instead of having four Naafis, and so on. It was all great fun, and we've all had those views of the Services, but that was *not* the root of the problem.

Therefore, what set the tone of the defence review you carried out?

Francis Pym had already given, on behalf of the Government, a commitment to a reduction in Defence expenditure in the current year of about one hundred million pounds. We had all agreed with that and it had been announced. I had to find that one hundred million. I can tell you that there was nothing left to save but the food of the forces! By the time the financial year has begun in the Ministry of Defence, there is virtually nothing you can save, except jet fuel and food. That one hundred million was an absolute nightmare.

11 The agreed determination of all members of the Alliance to increase their defence expenditure by 3 per cent a year.

12 Lord Rayner, managing director of Marks and Spencer, and 'Adviser to the Prime Minister on improving efficiency and eliminating waste in government', 1979–83.

It then became clear to me, as I tackled the problem in the first two or three weeks, that there was a very much greater one. It had been anticipated that the 3 per cent growth in defence expenditure was going to go on for a decade. The long-term costings were almost predicated on a 3 per cent growth right through the decade. No one had ever said *that* was the policy of the Government, although it *was* the policy of Nato, and far too much had been put in the programme. I thus became aware that there was a, literally, huge problem. I have to say the civil servants were aware of it too and so were the more intelligent members of the military.

Faced with two exacting demands, strategic commitments and no money in the Ministry of Defence to pay the bills, Sir John Nott proposed to let the axe fall on some sixty warships by 1984.

The decline in the imperial role had been particularly hurtful for the Royal Navy. The navy was the oldest instrument of empire, and for the British, visible sea-power had been almost part of the order of nature for centuries. The Chief of the Defence Staff, from 1979 to 1982, was **Admiral Lord Lewin**.

Argentina was considered very much a political matter and not one for military involvement. We had a chiefs of staff 'view' on Argentina, which we dusted off every time it came to the top of the Foreign Office agenda. We had warned successive governments of the problems of defending these islands so far away from the UK base. In terms of military priorities which, of course, ministers give us, it was very low on the list. Ever since 1966, when the Labour Government had decided that there would be no more 'strike' carriers, successive governments had told us that 'never again' would we be called upon to fight a limited war, without allies, outside the Nato area, or to fight a war outside the range of shore-based air support. This had been consistent for fifteen years. If we had asked for the material required to fight that sort of war, we would have been laughed out of court.

The prime minister herself mentioned subsequently the constant similarity in the reports over the years from the chiefs of staff. She quoted the September 1981 paper by the chiefs. They, 'having recognized the strength of the Argentine Air Force, concluded that to deter a full-scale invasion, a large balanced force would be required, comprising an Invincible-class carrier, four destroyers or frigates, plus, possibly, a nuclear-powered submarine, supply ships in attendance, and additional manpower up to brigade strength to reinforce the garrison. Such a deployment', the prime minister continued to quote, 'would be very expensive and would engage a significant proportion of this country's naval resources.

There was a danger that its dispatch could precipitate the very action it was intended to deter. That,' the prime minister concluded, 'was the advice that continually reached me.' There followed this, from the chiefs, in the same report, 'If then faced with Argentine occupation of the Falklands, on arrival, there could be no certainty that such a force could retake them.'

Was this not an acknowledgement it was necessary, and should be our ambition simply, to be rid of this commitment Britain could no longer discharge?

Yes. I think it should, politically. We were talking about deterring a *full-scale* Argentine invasion. You could deter an Argentine invasion by a much *smaller* force, by putting a token force down there. This was the advice we gave, and indeed it was the deployment we made, in 1977, when talks were going on in Buenos Aires, and intelligence told us that there might be some attempt at invasion if those talks failed. We deployed, on that occasion, two frigates and a nuclear submarine, which would have been enough, I would estimate, to deter an invasion *before* it was mounted. But the larger scale force is required if it gets to a higher level of Argentine readiness, and they have actually *sailed* an aircraft carrier, landing ships, and two thousand marines to carry out an invasion.

Do you agree that Argentine planning seems to have assumed that the real deterrent to their taking military action over the Falklands was whether they could hang on to the Islands once they had taken them? They appear to have thought their problem was not so much actually landing on the Falklands, but their calculation of our ability to dislodge them if they did so.

I am not sure that I am in the Argentine mind. That could well have been their feeling and also the reason they had not tried sooner.

And the 1981 defence review would have been more evidence that we would not fight or did not intend to fight?

At some time in the future. The 1981 defence review had not started to bite in 1982. It was a wasting away of maritime assets in the longer term.

None the less, Sir John Nott's view was that the concept of 'global reach' for the Royal Navy, implicit in the balanced naval task force, was nostalgia for the days of empire?

I am afraid this is nonsense. The 'balanced naval task force' went when the old *Ark Royal* paid off, in 1978, and we no longer had the Buccaneers and the Vixens and the early-warning aircraft of the strike carriers. We only had *one* then. You could not do much with one aircraft carrier, and she was a contribution to Nato. *That* was a balanced task force.

We then obtained the Harrier and, my goodness, it was a long fight in Whitehall to get the Harrier. There was a tremendous amount of opposition to it. Mr Healey had dictated, in 1966, that 'never again' would the Royal Navy operate fixed-wing aircraft. We wanted the Harrier to provide us with a rapid response to a 'shadower' in the North Atlantic, that came out and detected our position. We wanted to be able to shoot that 'shadower' down before it homed submarines, or Soviet surface ships, on us. It is very expensive to maintain a combat air patrol from a shore base seven hundred or a thousand miles away.

The second requirement of the Harrier was to identify surface targets detected by maritime patrol aircraft. Maritime patrol aircraft would be high up and would not want to go down and look at each surface contact. So you have the Harrier, that can nip out and say, 'That's a merchant ship', or, 'That's a Soviet cruiser', long before you could bring aircraft out from shore. If we had suggested we wanted the Harrier to provide air defence of a task force *outside the Nato area* we would never have got it. But that is how, in fact, we used it in war.

But had that defence review been implemented, and had the Argentines waited, we would not have been able to do in 1985 or 1986 what we did in 1982?

No. We would have had to have very much more luck. If the 1981 review had been carried into effect, *Invincible* would have been sold to the Australians. We would have had only two of those carriers available. One might have been deep in the middle of a refit, in which case we would only have one. We could not have done the operation with one.

In reaching his own conclusions about his defence review in 1981 Nott, clearly, took the view that it meant, decidedly, not equipping ourselves for another 'Suez', or post-colonial war, and that the financial imperatives pointed remorselessly, as he put it, to 'the need to end the task-force mentality' of the Royal Navy.

I think this is a post-Falklands thought. For fifteen years ministers had told us we would not have to fight that sort of war and so it was not on our list. I don't think ministers ever envisaged that the Argentinians would invade. Diplomacy would prevent them from invading. Because we told them we could not, or they had decided that they could not, mount the deterrent which the military had advised would be necessary.

But the navy has a sense of history. British history and 'the navy' have been indivisible. Do you remember Admiral Beatty, at the great Washington Naval Conference after the First World War, when the American Secretary, Hughes, proposed as part of a general international disarmament the 'scrapping in a moment', as I think the British Naval historian put it, 'of more naval tonnage than the cycle of wars and centuries had achieved'? It was said that Beatty was 'slightly staggered' and 'deeply disturbed'. He was 'observed to come forward in his seat' at this suggestion! What were your own reactions to Nott's defence review in 1981, and its planned reductions in the surface fleet?

Well, I was in a very difficult position. I was an admiral who was also chief of the Defence staff. During that defence review, I was the chairman of the Chiefs of Staffs Committee and *primus inter pares*, not an adviser in my own right. I was required to present the advice of my colleagues. If I was to retain their confidence, I had to be seen to be even-handed.

That defence review was rushed through at an enormous pace. Now, I had a very small central staff. The organization of the Ministry of Defence was such that the individual service staffs were very much larger, and stronger, than the central staff. My central staff could not really operate until the stage *after* the individual service staffs had prepared their positions. Only then would we be in a position to produce a consensus for the chiefs of staffs. We were not given enough time to do that. So the input from my central staff, or from myself, was not really sufficient. It was a very hurried, very superficial, defence review, politically imposed.

At one stage, the chiefs of staffs exercised their right for direct access to the prime minister. She listened to us very carefully. We had a two-hour meeting with her, and in fact the reduction was lessened a little. Mr Pym did not get enough money out of defence, and he went. My feeling is that Mr Nott was put in to cut defence expenditure, and he was determined to do it quickly. In the defence review, the navy suffered more than the other two services. The other two services suffered as well, and not enough attention is given to that. All three services suffered. I think it is quite wrong to express it as slashing at the navy and leaving the other two untouched.

From my own point of view I thought that John Nott had got it wrong. It was very difficult for me to say so and preserve support and confidence of the chiefs of staff. But I did not think it was so *radically* wrong as to be dangerous for the security of this country, or for our contribution to Nato; and, I thought, as the years went by, we might have time to redress the balance a little.

How was the eventual decision reached to get rid of the navy's big ships, like Invincible, *in discussion with Nott?*

I think we had only two meetings, at most, with Mr Nott. The final decisions were taken very quickly, and indeed, the First Sea Lord exercised his right of direct access to go and see the Prime Minister.

The other chiefs of staff[13] would not support him, because they felt if the navy got something back then *they* were going to lose something more. Again, at that time I was in the position of not being a separate adviser, I was only a 'consensus' adviser. Subsequently, I managed to change that. Mr Nott's proposal, in his White Paper, was that of the three carriers, only two should be maintained as operational. Certainly, the navy was working on the assumption that the third one would be kept in care and maintenance. Of course *Ark Royal*[14] was not completed then. Neither was *Illustrious*. The two carriers operational were *Hermes* and *Invincible*.

Now, Mr Nott in deciding to *sell Invincible*, had sought no advice whatsoever. The Australian defence minister had come to London on a personal visit. He had fought in Crete in 1941 and had been to a reunion of Crete veterans there, and he had come on to London to go to the Derby, being a keen racing man. He made a courtesy visit to Mr Nott. I do not know what happened during this courtesy visit, I was not present, but after that meeting, Mr Nott's office came to the decision that *Invincible* would be offered to Australia.

Now, my Australian opposite number, the Chief of the Defence Staff in Australia, was a man I had known for over forty years. We were in destroyers together during the Second World War and he is the godfather to my son. I immediately corresponded with him and suggested that, if he wanted a carrier, *Hermes* was a much better bet. She fitted in with their material very much more. Unfortunately, I was not able to persuade him that *Hermes* was the one he should go for.

Didn't John Nott call the navy's bluff by saying, in effect, that the navy vote could not be justified outside the Nato area? In essence, wasn't that the decision he took?

No, I do not think that is so at all. He thought the balance of the navy, as between surface ships and submarines, was wrong, and that we should give priority to submarines. This is a perennial argument. 'What is the right balance?' In peacetime, in the run up to war and in preventing war, surface ships are very much more use to you than submarines. If you get as far as war itself, submarines are of more use than surface ships. The balance of expenditure between the two is extremely difficult to strike. All I can say to you is that to meet the political commitments successive governments have placed upon us, in peacetime, *always* requires us to have more surface ships than we actually possess.

13 Field Marshal Sir Edwin Bramall, and Marshal of the Royal Air Force, Sir Michael Beetham.

14 That is, a new, smaller, *Ark Royal*, not the large strike carrier paid off in 1978.

In protest against the defence review of 1981, the minister for the navy, Keith Speed, tried, and failed, to change the policy. When asked by Nott to submit his resignation he refused and was thereupon dismissed, following a personal audience with the prime minister. His going was a repetition of what had happened after Denis Healey's major review under Labour in the 1960s, when the big aircraft carriers were sent to the scrapyards, and Christopher Mayhew quit the government. Keith Speed was destined to be the last of the navy ministers. As he departed from the Ministry of Defence in Whitehall, the corridors and lobby were filled with waving, cheering, naval and Royal Marine officers who worked in the ministry. He was seen into his car by the First Sea Lord, Admiral Sir Henry Leach.

Unlike the occasion of the 1966 review, this time it was a Conservative Defence Secretary in a Conservative government, pledged to strong defence policies, who had drawn the sword and made cuts even more dramatic than Healey's fifteen years earlier. **Sir John Nott**'s action and analysis, made manifest in his defence review in 1981, stirred strong conflicts of emotion and reason in the party and the services.

I realized that I could not leap into this too quickly. So Sir Frank Cooper[15] and the staffs started to prepare papers for me on how we were going to solve the problem; how we were going to cut back in the medium term on defence and bring the projections back to *nil*-growth. I played it fairly slowly, initially. It was only after I had been there four months that I sent a minute round the Ministry of Defence saying that we must have an internal review, and a major one. Because I had been in Bermuda just after the note went out they called it, as I remember, the 'Bermudagram'.

I had not intended, of course, that any of this should involve drama. I had intended it should be an internal review of the problem. But as soon as elements in the Forces realized that this was going to be a very painful process, they started fighting me in the media and in the House of Commons. So quite quickly I found myself in a public punch-up with the Conservative Party, and with the service 'lobbies', in a way which no secretary of state would wish. That made the whole thing very much more difficult. The discussions eventually led, with the high profile it had all acquired, to Keith Speed's resignation.

In a way, I needed another month or so to complete the process. But I realized that unless I got it out of the way, I was going to *lose*. There was great pressure, therefore, to get the thing announced and agreed. And we *did* get it announced and agreed. My Cabinet

15 Permanent under-secretary, Ministry of Defence.

colleagues, including my predecessor, Francis Pym, who was still a member of the relevant Cabinet committee chaired by the prime minister, were very supportive of the recommendations I had made. They were exceptionally difficult recommendations. But every step I took was taken with the full agreement of my Cabinet colleagues.

One or two of the things you have said might suggest or confirm what your critics believed, that you were a man in a hurry. Do you feel that you produced an intellectually coherent strategy in that defence review of 1981?

Well, you are quite right. My critics *do* say I did it all far too hurriedly; that I did not listen to professional advice, etcetera, etcetera. It simply is not true.

It *was* done in rather a hurry. It was done in a hurry because, as a group of people, we did make up our minds, about what had to be done, fairly early. There came a point in time where I could not go on having meetings with people who did not agree with the conclusions. I knew perfectly well what their objections were; but there was no way in which we could go on, week after week, hearing the same objections over and over again. So the thing had to be announced. We had to conclude it.

And of course it is not true that I did not take professional advice. Apart from one section of the Ministry of Defence, centred mainly around the Admiralty Board, in the Central Military Staffs – not every individual member – and in so far as there could *ever* be a consensus among the military about a forward reduction in defence expenditure, I think there was a feeling that this was the best we could do.

Now, intellectually, the White Paper is still on the record. It is there for everybody to see. I doubt if more than a hundred people have ever read it, but it is there to be read. I happen to believe that, intellectually, it stands up very well to the circumstances which required it.

Even after 1945, which marked the end of British naval mastery, and during the long recession which followed, bases and personnel had been cut, rather than ships. The Royal Navy still deployed a considerable force of surface warships and it still showed the flag in all the oceans. Aircraft carriers, scrapped in successive defence reviews, were reincarnated in the form of the smaller through-deck cruisers, with their Harrier jump-jets. Only with Sir John Nott's review, which proposed to concentrate the navy under water, and bid farewell to the long tradition of the ocean-going surface fleet, by now enshrined in the issue of the 'task force', did the great vicissitudes come for the senior service. What was the nature of the formidable opposition these proposals aroused, and why was it so hostile to this particular defence review? Unsurprisingly, John Nott's principal adversary was the First Sea Lord, **Admiral Sir Henry Leach**.

I think largely because it was probably the most savage, in terms of cuts of defence overall, that had ever been perpetrated. In its more detailed application it was particularly savage on the navy. The navy, in crude terms, was cut by more than twice the army and more than seven and a half times the air force. Now that is not exactly the way to maintain a balanced, overall defence capability.

You can counter that argument, with other allegations that the navy was 'out of balance', meaning 'too big', or 'too something or other'. That is an argument, although it is not one to which I personally subscribe. I think one has to view it against the background that we are an island still. Just. We are surrounded by a thing called the sea. There is a great deal of sea about the world, 'more than 75 per cent' and all that, and we are pretty dependent still on free use of the sea for the bulk import and export of the commodities that we badly need, and do not have here.

It was part of the debate at the time that Nott had, in effect, 'called the Royal Navy's bluff', that you could not justify the vote of money for the Nato role alone, and yet that was 'the future', and the thrust of our defence policy?

I would dispute that, and indeed I did at the time. I don't think he ever actually put it like that to me. He put a number of things to me, but they were, usually, completely off the cuff. I mean, the whole thing was done in a most *ad hoc* way. It was sort of 'back of an envelope' stuff, and there was a great deal of preconception about it.

I don't want to 'go on', but another thing, for example, was a precedent of very considerable magnitude. The decision had been taken, absolutely correctly, to go for Trident as the successor to Polaris/Chevaline,[16] as the national independent strategic nuclear deterrent. The warhead apart, virtually the full cost of Trident was placed upon the navy, without any subvention from defence as a whole to the naval budget. That had not been done before. It largely emasculated the navy, or would have done, if it had been carried through. This really compounded the felony. Not only was the navy cut by the figures I've given but those cuts were exacerbated by the imposition of Trident, albeit that I am an unswerving proponent of Trident.

16 The British-designed and -manufactured nuclear weapons for Polaris missiles.

The aircraft carrier was a symbol, was it not, of the navy's ability to perform a world-wide role. You speak about these things being done 'on the back of an envelope' in the 1981 defence review. How was the decision taken to sell Invincible, *the through-deck cruiser or little aircraft carrier, to the Australians, and to send* Hermes, *the other aircraft carrier, for scrap?*

I never knew. I could never get any explanation, because there was no sense. When, for example, the Australian defence minister and their chief of naval staff, who was an old friend of mine, came over to discuss this matter, I was put in to bat by John Nott after a friendly lunch, and this came as a complete surprise. It was an absurd situation. We sat across the table, and the Australians were saying, 'Well, why should you want to keep this thing, because you want to let us have it' and so on. It was really an absolutely vacuous discussion. I just cannot tell you. There was no rational philosophy, except for this driving thing of saving money. What was fundamentally wrong about doing it by that sort of method was that it was not backed by professional argument at all.

After the Falklands war was over it would have been dead easy for me to have spent my last six months in office saying, 'I told you so.' However, a very large number of the things that I advised, to the limit, ultimately, of crossing the road to Number 10 with John Nott – because I wanted to say it in front of him and to his face – were borne out in the Falklands war. A considerable number of them, something like two thirds, were then reintroduced. *Invincible* was a classic case in point.

Invincible *is of interest when one comes from the general problem, as you saw it, with the 1981 defence review to the specific one of the Falklands war. The only use for the aircraft carrier is for the landing or withdrawing of forces against opposition outside the range of land-based airpower. That was the Falkland Islands in a nutshell, was it not?*

I would not say it is the only one, but you are absolutely correct that it is a major one. If, for example, the Falklands crisis had occurred let us say two years later, *Invincible* would have gone, *Hermes* would have been scrapped. We would have had *Illustrious*, and I doubt that we could have expedited the in-service state of *Ark Royal* sufficiently, so we would have had only one. In those circumstances, and if we had not had even that, I would not have advised the operation was even on. It would not have been a practical proposition. It would have been suicidal.

Metaphorically, the white ensign and your personal battle colours are flying at this moment, are they not, above the Ministry of Defence, and against the whole thrust and intention of the 1981 defence review?

Absolutely. I think it was ill conceived and ill conducted.

Before the conflict itself, therefore, the Falklands commitment had become invested with no little symbolic importance for the Royal Navy.

In what is regarded as one of the greatest of British state papers, written in 1907, Sir Eyre Crowe of the Foreign Office had defined Britain's strategic aims and interests as an insular and naval state in a sentence of limpid simplicity. 'Great Britain', he wrote, 'is the neighbour of every country accessible by sea.'[17] Did **John Nott**, in 1981, intend to take account of Britain's almost wholly changed circumstances after the Second World War in that same masterful way?

Well, you know, I would need two hours, that's the trouble, to deal with this question, and I've got to deal with it in two minutes. But my answer is like this. First of all, let me say, that I think the Royal Navy, at that time, was the finest of the three services. They change. My family have been in the Royal Navy, it is a tremendous service and in it there are many very intelligent people. But, you know, in the business I am now in, which is finance,[18] a chap, when he has been in a top job for five or six years, has been in that job long enough. The difficulty with the services is that people get to the top after *forty* years. How do you get original, fresh, radical thinking into the top echelons of the Ministry of Defence? Fresh, radical thinking tends to reside rather more amongst some of the younger military people, in a very hierarchical arrangement, and among the civilians, than it does at the top.

In answer to your question, I saw the main strategic priority of the United Kingdom as the defence of the British Isles against a Soviet threat. The principal defence requirement of this country could change. However, in the foreseeable future, I believe for the next ten, twenty years, as long as we can really plan, the only real threat to the freedoms of this country comes from the Soviet bloc.

I do not deny that there may be other little Falklands which will pop up all over the world, and that there you want a different kind of Royal Navy, the sort of navy that we nearly had for the Falklands. But you have to *decide*. Are you going to equip your forces to meet the Soviet threat, and provide 'deterrence', or is it for these other purposes?

How far would it assist our understanding of events to appreciate the relationship, and common interests, between the two navies, the United States Navy and the Royal Navy?

17 'Memorandum on the present state of British relations with France and Germany', 1 January 1907, FO371/257.
18 A director of Lazard Bros from 1983.

I think it was exceptionally close. We always had American naval officers in the Ministry of Defence, and there were many British naval officers serving with the American Navy. This close relationship developed, partly, out of the strategic nuclear forces and our relationship with the Americans on Polaris.

The relationship between ourselves and the United States has two actual foundations, today. One is the intelligence relationship, in which the navy is marginally involved; the other is the nuclear relationship. In both cases the Royal Navy's relationships with the United States are probably closer than those of the other services.

In addition, of course, the Royal Navy remembers the great days, in the early part of this century, when we had the largest, greatest navy in the world in terms of hulls afloat. If you look around, now, it is only the Americans and the Soviets who have got this great display of power. And if you were a naval officer you would look to the American carrier task force as being one of the wonders of the world. Indeed it is. It costs, I think, around sixty *billion* dollars. But if you were a naval officer, you would find attractive the American task force concept, the whole concept of horizontal escalation – in other words, the Soviets attack you 'here' and then you send the American Navy around the rear to attack it. The whole thing is simply romantic beyond belief. How could it be that you would not admire and wish to work alongside the United States Navy?

The fact of the matter is that the Royal Navy is superbly good at its job and particularly at anti-submarine warfare. The American carrier groups are vulnerable to submarines. The role that the anti-submarine carriers, our small carriers, play in the protection of the American carrier task groups is really very vital. The American Navy really does need *Invincible* and *Ark Royal* to protect its assets. So there is a sense of need and admiration which goes both ways.

When I was there, I sometimes wondered to myself whether the Royal Navy was not almost a subsidiary company of the American Navy. But at least there are a few people asking questions in Whitehall about these traditional concepts. There is nobody asking these questions at all in Washington. The American Navy is totally in control of the Administration.

But if it was your view that the concept of 'global reach' for the Royal Navy, the need for 'a balanced naval task force', was 'nostalgia' for the days of empire; that it makes, I think you said, 'for a good-looking navy, but little else'; was not the balanced naval task force what was needed to retake the Falkland Islands?

Yes, most certainly. The balanced naval task force was exactly what you'll need for the Falkland Islands, and it may well be what you need for similar 'brush fire wars', low intensity emergencies, in the future. I do not deny that, if I was a member of the Admiralty Board myself, I would say, 'This idiot John Nott sees everything in terms of deterrence against the Soviet Union, and he doesn't understand that when he's gone, and defence secretaries change every few days, there will be some other brush fire war, and the Cabinet will require us to send a balanced task force to deal with the thing.'

So there is no black and white answer to these problems. I did not believe we had the economic resources to do both.

John Nott's defence review, in 1981, therefore continued the logic of imperial and naval retrenchment which had been the undertow of British policy and in motion over many years. Adjusting national policies to resources is the basis of any sound strategy. But it was at this point, in 1981, that the knitting of defence and foreign policy concerning the Falklands simply unravelled.

As early as the 1960s Britain's withdrawal from the Simonstown base, and the retirement of the resident South Atlantic squadrons, also removed the credible deterrent to a full-scale Argentine invasion. Thereafter, deterrence consisted of inculcating in Argentine minds the belief that the Islands *could not be held*, and that Britain could, and indeed would, repossess them with reasonable certainty. Since the 1970s, the chiefs of staffs had made it clear that a large task force, including aircraft carriers, would be required for the purpose. But Sir John Nott's review, rooted in the insistence that Britain 'no longer had the resources' for all its commitments, was now a declaratory policy of 'the need to end the naval task force mentality'.

Britain had been relying increasingly on bluff in the South Atlantic. The bluff was the ice-patrol ship HMS *Endurance*, a tripwire which, over the years and in succeeding defence reviews, was becoming a silken thread. One additional consequence of Sir John Nott's review was that *Endurance*, which had been threatened with a Treasury death in 1974, but reprieved, *would* now be withdrawn and not replaced. Both tripwire and task force were going to melt away. Following upon these declared intentions, in 1981, what was to forestall Argentina taking military action if her ambition was not satisfied by negotiation? **Admiral Sir Henry Leach** was then First Sea Lord.

In theory, deterrence rested on forty Royal Marines forming the garrison of the Falkland Islands. No change, because as part of that defence review *Endurance*, the ice-patrol ship, which is only normally deployed there for half the year anyway, would have been withdrawn, and disposed of, without relief. I say 'in theory' because the actual savings on *Endurance* – it might have been three million – was peanuts compared with the overall figure. Nevertheless, one was down to groping for *peanuts*. And so *Endurance* was put up.

Was she put up over your dead body?

No. Not at all. Because *Endurance*, in terms of straight naval capability, has very little.

But she was the symbol of our presence?

Yes, she was, but that's a political matter.

You did not believe in symbols?

Up to a point. But, when the chips are down, and you have to pay through the nose for those symbols, then you have to cut your cloth again. And I was desperate. What I did feel, fairly strongly, was that if *Endurance* had gone it would only be a matter of a year or two before we would have to deploy a frigate down there, at least from time to time. So, you know, it's swings and roundabouts.

You wanted frigates, not 'symbols'?

I wanted a balanced navy of a size that could continue to perform its tasks. Just that. There was a lack of understanding – the understatement of the year – by my defence secretary of the role, the use, the value, and the need for surface ships. He was advised by the chief scientific adviser of the day,[19] who was a friend in many ways, and who was sound on the strategic deterrent. But he too thought you could win the next battle in the Atlantic by long-range maritime patrol aircraft and nuclear submarines. He had never even got his feet wet in any form of conflict, and he simply did not know what he was talking about.

The announcement that, after twenty-seven years of continuous Antarctic patrol, HMS *Endurance* would depart in March 1982, and not be replaced, was construed by Argentina as a deliberate political gesture, a calculated diminishment of British interest in the Falklands commitment. For that reason the decision to dispense with this minimal British 'deterrent' was opposed by the Foreign Office. Despite Lord Carrington's protests, the withdrawal of the ship was confirmed to Parliament in the summer of 1981. This argument was still continuing six weeks before the war, when, as late as February in 1982, John Nott declined to reverse his decision.

Whitehall, with its long history and tradition, exists for the purpose of making coherent policy. But there appears to have been some particular

19 Professor Sir Ronald Mason.

difficulty, at this time, in coordinating the views of the Foreign Office and the Ministry of Defence. How did the issue of *Endurance*, whose planned withdrawal in the 1981 defence review was subsequently described by Franks as 'inadvisable',[20] present itself to **John Nott**, the secretary of state for defence?

Simply because it was top of the list, after the royal yacht *Britannia*, for scrapping by the Royal Navy. I think this was a tactical move on their part. When I asked them how they intended to reduce their financial commitments to the money available, the two ships *they* put at the top of their list (although you don't hear much about that because I *did* seek from them their opinion of the priorities), were *Britannia*, first, and HMS *Endurance*, second. I said I thought it was not reasonable that we scrap *Britannia*. I thought that was just too difficult, politically. But I thought *Endurance* had no real defence requirement. It certainly had some visible value as a deterrent in the South Atlantic. I felt that if it was either a frigate, or *Endurance*, I had to choose in favour of a frigate, which is what I did.

Your service advisers did not urge upon you the vital nature of Endurance*? They acquiesced, which seems odd when it is the Foreign Office which is pleading with you to keep it?*

Some service advisers of course were advising me that we should double the size of the fleet; double the size of the air force, and the army. The predominant mood in the Ministry of Defence is to spend more money. Clearly, in terms of the Royal Navy's priorities, they were not to reduce further the frigate force. Between a frigate and HMS *Endurance*, they would have chosen a frigate. Quite rightly.

Does that canvass your arguments for resisting the case made for keeping HMS Endurance *as a symbol of minimum deterrence in the South Atlantic?*

I think that if I had not been at such a difficult stage in the defence review, where certain elements in the Ministry of Defence were fighting me over this problem in public, through the naval lobby, and in the House of Commons and through the press, it might well be that it would have been easier for me to have said, 'Look, we *must* keep HMS *Endurance*', for reasons which were being made clear to me by the Foreign Office. That is, it is an important symbol in the South Atlantic.

But if we did that – and *Endurance* was due for a refit; I think the cost was something like three or four million pounds – it did mean that we were going to have to have another frigate in the stand-by

20 Franks Report, para. 288.

squadron. But the mood of the times was such that 'yet one more frigate' was the straw that was in danger of breaking the camel's back. Publicly. Therefore one took the view that since *Endurance* had no defence requirement in terms of our *priorities* as a country, the *Nato* priority, it was better to scrap *Endurance* rather than go for another frigate.

The admirals wanted fighting ships, frigates, rather than *Endurance*, a 'symbol'. The defence secretary believed that the attachment of the Royal Navy to a long tradition was distorting Britain's strategic planning, and therefore considerable cuts should be made in the surface fleet. Having wound up Simonstown and quit the Gulf, the only place where Britain might still have need for the 'balanced naval task force' in supporting landings or withdrawals of forces, *within Nato's defined area*, was northern Norway. The secretary of state for defence was among those who felt surface ships thus deployed would stand little chance of survival against the stand-off missiles of the Soviet Backfire bombers, thus reinforcing 'the need', as he put it, 'to end the task force mentality'.

In this manner the low-rated Falklands obligation suddenly acquired a different emphasis in its importance to the senior service. The future of the Royal Navy in its global role of sharing burdens with the Americans 'east of Suez' was at stake. Sir Henry Leach seized his opportunity in the Falklands to prove the Navy's ancient, and natural, strength.

In 1981 the Falklands policy fell between two schools of thought and two views of Britain in the world: the naval argument, which holds that the Soviet challenge to Britain's interests is not confined to one region, and the case for the defence of Europe embodied in the continental commitment of the Army of the Rhine. But in making a choice, John Nott's 1981 White Paper only managed to state a preference. In its determination to 'put an end to the naval task force mentality' it offered no solution to Britain's practical dilemma of staying on in the Falklands.

I think that our role is deterrence, on the central front, and clearly, therefore, an independent nuclear deterrent, which I put almost more important than anything. That means Trident. It doesn't mean anything else. Almost as important as those two, no less important, is our role in the North Atlantic.

My quarrel with the Royal Navy, in detail, is – of course I want a big navy, I want a good-looking navy, because if you don't have a good-looking navy you can't recruit – but my view is that the balanced naval task force is *not* the correct Nato specialization for the United Kingdom. It will be three weeks earlier, in this ghastly third

world war – before the American Navy are ever there in real force –
and the containment of the Soviets out of northern Norway, the defence of northern Norway, is our first priority. I simply do not believe
that HMS *Invincible* and HMS *Ark Royal*, with five frigates, is the way
in which we can contain the Soviet Union. What we want is different
equipment. This is where the difference between myself and the navy
lies. It is not that we don't both want a large, good, balanced navy *if we
could afford it*. But it is not the first priority, in my mind, for the United
Kingdom. The navy are perfectly entitled to take a different view.

*'The need to end the naval task force mentality', as you put it – to what extent do
you think that that became embodied for the Royal Navy in the Falkland Islands
commitment?*

Yes, it did. The Falkland Islands commitment would certainly
require a balanced naval task force to provide deterrence to a threat to
the Falkland Islands.

*Therefore the question must be: without the balanced naval task force, what, in
your view, constituted deterrence to an Argentine invasion of the Falkland
Islands?*

Well now, of course, we know. That is, a proper airfield, and in-flight
refuelling, and the ability to reinforce the Falkland Islands within
forty-eight hours by air.

All of which had been turned down by previous governments?

All of which had been turned down by previous governments. I mean
there is no conceivable way, unless we'd gone completely crazy, that
you would keep a couple of aircraft carriers and supporting frigates
for that. By the time you've protected two aircraft carriers, you've
actually answered for about half the Royal Navy's surface fleet – just
to protect the two carriers.

There's no way that you would have two carriers to defend the
Falkland Islands. You would defend it by aerial reinforcement, and
submarines of course.

*But the Falklands crisis followed so soon after the announcement of the initial
conclusions of the defence review in 1981 that it has sustained controversy as to
whether those conclusions were well founded. What view is justified?*

Well, certainly, the Falkland Islands event proved that the defence
review was mistaken. Of course.

*How far should historians see the Royal Navy as perceiving an opportunity in the
Falklands crisis?*

Oh, the greatest possible opportunity. It was the answer to Sir Henry
Leach's prayers and he responded magnificently. I am delighted, for

him, that he could show that the Royal Navy could 'do it', in its traditional way. It proved his point. It did not actually deny *my* point, but it certainly proved his. I was arguing on an entirely different basis. I was arguing in terms of priorities for the nation, not whether the navy could do the task assigned to it.

In coming to the conclusions of his White Paper in 1981, Sir John Nott took the view that Suez, in 1956, was a watershed for Britain and that its strategic and economic lessons were of lasting significance. That meant, emphatically, that Britain would not equip itself for another 'Suez' or post-colonial war. This was a conclusion to which Argentina paid attention.

As Clarissa Eden said, the Suez Canal 'flowed through the living room' of 10 Downing Street when Anthony Eden was there in 1956, and it was still much more than a trickle in 1982. The name was on the lips of all the actors in the Falklands drama. At Suez, Britain had been brought to its knees by the United States, the arbiter of its future. When Argentina invaded the Falklands, Argentine hopes and British expectations were fixed, with the Ancient Mariner's glittering eye, on the attitude and responses of the United States.

7

Haig in a Poncho

The prospect of Britain going to war over the Falkland Islands astounded Washington. It took its place amid the doings and undoings of a time already overcrowded with the outlandish. A decade before Argentina landed at Port Stanley, the Americans had landed on the moon. The British Government's readiness to risk all, and fight a war in the American hemisphere, for what President Reagan called 'that little ice-cold bunch of land down there' was greeted, at first, with something of the same eye-rubbing sense of improbability.

There is little in the historical record to suggest that Britain's colonization of the freezing South aroused close American attention. What there is discloses, however, that in 1832, a year before Britain resumed her since unbroken occupation of the Falklands, an American sloop, the *Lexington*, arrived and 'dispersed' Argentine colonists. Like Britain, the United States did not recognize Argentina's right to inherit from Spain in the hemisphere. Earlier in the nineteenth century there was an implied challenge to Britain by John Quincy Adams. Adams, the sixth president, was secretary of state to President Monroe and fathered the policy which denied the right of interference by European governments in the affairs of the American continents, called the Monroe Doctrine. When Britain was opening up sub-Antarctica and found the South Shetland Islands, Adams wrote to Monroe in 1819. There was, he said, an excellent opportunity to profit by these discoveries, 'since the British government and people at this time are fully occupied in the discussion of Royal fornications and adulteries'. But that is as far as it went. British governors thereafter wore their plumed hats in the Falklands unchallenged by the moral precepts which steered American foreign policy and those hallowed 'self-evident truths', which had long since included the evils of 'colonialism'.

By the 1980s, Latin America, with its crises of democratization and debt, had all the turmoils under heaven. Suddenly, over the Falklands, the Americans were called upon to choose between one of two 'special' relationships. To no little British alarm and indignation, this choice was at first deferred. The United States assumed the role of mediator between Argentina and Britain. How far was this American stance dictated by knowledge of British ambivalence, spanning many years, over the Falklands, and to what extent was Washington's approach governed, in this dispute of such long standing, by a belief that a chance had now come to settle it, once and for all? The pivotal figure in weighing these considerations was President Reagan's secretary of state, **General Alexander Haig**.

Our own, very hasty, recapitulation of British attitudes on the Falklands suggested that there had been, of course, differences of opinion, depending on the party in power. The Labour Government had, previously, at least flirted with the concept of relinquishing sovereignty, only to have that prospect overturned in Parliament. That led to a plebiscite which resulted in reaffirmation of continued allegiance to British rule by people who were, essentially, ethnic Britons. There was also a litany of alleged insensitivities provided, *ad nauseam*, to the United States by Argentine officials, here in the embassy, and by other 'Latinists' who had followed the issue. That tended to suggest that the United States could assume a 'good offices' role, a role of impartiality, with some prospect of success.

But the dominating concern I had was that this incident, whatever its merits and antecedent history, had to be resolved on the basis of the rule of law. The successful seizure of territory by force, in lieu of negotiations, could not be allowed to become the lesson derived or the final conclusion drawn. With the history of western weakness in the recent past it would probably have sent a very serious signal around the world, especially to the Soviet Union.

What, essentially, obliged the United States to adopt its even-handed approach, studied neutrality, at the outset?

Certainly the United States had split interests. It had additional considerations that had to be weighed. There was the issue of our role in the hemisphere, and our future relationships there. It was clear from the outset that the hemisphere, at large, would be supportive of the Argentine position; as it proved to be, with varying levels of enthusiasm. Those that were *close* to Argentina, and fearful that this victory would lead to other uses of force by a Junta that had long-standing disputes with them, dampened their hemispheric solidarity. The farther *away* they were, the more ideologically supportive they were of the Argentine action. So that was an issue – our long-term relationships, and our ability to lead in the hemisphere.

The second issue, of course, was the unity of the Alliance. It was very evident that the British Government, while enjoying broad sympathy for their plight, could not be assured of unity, because there were 'special relationships' with the Argentine, and the Argentine people, among a number of key allies: notably, Italy. Our evidence, and our soundings in Nato capitals, suggested that support for military action by Britain would be lukewarm at best, and probably unravel in the final analysis.

Thirdly, there was the major problem. That was the Soviet Union's perception of the West when faced with an aggression which, no matter how ludicrous in the context of East–West relations, could add further to the erosion of credibility of our overall deterrent, depending on where the United States stood. If the US aligned itself, from the outset, with Great Britain, either because of our traditional relationship with Britain, 'the special relationship' as it is referred to historically, or on the broader grounds of being an advocate for 'rule of law', it offered great opportunities for Soviet mischief-making either directly, or through their Cuban proxies, in Argentina.

All of these things contributed to the conviction, at the outset at least, that until an honest, genuine effort was made and seen as such, the United States was better served by an impartial position and could serve all of the parties, including Great Britain, more effec-tively from such a posture.

By the 1980s, the original theme of the Monroe Doctrine in American policy was overlaid by 'the major problem' which gnawed away at American composure. The vigilant American opposition to any increase of Soviet influence in Latin America, and its determination to exclude Communism, were among the reasons that Argentina considered it might have the acquiescence of the United States in a forward policy over the Falklands.

Under President Carter, a policy purporting to serve the cause of 'human rights' had been installed almost as a new commandment. The Reagan Administration took the view that it had assisted to power in Nicaragua, on the American doorstep, a government led by the Ortega brothers and organized on avowedly Marxist-Leninist principles. Among those who believed the president should not, therefore, prejudice American influence throughout Latin America by siding with Britain over the Falklands was America's ambassador to the United Nations, and a Latin American specialist, **Jeane Kirkpatrick**.

In an influential essay,[1] which had done much to secure her a high

---

1 *Dictatorships and Double Standards* (Commentary 1979).

position in the Reagan Administration, the ambassador had argued that a distinction should be drawn between 'authoritarian' and 'totalitarian' governments. In this context, Argentina was important to Mrs Kirkpatrick's thesis. Jeane Kirkpatrick had Cabinet rank, and the ear of President Reagan. As a basis for American foreign policy, how were her arguments to be understood?

I think they have been very badly *misunderstood*. I was not, in the first instance, concerned with the distinction between authoritarian and totalitarian governments. I was concerned with a particular type of US foreign policy which, I thought, had reached fruition under the Carter Administration. I may say that I had no predisposition to dislike or criticize, having been an active, and lifelong, Democrat at that point. There was not a scintilla of partisan zeal in my reflections.

I had watched situations develop which I thought were very dangerous for the United States and the West. In Iran, we had seen the United States Government play an active and important role, and the British Government also played some part, in finally bringing down the Shah and the arrival of Ayatollah Khomeini in power. In Nicaragua, we saw again the United States active, I think more crucially, in the departure of Somoza and his replacement by the 'Sandinistas'. Both these things purported to be serving the cause of human rights. There is no doubt that President Carter, specifically, and Cyrus Vance, the secretary of state, wished to promote more moderate, less repressive and more liberal and democratic governments in the Third World.

It did *not* lead, either in the case of Iran, or Nicaragua, to moderate, liberal or democrat governments. It led to the replacement of one kind of authoritarian regime by Khomeini and by the Ortega brothers. Not only were these leaders not what our policy had in mind, they were *more* repressive to those who have the misfortune to live under them, they were hostile to the West, and more difficult to dislodge. I also noted, in the Carter Administration, there was a generalized tendency, discernible in documents and public appearances, to systematically *prefer* left-wing Marxist dictators to, if you will, right-wing authoritarian dictators. I suggested that, not only was it not progress when the US government succeeded in dislodging a government like that of Somoza, let us say, in favour of one led by the Ortega brothers, it was exactly the reverse.

To what extent did you believe that the United States could establish some new policy design in Latin America based on a distinction between 'good' and 'bad' dictators?

Not at all, not at all. I do not think there is such a thing as a 'good' dictator, let me say, and if you would read my article, which most people have never bothered to do, you would see that there is no suggestion there that there is such a thing as a good dictator. There is only a suggestion of lesser evils, and the greatest virtue of the lesser evil is that the 'authoritarian' dictator is more likely to self-destruct, to be liberalized, and be transformed into a democratic government. There is no sense in which I had ever any notion of the US building of foreign policy or Latin American policy on a distinction between authoritarian and totalitarian dictators.

But the essence of your position, am I right, is that the 'authoritarian' government, unpleasant though it may be, was capable of evolution towards democracy, whereas the 'totalitarian' Marxist framework was irreversible?

Precisely, precisely. And it should not be considered 'progress' to displace the first in favour of the second.

How far was this argument determined for you by the fact that many respectable Pan-Americans were against American intervention in the hemisphere, as with Central America, and that, therefore, the time had come to call in forces at work in Latin America itself to redress the imbalance?

Not at all. The respectable Pan-Americanists were *all in favour*, at that point, of US intervention in Central America. But they were in favour of the kind of intervention that was bringing the Ortegas to power. I did believe then, and I do now, that it adds up to a growing security problem for the United States, of such a nature that it could, if continued, inevitably reorient US policy away from Europe or the Pacific to the defence of the United States in our own hemisphere.

One of my good political friends was the late Senator 'Scoop' Jackson of Washington. Scoop Jackson said, at about that time, that our European friends should understand that if there were ever a choice between defending the United States on our Mexican or Southern border, and defending Europe, it was *no* choice. Every country must first defend itself.

For the Americans, therefore, the shadows of the sovereignty battle over the Falklands fell all across Latin America, and they upset carefully designed American plans and priorities. A war for President Reagan's ear was waged not just by Argentina and Britain, but by 'Atlanticists' and 'Latinists' within the American government.

After the Argentine invasion of the Falklands, the Americans elected to be impartial, the friend of both countries. This accorded with Argentine calculations. But impartial negotiations are seldom success-ful. The British, who considered that a dictatorship should not be appeased, bent all their efforts towards breaking down this public posture of neutrality which, at the beginning, **Alexander Haig** had felt obliged to adopt.

The motivation was not to assume neutrality because of political expediency, or even a concern that our failure to do so might rupture Latin American ties, but, more importantly, it was a position from which we could influence events. From the outset that was the primary motivation, certainly in my own case, and I think in the president's case.

But looking back in great wisdom and hindsight on 'even-handedness' as a basis for negotiations, do you think it made it more difficult to succeed? In this sense, United States neutrality upset the British, who felt the United States was prepared to abandon or betray shared values, and there was a principle at stake; and also it encouraged the Argentine military Junta to be more obdurate?

I would challenge the thesis that it, in any way, encouraged the Argentine military to be more resistant to a peaceful settlement. Not at all. Precisely the opposite. It was never portrayed to the Argentines for a moment, for example, that the United States considered that Great Britain would not fight if forced to, or that we would end up supporting them if that were the outcome. That was understood from the first hours of any interchange between either government.

The clear problem was this. We felt, and I think history will sustain it, that Britain had an obligation, after one hundred years of dispute, and a somewhat less than consistent position by various British governments on this issue, to see whether or not a fair settlement could be made. A settlement in which the issues of the rule of law, and the subsequent surfacing of self-determination as the key factor, could be realized without bloodshed.

But did not repeated declarations by the United States that it was the friend and ally of both parties mean that you were unable, as the British felt, to make it clear to Argentina in time that the United States was already on Britain's side because of the Argentine invasion, and would support Britain in the event of further hostilities?

Quite to the contrary. I think it was the knowledge that the United States would be a reasonably objective observer that gave us any credibility at all. Had we *not* been viewed by Argentina as an impartial adjudicator, offering our good offices as such – we were not *really* an adjudicator, of course – then I do not think there would have been any chance of a negotiated settlement. None.

How strong was the belief in the Administration that the purpose of your mediation was to save Mrs Thatcher's face, whereas in Britain it was widely regarded as an issue of principle? How difficult was your task in making that clear?

I do not think it was difficult at all. There may have been circles in Britain, opposition party people, that may have drawn that conclusion, and clearly it was not an irrelevant aspect of the thing. After all, Mrs Thatcher's government was very compatible with the Reagan government, and had been a very strong supporter. But the issue was not any partiality towards the Thatcher government, or even the 'special relationship'.

The issue was whether the United States stood for the principle of the rule of law, and whether, in the final analysis, the British obligations with respect to that principle were not going to be clouded by a preoccupation with holding resources, regardless of the justice of the case; whether *that* was Britain's 'matter of principle'.

It became clear, even though it may have been very discomforting for Mrs Thatcher to have *delivered*, that her 'bottom line' surfaced as being simply self-determination, *not* a desire to hold an appendage of the British Empire. When *that* issue stood alongside the Argentine unwillingness to make a compromise, and a compromise in which self-determination could be realized, under reasonable, objective, and fair terms, it became clear also that the United States would have to side with the rule of law and what was, clearly, a more sustainable position.

Calculation, or miscalculation, by Buenos Aires of the American interest, together with Washington's *declaratory* policy of 'even-handedness', led Argentina to gamble that Britain would not have American support in a showdown.

Britain and America quickly discovered that there was no place where their interests were more divergent than in Latin America. The Latin American orientation in the state department was a strong one, and it was not on Britain's side. Argentina was much more important to America than to Britain. Indeed, the underlying American attitude was the one so often articulated in official circles in England, that a tiny minority of Falkland Islanders could not be an obstacle, provided they were properly treated, to relations not only with Argentina, but with the whole of Latin America. A declaration of support for Britain, from the outset, was opposed because it risked America paying a permanent price throughout Latin America. The British view was that *only* a declaration of support for Britain at the outset might have given Buenos Aires pause.

The latest, and what proved to be the last, round of British and Argentine talks, in February 1982 in New York, had found no way forward. **Thomas O. Enders**, the assistant secretary of state in the state department who dealt with Latin American affairs, had been asked by the British to use the occasion of his forthcoming official visit to Buenos Aires[2] to warn that Britain would find it politically impossible to continue negotiating against a background of threats, and to encourage the Argentine to 'keep things cool'.[3] Enders was aggrieved it might be thought that Argentina could have been encouraged, in the absence of more explicit American warnings.

We were contacted by the British government, prior to my trip. They raised their fears about the unproductive character of these talks, and that they might be broken off. I raised that fear with the foreign minister of Argentina, saying that the United States did not intend to change its historic view – which was not to take a position, one way or the other, on the territorial dispute. We wanted countries with which we had friendly relations to solve that problem, but we were concerned that the talks appeared to be headed nowhere. Costa Méndez did not commit himself, although he was not negative.

We are approaching that period when it appears to have been very difficult to convince people of the seriousness of British intentions. Charged, as you were, with the conduct of Latin American policy, did you find it difficult to say in Buenos Aires something which may have been seen by the Argentines as loudly disagreeable?

No. Like everything else, people listen to what they *want* to listen to. Mr Costa Méndez commented on this afterwards, and he said, 'Yes, the Americans did bring it up with me but they said that their attitude was hands off.' What I said to him was that we were 'hands off' *on the basic dispute*, but that we hoped they would get on with the discussions with the British. That is what he was non-committal about, although, as I say, not negative. He said they were 'working on it' and they 'hoped to have something'.

In retrospect, do you agree it is possible that the Argentines were guided by an ambiguity in your position? They are not quite sure how you will behave? They felt they could rely on a benevolent American neutrality?

All throughout this unhappy story those responsible in Argentina proved extremely difficult to convince of what was going to happen in the future. We made very explicit statements to Argentine leaders at a

2 In March 1982, three weeks before the Argentine invasion of 2 April.
3 Franks Report, paras 142–4.

large number of points in the course of this thing. Perhaps the clearest statements of all were made by Haig to Galtieri, and then to the foreign minister, Costa Méndez, in the course of our final rounds of negotiation of the draft settlement plan. Haig said, in many different ways, as we had said earlier in many different ways, that if the mediation were to fail the United States would come down firmly in support of a friendly country, and a close ally, which had been the victim of an unprovoked act of violence. This corresponded to our international obligations, and to our basic view of the world.

When that actually *happened*, the Argentines were deeply shocked. They expressed their shock in a very large number of ways. They regarded themselves as betrayed.

I had another instance of this kind in the first set of meetings we had with the Junta. Haig said, 'Look, the British are preparing for military action. I am a military man, as you know. I do not *know* what they are going to do, but I think that they would do the following. This is what *I* would do as a military man . . .' And he described a plan of action that involved the South Georgias, and ultimately the action against the Falkland Islands themselves. It was very similar to the one that was, indeed, adopted. Anaya,[4] I remember, said to him, 'You are entirely wrong, Mr Secretary. That will never occur, because the British, basically, are interested only in commerce. There is oil there. The British will protect their oil. The way to protect that is to enter into an agreement with us. They are not interested in anything else . . .' Haig looked at him in disbelief, I remember, and said something like, 'You have to know, Admiral, that I have no idea whether the British think there is any economic use to these Islands at all, but they *are* interested in the same thing you are – honour.' And they broke off.

Then, when the British finally *arrived* in South Georgia, Anaya came back to us – I remember it was a very tense moment – he lifted his finger, and pointed it at Haig, and said, 'You are a *spy*. You *knew* what they were going to do all along, and knowing that, you negotiated on false pretences with us.' That was a very tense moment.

Throughout this crisis, the Argentines did not respond to the most direct statements, either when made by you, or by us. There are some other things we found out, afterwards. We found out that Mr Galtieri, shortly before he became the leader of the Junta, had been up that winter as a guest at luncheon at the Argentine Embassy in Washington. The guests included myself and Ambassador Kirkpatrick. It is rare for a Washington luncheon to turn out with as many people.

4 Admiral Jorge Anaya was commander-in-chief of the Argentine Navy.

Afterwards, we learned that General Galtieri thought this was a sign of particular favour that indicated a degree of support *planned* by the American Administration. Clearly, it was not intended to do so.

But why should he not have seen it like that?

I think the answer is that all through this crisis I think the Argentines clung to something which we found unshakeable. They clung to the notion that the United States would *not* come down on the side of its British friends. And the United States did.

Some of this delusory confidence was reposed in the historical outcome of the Suez crisis in 1956. The greatest and most demoralizing of the challenges to Anglo-American unity since World War II ended with an intervention by the United States which forced Britain, and France, to yield.

The Falklands touched something of this old raw nerve in all the players. Given the possible parallels, a major Argentine miscalculation was to misjudge the evolution there had been in American reflections on Suez. It was this which enabled Haig to say to the British at the beginning that, while *publicly* neutral, America was not, at heart, impartial. What was it about Suez that had come to guide the thoughts of the secretary of state, **Alexander Haig**?

I think Suez was one of the great blows to Western unity following World War II. It was a major contributor to the ultimate withdrawal of de Gaulle from the integrated aspects of the Alliance, combined with some other subsequent nuclear-related questions. It certainly had a devastating impact on the British Empire and attitudes in London, with respect to not only decolonization, which I think the British Government had long since accepted, but, in some instances, the manner in which it would be done. It raised doubts about a heretofore very close bond between Washington and London. In strategic terms it was one of the major bench-marks after the Second World War; and not only in Alliance relationships but in East–West relations also.

Armed with these reflections, Haig gave a decisive lead in making sure that Britain would not become separated from its closest ally, as had happened at Suez. But the difficulty he had in producing a unified American approach meant that American support was to a degree equivocal, and not to be taken for granted. This, in turn, stiffened British resolve not to compromise concerning a matter of principle.

For its part, Argentina had some reason to believe that it was viewed by President Reagan as a valuable potential ally in a struggle whose epicentre was El Salvador and Nicaragua. Argentina had been giving support for American covert operations there, and for the anti-Communist stance throughout the hemisphere. Between June of 1981 and February of 1982, a few weeks before the war, several visits were made to Argentina by a ubiquitous figure often charged with special missions, a former deputy director of the CIA,[5] and today America's ambassador to the United Nations, **General Vernon Walters**. President Reagan had come to office with a new emphasis on American relationships with Latin America. What was it that General Walters, who, incidentally, speaks Spanish, set out to achieve with Argentina?

I was trying to encourage and promote the sense that we have of belonging to the oldest regional organization in the world, the Organization of American States, and basically, as you know, because they had a certain commercial relationship with the Soviet Union, to make sure that that did not lead them astray. There has been a myth, popularly circulated, that *I* gave them permission to attack the Falkland Islands, which is absolute bunk. Neither President Reagan, nor the US Congress, nor anyone else could give such a permission.

However, there is a good deal of interest in whether they may have inferred, from the new interest that you were taking in them, that you would acquiesce in a more forward policy over their long dispute with Britain over the Falkland Islands?

Well of course. I'm more aware than most Americans of this, because I have been a student of Latin American history for a long time. Let me assure you that I was extremely careful *not* to give them anything that they could infer, or anything that the US Government did not intend.

In which case, how does one account for the illusion, something in which they had put so much faith, that the United States would remain 'benevolently neutral'?

It was not so much *that*, as an absolute conviction that *Britain* would not fight. There were a number of Argentines, not all of them military, who had served in Britain and had said, 'Oh, this will just be another Suez. There will be such an uproar in Britain that they won't do anything. They will go to the World Council of Churches, the International Red Cross, the UN Security Council, and various other things, *but they won't fight.*'

That is certainly something that both Haig and I tried to disabuse them of: the difference being that the Labour Party in Britain in 1956 was not anxious to take action against Colonel Nasser, but against the Argentine Junta, and military men, it was quite a different matter. I think they misread opinion in Great Britain altogether.

5 1972–6.

How well did you know General Galtieri?

Not terribly well. I read various articles that say I was some kind of old drinking buddy of his. It is absolutely false. I think the first time I met him he was a brigadier general. I knew him and I liked him. He is a gregarious, outgoing and pleasant man. But you see, every Argentinian is brought up to believe that these are *his* Islands – not just Galtieri, not just the military Junta, but everybody. There is a law, I believe, that you cannot bring a map into the country that shows them as being other than 'the Malvinas'. This is not just the military Junta, it is a deep felt national cause.

After it was all over, Galtieri talked of 'the many joint plans' for the continent which he shared with the Reagan Administration. During your various visits there, did you canvass ideas or try to rally support for the idea of a security system in the South Atlantic?

I did not, personally, no. I am sure there were other people doing that. You know there is a major US Command in Panama which is charged with all these security problems, but I was not privy at that time to the particular planning they may have been engaged in.

Would it be true to say that the United States has long desired that there should be something like that in the South Atlantic?

I think the importance of the sea lanes of the South Atlantic is as important to our Nato allies as it is to us. Argentina is a terribly important country to us, in so far as the American continent is concerned. I have very good friends in Argentina; I have great admiration and liking for the Argentines. Of course, Britain is an indispensable partner in maintaining world peace.

But, you know, this was a very caring experience for us. Basically, what it amounted to was that we were forced, without any consultation, to choose between the Organization of American States and Nato. I think we decided that on the basis of the importance of deterrence.

There are so many misunderstandings. Argentines asked me, 'Why are you letting the British use Ascension Island?' I said, 'You've got that upside down. It is *their* island which they allow *us* to use.' But for me it was a very painful episode altogether. Argentina and Britain are two nations which, by every normal standard, should be friends. They are both important to the free world. I have had a great deal of experience in Latin America and I went to school in England[6] and so forth. I hope that some way can be found to solve this question and

6 Stoneyhurst College.

preserve the honour of all concerned in a peaceful way. And the sooner the better as far as I'm concerned.

But there was no question that the United States was taking a position on the sovereignty of the Falklands. The idea that there was some kind of American quid pro quo, 'If you'll sign this defence agreement with us then you can take the Falklands/Malvinas', is buck. There was no such thing.

It was the British ambassador to Washington, Sir Nicholas Henderson, who thought, 'The Argentines may have felt they had a degree of United States acquiescence in a forward policy over the Falklands.' You, perhaps more than anybody, can attest whether that may have encouraged Argentine intransigence or emboldened them in an impetuous decision?

You are asking me to give an Argentine perception and I cannot. All I can tell you is that I am certain that, at no time, did the United States indicate *any* acquiescence in any plans for the use of force to change existing boundaries.

But, in a rapid solution?

When the problem arose we certainly exerted ourselves, and General Haig expended a great deal of personal capital, to try and achieve a peaceful solution.

Not the least of the ironies which followed the Argentine invasion of the Falklands was a reversal of the historical British and American attitudes that had been taken up during the Suez crisis in the fifties. This time it was the British who were insisting on the moral principles of self-determination, the seed so heavily sown by the United States, and who sought to count the Falklands as part of President Woodrow Wilson's harvest. It was the Americans, with their global responsibilities, who were inclined to take the more worldly view.

For Britain the main objective of any mediation was that aggression was not to be rewarded. The future could be negotiated only after an Argentine withdrawal from territory it had seized illegally. But the Americans concentrated their intervention on the future administration of the Islands, with consequent doubts surrounding the purpose of the American mediation. A leading part was played in this diplomacy by the assistant secretary of state for Latin American affairs at the state department, **Thomas Enders**.

All the way through, the British, and the British Prime Minister in particular, were sceptical of this effort by the United States.

I'm not sure if that is a scepticism that you feel was justified?

Let me put it this way. We were operating from different points of view. We shared the British estimate that it was an exceptionally difficult thing to do. We were anxious ourselves to avoid the war because we thought, among other things, in addition to the principle involved, that we would be the unique losers from the war. When it did occur, it would be hard to say that British interests throughout Latin America, which are not large, were damaged. It was *American* interests that were damaged. I would even say that there was a certain admiration for Britain, given its fine performance in the military action which followed.

We discussed all this, quite openly, with the British representatives beforehand. I think they were under no illusions as to how we saw our own position, and why we thought it important to make this exceptional effort to bridge the gap. What I am saying is this: the British *did not actively seek to reach a negotiated conclusion* to this. The British Government overall, whether at the Cabinet level, the level of the prime minister or of Nicholas Henderson,[7] obviously lent themselves to the effort the Americans led, and insisted upon so much. I am not sure that our basic judgement as to what would happen with Argentina was all that different. But the British took *no* initiatives, and we took many.

In view of what you've just said, and after the failure of the Haig, the Peruvian, and the UN efforts, the British proposal of May 17th is worth going through, if I may read the eight points to you. 'The Government of the UK has agreed to the non-reintroduction of British administration to the Islands. They have agreed to a short interim period, with a specified target date, for the end of negotiations. They have agreed to a UN interim administration of the Islands. They have abandoned their demands for Argentine recognition of British sovereignty over the Islands. They've agreed to a parallel withdrawal of forces, rather than prior Argentine withdrawal. They have agreed that on the Consultative Council there will be two representatives for Argentine residents and six representatives for eighteen hundred British residents. They have agreed to the verification of force withdrawal by the United Nations rather than the United Kingdom.' Of which the British Ambassador to the United Nations, Sir Anthony Parsons, said, 'These concessions go far beyond what most would have expected, and they will be considered a complete sellout by many in the House of Commons.' That was handed around by him in the United Nations the day before the British landed to repossess the Falklands.

Go back and see the terms in which the British responded to the Haig proposal, the elaborate one, the one that Costa Méndez rejected, and

7 British ambassador to the United States.

then to the statements made by British representatives, or the instructions given to British representatives regarding the *second* Haig effort, the one through Belaunde,[8] the one that came to grief on the *Belgrano*. We did not find the British Government taking any initiatives at all with us on the subject. We found ourselves pursuing them. Haig found that, little by little, he was confined to dealing with Nicholas Henderson – not that Henderson is not a very substantial figure, but he was an instructed ambassador – rather than with a principal. He found that he was being edged away from those directly responsible for decision making.

In the two sessions that Haig had with the British Cabinet, led by the prime minister, no British proposals other than for settling on their own basic position were put forward. As I say, I think that I would characterize this as a British willingness to listen, be drawn along in a process, but not as an active British search for a solution.

The British and Americans were indeed, as Enders said, operating from different points of view. While Al Haig was consistently adamant that Argentina was guilty of aggression and should not get away with it, the Americans also wanted a deal. Britain was unyielding on the issue of principle at stake. 'Even-handedness', or complete impartiality, on which the American mediation stood, could not make it clear to Argentina convincingly, or early enough, that in the event of general conflict following the invasion America would back Britain. In this sense, it is easy to say America's diplomacy hindered a solution. But, quite apart from the crucial role of the United States, there was a governing reality: Argentina's view of Britain and of the prime minister, to which Vernon Walters has referred. General Galtieri, the leader of the Junta, expressed this opinion during the American mediation to **General Vernon Walters**, who accompanied Alexander Haig on his 'shuttle diplomacy' in Buenos Aires.

> They had this view of Britain as a sort of fallen major power. At one point one of them said to me, 'It is a world in which there are two major powers, and everyone else is equal.' And I said, 'No, everyone else is *not* equal.' That did not have any impact, I regret to say.
>
> *But why do you think you were unable to disabuse them? It's absolutely critical, isn't it, in understanding what happened?*
>
> At the very first meeting between Haig and Galtieri, at which I was present, Haig told them with great emphasis that if there was no

8 President Belaunde of Peru – the so-called 'Peruvian initiative'.

negotiated solution there would be fighting, and that the British would win. They doubted that. They went into this business of 'Everybody's equal.' Haig said, 'No. The British have a career army in which almost everyone has been shot at in Northern Ireland, and they're used to having hand grenades thrown at them . . .' – as used as you ever *can* get to that sort of thing. They just fell back on, 'You are worrying about nothing. The British are not going to fight.'

When we came back from that meeting to the hotel, Haig said to me, 'Go back, and see Galtieri alone, and repeat this to him.' I did.

In Spanish?

In Spanish. No one else present. I said, to Galtieri, 'General, they *will* fight, and they will win. They have technical means that you simply do not have. They have an experienced, career army in which everybody has been shot at, and everything else. You've got seventeen-year-old conscripts, some of whom come from tropical areas to this very cold, very unpleasant, very windy climate.' But he was absolutely, viscerally, convinced that the British would not fight. At one time he said to me, 'That woman wouldn't dare.' I said, 'Mr President, "that woman" has let a number of hunger strikers[9] of her own basic ethnic origin starve themselves to death, without flickering an eyelash. I would not count on that if I were you.'

After three weeks and two visits to Buenos Aires, with Walters, Haig's mediation failed when Argentina rejected his proposed settlement terms.

The final proposal – to this day I will not understand why it was not accepted; I really cannot believe that the British agreed to it, but they did – was that the fleet would stop,[10] the Argentines would evacuate the Islands in accord with the UN resolution, a tripartite administration would be set up in the Falklands. The US would be present at the request of the Argentines, as a sort of guarantor. Three flags would fly over the islands until agreement was achieved as to their final disposition, between Britain and the Argentine Republic. A date was set. It was to be, at the latest, by the end of June 1982.

I thought, if anything can be accepted, *this* will be. It was not. I could not *believe* that they had rejected it. I could not believe that we *obtained* this proposal.

When the 'crunch' came, did it appear to you, in contrast to the British, that the Argentines never knew their 'minimal' position?

9 IRA hunger strikers in Northern Ireland.
10 That is, the British Task Force sailing south.

Their position was the transfer of sovereignty. I don't think they contemplated anything less than that. There were various 'drifting' solutions like leaseback, ninety-nine year leases, and so on. I do not think any of those were seriously considered by Argentina. My own personal feeling is that there was no one in a position to *make* that agreement. No member of the Junta, or maybe even the three of them together, had enough power to make that concession.

In which case, they were simply not capable of taking a proper decision?

They thought they had taken it when they moved into the Falkland Islands.

Haig's mediation secured a role for Argentina in the future administration of the Falklands, had the Junta been prepared to withdraw their invading force. Because they were not, it opened the gates to war. At this prospect, American alarm and desire for a diplomatic solution increased.

Enders has referred to Haig, thereafter, 'being edged away' by the British. Indeed, as the probability of Haig's failure became apparent, Britain turned from him, in the final phase of diplomacy over the Falklands, to Pérez de Cuéllar, the Secretary General of the United Nations. At the UN, the British Ambassador, Sir Anthony Parsons, had secured a spectacular diplomatic victory the day after Argentina's invasion with the acceptance of Resolution 502, which called for immediate Argentine withdrawal. However, the American secretary of state's efforts never, in fact, ended. On 30 April, Haig announced that, Argentina having failed to accept a compromise, America would support Britain. We are left with the controversy and such mystery as by now surrounds the Peruvian initiative of Sunday 1 May 1982; whether the sinking of the Argentine cruiser *Belgrano* the following day also sent to the bottom a last promising opportunity, short of the war that followed.

The first thing to be said about the Peruvian initiative is that it was not Peruvian, but American inspired, as the former assistant secretary of state, **Thomas Enders**, makes clear.

We drafted that proposal and negotiated it with the British. It was less good, from the Argentine point of view, than the one that Costa Méndez had rejected the week before, and we had of course simplified it.

Less good because it restored the question of some test of Islander opinion, their 'views' and their 'interests'?

That's right. There was a distinct shading of the proposals this time, given what we thought was a changing military balance. Once again, our impression of the British view of this initiative was 'Try it on the Argentines, and see what they say.' Them first, in other words. Belaunde made it his own. Haig and I had drafted it, at Haig's house in Washington, on an early Sunday afternoon and we passed it on to Belaunde in those terms. He contacted Galtieri.[11] Galtieri said, 'It's interesting', and, 'I'll have to take it up with the Junta and others', and, 'Let me call you back.'

For the first time, speaking personally, in this whole crisis, I thought maybe something might happen. I confess that I had no particular basis for it other than I was tired, I suppose, like everybody else, with *nothing* happening. I allowed myself a moment of optimism, and went jogging for the next two and a half hours. I came back to Haig's house to find that Belaunde had called him up and said, 'It's all off', because of the *Belgrano*.[12]

Now, frankly, those who have made a conspiracy out of this, on the British part – that, I really do not see. Because we had no commitment, on the part of the British, that they would accept this outline as a basis for negotiations, if we got the Argentines to agree to it, or Belaunde got them to agree to it. But they did not say the opposite either – that they would reject it. They sort of left the door open, which seemed to me something very much like what was going on before. The British did not appear particularly eager to have another round of discussions. We had to sort of shove and push to get them to take another text.

All the time, of course, the British fleet is rolling around in the South Atlantic, with thousands of men, and with winter coming on?

That's right. The British were following a very clearly laid out plan.

And thought that negotiations were now prevarications; an extended negotiation which had already failed? Because they saw nothing new in the Peruvian proposals, which to use your word was only an 'outline'?

They were not eager to do this. I think we got their tolerance for this effort by shading the terms. But we certainly did not get their agreement to it. So those who charge bad faith, in the British case, would have to make the case somehow that this Belaunde proposal was a positive result of British initiative or activity. It was not. It was ours.

11 There were telephone calls between Haig and the Peruvians and between the Peruvian president Belaunde and Galtieri on 1 May. Francis Pym met Haig and discussed the Peruvian outline on 2 May in Washington. Two hours earlier the war Cabinet in London authorized the attack on the *Belgrano*, which was sunk twelve hours later.

12 3 May, at 0200 Washington time.

The original British position was not really changed in the course of this crisis. *We* were the ones urging some kind of peaceful settlement, trying to find common ground. We were not sent away from our meetings with the prime minister and the Cabinet with a British mandate to find an outcome, within such and such parameters. We did not receive that. We received, of course the clear British position. 'The Islands must be returned and their future must be subject to the will of the inhabitants.' I think the British position, frankly, was coherent all the way through. Britain did not vary at all, really, from its position.

Was American support for Britain inevitable?

Yes. In fact it was made easy, in this case, although hard as a matter of practical politics, because the principle of the use of violence to settle a territorial dispute was so clear.

Sir Nicholas Henderson wrote subsequently that American support was not inevitable: 'It had to be argued and fought for all the time.'

What do you have ambassadors for?

But no amount of bargaining over the future administration of the Islands could obscure the question of principle, could it? Yet the American negotiation did seem to concentrate on that aspect rather than the principle?

We sought a compromise that would prevent the war. I think the real answers to all this lie not so much in the failure or success of the negotiation but in the structure of Argentine politics. The Argentine leaders had put themselves in a position from which they believed, and quite possibly they were right, there was no retreat, without the destruction of their regime. Unable to retreat, they were then beaten. That destroyed them. They undoubtedly saw some of that coming, to judge from our own contacts, as we discussed the mediation with them. But they preferred to do it that way, and be destroyed that way, than to do it the other way. That was the choice they made.

The Peruvian initiative was an unwelcome distraction as far as the British were concerned. Following Haig's failure, the focus of negotiation had moved to the United Nations, where Britain, in intense discussions, was backing the efforts of the secretary general, Pérez de Cuéllar. Thomas Enders acquits Britain of sinking a likely *agreement* in the American proxy of the Peruvian initiative. Argentina's rejection of the outcome of Haig's own mediation, his first and more elaborate peace plan, proved to be the watershed. As the former Argentine foreign minister Oscar Camilion has conceded, Argentina was never able to determine its minimum aspirations, and so Haig's negotiations failed.

That Argentine rejection meant also, of course, that Britain's final position was never really tested.

America came down openly on Britain's side only when it had been demonstrated that Argentina was incapable of coming to a reasonable decision. This conclusion was possible only when the nature of the Junta, as a committee of limited agreement, was revealed in the course of his negotiation to **Alexander Haig** himself.

As is so often the case, what was apparently a failed effort served an absolutely invaluable purpose – and not only here in the United States – of revealing a set of judgements that right was on the side of Great Britain. It also, I may add, provided the same kind of opportunity in British political circles.

I have to tell you that, rightly or wrongly, my impression after my first meeting with Mrs Thatcher, in Number 10 Downing Street, following the outbreak of the crisis, was that she was, with the exception of her minister of defence, and the chief of the defence forces, Terry Lewin, somewhat isolated within her Cabinet. I could only assume that that was a microcosm of a potentially less than united British opinion. The actions in the 'good offices' effort not only permitted the United States to sort *its* thinking out, with respect to who was right and who was wrong; I think it also permitted time for *Mrs Thatcher*, in another, more subtle, way to continue with the actions that were necessary in order to have right prevail. Even though it was the use of force, it may have been far more difficult for her to have assembled, in such a remarkably short time, what she assembled and dispatched to the scene.

If you felt Mrs Thatcher was 'somewhat isolated' in her Cabinet over the wisdom of trying to repossess the Falklands, did that encourage your belief in the necessity of a negotiated settlement – that the military risks were so great for the British, the chances were that a negotiation was going to mean, 'For God's sake get us out of this!'?

There were many in the United States, and very close to the president and the Cabinet, who believed that Britain did not have the military capability to succeed. I was never in that camp. I felt, from day one, that if Britain set its mind to it, it could, very efficiently, retake the Islands. There was some doubt in my mind, in the early stages, whether the British political will, or European political will, would tolerate such an action. After all, if you look back over history, you could find a lot of justification for those concerns.

The British view, I think, was that when your own mediation ended, that was indeed the end of it. If the United States could not succeed it was improbable that

*others could. What, therefore, is to be said of the Peruvian initiative, which came
at the eleventh hour, and which is referred to by some as 'Haig in a poncho'?*

Well, it was evident to me that there was still a strong appetite, in
London, for a negotiated settlement, even *after* the failure. Not on the
Peruvian initiative, but on an initiative of Foreign Secretary Pym,
when he informed me on that Sunday meeting, following the collapse
of *our* efforts, that Britain was immediately exploring and moving into
a Mexican initiative. That fell of its own weight in a matter of hours.
The Peruvian initiative, which *followed* that, came May 1st. It was
simply a repackaging, in simplified terms, of the final proposals we
had discussed in Buenos Aires.[13]

*What view do you believe historians will be justified in taking about the
Peruvian initiative? Can it be said that the sinking of the cruiser* Belgrano *by
Britain thwarted, or frustrated, a promising negotiation?*

No. I never had that feeling. By the time we withdrew from the effort,
and before I recommended to President Reagan that we do so, I and
my colleagues had to convince ourselves that there was no further
hope. That scepticism about further hope had nothing to do with the
attitudes of one or other high Argentine official with whom we had
been dealing: especially Galtieri who, I think, *would* have settled the
conflict early on, had the structure of the Argentine government
permitted a negotiated settlement. But, as I've said many many times,
you had a form of government that was neither a dictatorship, in
which you only had to convince one man, nor a democracy, in which
consensus would normally be counted on to carry the day. Here you
had an oligarchical structure of many heads, in which everyone could
say 'No', or anyone could say 'No'. Therefore, each issue was subject
to a one-man veto within that Junta. And the Junta was more than just
the hierarchy you saw at the surface. It involved the whole structure of
the armed forces, the corps commanders, and I'm not sure that even a
special *division* commander didn't have a voice.

It was clearly the pattern of things. We had achieved, after the most
anguishing negotiations, an agreement in principle by Galtieri and
the foreign minister, Costa Méndez, only to have it totally withdrawn
and reversed by some hidden hand. That could only have been a
structure of the kind I have just described.

Because government in Argentina was intrinsically unstable, it needed
the unifying achievement of the Falklands invasion. For the same
reason, the Argentine generals and admirals could not accept Haig's

13 That is, Haig's settlement proposals, rejected by the Junta.

proposal without bringing about the downfall of their regime. Unable to call off their invasion forces or survive their defeat, there seems little reason to doubt Enders's verdict that they then preferred to go on, and be destroyed. Argentina made bonfires of the olive branches. Just as Blücher is inclined to be left out of the hagiography of Waterloo, so are the Americans from the Falklands. Almost to the end, Britain entertained lively suspicions that the United States might repeat its role at Suez. But a crucial difference in 1982 was the Nassau agreement of the 1960s, which gave Britain Polaris.

In consequence, diplomacy was underpinned by everyday, practical, working relationships. These have a unique intimacy in the strategic and intelligence fields, and particularly in the case of the former, between the Royal Navy and the United States Navy. Practical American help to Britain began at once, and therefore long before the final failure of General Haig's mission in Buenos Aires. In the Pentagon, Britain had an ally of incalculable importance in the defence secretary, **Caspar Weinberger**, who had said to the ambassador, Nicholas Henderson, simply, 'Tell me what you need.'

To what extent was American assistance the result of the close dovetail of those long-standing cooperative arrangements?

I think that was a very important aspect to it. In other words the framework for close collaboration and discussion, and the friendship that existed at various levels of the Defence Ministry and our Department of Defence, enables us to be effective very much sooner than otherwise might have been the case. The basic policy decision was made here,[14] immediately, that we would do everything we could to help in what we recognized was a very difficult logistical and military task. The various arrangements you cite certainly made us more capable of 'delivering' and carrying out that policy quickly. Speed was the whole thing.

I think the Argentine Junta looked at the map and concluded it was absolutely impossible for anybody to fight a war at that distance, and with no more than the resources Britain possessed. They thought it was perfectly safe, so far from home. That was the critical factor. Mrs Thatcher's immediate decision to ignore the map, if you like, and simply to say that the possibility of defeat did not exist – well, we admired that very much. We felt that was the kind of decisive, vigorous, defensive action which should be supported.

It is important to establish the scale of the help given. Both sides, in Britain and the United States, have had reasons to be reticent about this; the sensitivity of countries in Latin America, and Whitehall's respect for that sensitivity.

14 That is, in the Pentagon.

I think there is no way of hiding the fact that we did everything we could and that it was a substantial contribution. But Britain's effort was enormously effective and very quickly assembled. We worked together as closely as we possibly could.

What stood out for you in the military assessments of whether Britain could win a conclusive victory in the South Atlantic?

I think what stood out was that the recognition came immediately from Britain that this was an expedition which had to be undertaken and an aggression which had to be resisted. There were immense logistical difficulties in the way of that. Seven thousand miles, with only one effective base, at Ascension Island, in between. There was no real British preparation, since it had not been foreseen, but a complete willingness to set aside these difficulties and indeed take the position that the possibility of defeat could not even be contemplated. All that stood out in my mind. It was a very bold, firm and decisive action, and it contrasted very much with the many long years in which a great deal of the West, the United States included, had always allowed contemplation of all of the things which could go *wrong* to block the course of action.

But how seriously did your military advisers doubt that this operation could succeed at that distance?

I think the common military advice was that it could not possibly work.

Therefore should we see the degree of support that the United States gave as crucial, because it was born of a sense of real doubt that the United Kingdom could pull this off, and you could not risk the defeat of your principal Nato ally?

No. I think that it was different than that. And I do not think the United States support *was* crucial. It was helpful, I hope, and effective, and most of all it was delivered in time and very much more quickly than had been thought possible. That was the principal contribution. I do not think that it was vital to the victory. I think it was *important* to the victory, but Britain's contribution – the actual fighting – was obviously the decisive thing.

Our support was based on a number of factors. Some people have even described it as romantic rather than practical. But the fact is it was based, not on the fear that our ally would be defeated, but a fear that aggression would succeed, and a resolve that the very strong, decisive and admirable actions that Britain was taking should not go unrewarded.

The whole Anglo-American relationship was at issue over the Falklands, as it had been at Suez. Argentina believed, and Britain itself knew, that the United Kingdom could not enter the American hemisphere without a friend. The friend was proved to be the United States.

It was Lord Nelson's opinion that ships of the Royal Navy were the best negotiators in Europe. The declaration, finally, of the support of America was the turning point as Britain sent the task force south to attempt, in the end, the most difficult military operation it had undertaken since the end of the Second World War.

8

Bloody Constraint

On 2 April 1982, Argentina invaded the Falkland Islands. At Westminster and in Whitehall, torpid detachment induced by some seventeen years of negotiations gave way to the pain of a humiliating disaster. Three years before Argentina raised its flag over Government House in Port Stanley, the foreign secretary, Lord Carrington, had circulated a warning to the prime minister and other members of 'OD', the Cabinet's defence committee.[1] The game in the Falklands was almost up. Either to go on playing for time, 'without making any concessions on sovereignty', or to choose 'Fortress Falklands' by calling off negotiations, 'both carried the serious threat of invasion', Lord Carrington's memorandum said. Whereupon the opinion of Parliament had thrown out leaseback, the last alternative left.

The arteries of the Falklands diplomacy had remained elastic during year upon year of talks, as long as the Foreign Office could discover fresh proposals to drip into them. They had finally hardened. **Richard Luce**, who resigned subsequently, together with Lord Carrington, was the minister of state at the Foreign Office who watched over what turned out to be the last agonies of the Falklands diplomacy, before invasion and war.

We knew before the talks took place in February 1982 what the Argentines were going to propose. Lord Carrington agreed that I should accept their concept of a 'negotiating commission' which would look at every facet of the Falkland Islands problem, including sovereignty. However, I was to make it absolutely clear to them that, as far as sovereignty was concerned, there would be no change without the consent of the Islanders and of Parliament. Against that background I was given the broad brief to go into negotiations, to keep the

1 Franks Report, para. 75.

dialogue going and, to be quite blunt about it, if things were getting difficult, we would just have to buy time.

What was putting us in a very difficult position was this pressure on 'time'. Acceptance of the negotiating commission meant we must have regular meetings, every month, conclude everything and reach an agreement by the end of 1982. Knowing what Island and Parliamentary opinion was, and how difficult it would be to find a solution, this squeeze on 'time' placed us under very difficult pressure.

Skilfully though you managed to keep those last talks with Argentina going, in New York, on February 26th and 27th 1982, and to which Franks in his report pays tribute,[2] we were, in fact, just stringing Argentina along?

There is no doubt about it, that we had to buy time at that stage. I say, quite bluntly, that we were boxed in. Leaseback had not made any progress, and we saw no easy way out. We hoped, *I* hoped, that perhaps the Argentines would come forward with something positive out of the negotiating commission, which might lead us to a new way forward.

There was no indication of what it might be as a result of my February talks. My opposite number was the deputy foreign minister Enrique Ros. I thought he was perfectly sincere. I think he genuinely hoped – although he was taking a lot of instructions all the time from Buenos Aires during our talks – that this negotiating commission *would* make progress. He lost a lot of face afterwards because his own government more or less disowned him.

There was no sign, in their representational behaviour, at those February talks that, if we turned up empty handed, they were just going to snap?

No, because I had agreed the main body of their proposal, which was the negotiating commission. So they had achieved their objective in getting that set up. There were, of course, these major differences on timing. I could not concede that we would immediately embark on this, because I would have to carry the Islanders, I had to carry my government, and I had to carry Parliament.

But Argentina goes to the talks in February, having got Britain to agree to the mechanism of a negotiating commission whose sole intention was to bring about an early settlement; whereas we saw it as the possibility of more years of negotiating?

Again, I put it bluntly. I think it is perfectly fair to say that all we could do was buy time. We had run out of any innovating ideas. Of those, leaseback had been the most important.

2 Franks Report, para. 297.

That brings us to the crisis on South Georgia from March 1st to March 22nd, and what began with the landing of a party of Senor Davidoff's scrap dealers. Mr Davidoff treads a path that leads to war. Why?

Like so many wars, including the murder at Sarajevo, in the First World War, it starts as a small incident that sparks something bigger but is not, in my view, the cause of it. It is certainly right that it escalated the whole thing, and led to the conflict.

I had heard that Mr Davidoff had an understanding with the distinguished company based in Edinburgh, Christian Salvesen, that he would carry out a sub-contracted scrap metal exercise on their behalf. When he landed I was deeply concerned at the *way* this happened. Nevertheless, when I was informed that, quite clearly, he had this contractual arrangement, it seemed to me that the problem really lay in the fact that he was there without clearance from our embassy in Buenos Aires. The important thing therefore was for him to get his papers in order.

That was your prime concern? His papers were not in order?

My concern was to smooth this one over. If he had not got this contractual arrangement with Christian Salvesen, I think we would have been even more concerned. But we were very worried about the position. *I* thought it was a provocation. The advice from our ambassador[3] was 'Look, I think we can seek a way through this one, because all we need to do is to try and legitimize his papers, as there is already this agreement.' So there was *that* factor to take into account.

I remember the telephone call at my house, on that Saturday afternoon, telling me of the Davidoff incident. I was already pretty worried about the Falkland Islands, so was Lord Carrington, and this thing did not help.

How was the incident put to you on the phone?

I was told that they had *not* got permission to land, and it was a provocation. The advice was that we should try and sort out the problem of Davidoff's papers and see whether we could legitimize his presence. It made sense to see if we could devise a formula which would allow him to do that. It was not, after all, a military invasion, which would have been quite a different picture.

However, there was that ambiguity, whether some of the scrap merchants were, in fact, military personnel?

Yes indeed. I think some *were*. That, of course, added to the tension.

3 Sir Anthony Williams.

What part was played in your mind by your knowledge that the government's intention was to withdraw the British Antarctic Survey from South Georgia, which would have left no British presence on the Islands, and none at all in the longer term, therefore, except Davidoff's scrap enterprise? Thus conforming to Argentina's process of establishing her presence on all the islands. She had done it in the South Sandwich group in 1977, and might now be proposing to do it on South Georgia?

We were conscious that tensions were very high and something silly might happen. I am trying to strip the benefits of hindsight from the reality of the atmosphere of that time. We knew of course that, on Southern Thule, they got away with it. They laid claim, and no reaction took place. Nevertheless, the fact that Davidoff did have this special scrap metal relationship, and had every right to undertake this exercise, *subject to his papers being cleared*, did put a slightly different light on the whole thing.

HMS Endurance *at this time was on her farewell commission, and due to be withdrawn on the 15th April 1982. There were last-minute, feverish, representations by the Foreign Office to have her reinstated. What led you to make those representations?*

In the end it was too close to the invasion,[4] and far too late in any event. I did persuade one of my ministerial colleagues in the Ministry of Defence to agree with John Nott that *Endurance* should not be withdrawn, and that we should announce the fact. Lord Carrington had been deeply concerned about the effect of the 1981 defence review on the Falklands, and some of our other commitments. Principally, I have to say, because of the symbolic aspect of *Endurance* and that her withdrawal would make our position harder in terms of discussions with the Argentine.

The position of the Treasury and the Ministry of Defence was one that had made our job more difficult. Lord Carrington had tried very hard with colleagues in government to get across the message that we must not change our posture on the Falkland Islands and give the wrong signals. He kept that position very strong but, sadly, did not make much progress. *Endurance* was still down there, of course. But it was very late in the day and, to my mind, at that stage it was the very least that should happen.

Endurance had a very tough time because we sent her sailing down to South Georgia after the prime minister's decision,[5] and then she

4 Lord Carrington wrote to John Nott on 24 March, seeking agreement to keep *Endurance* on station for the time being (Franks Report, para. 189).

5 That is, the decision to sail *Endurance* for South Georgia, to take the scrap dealers off the island if Argentina did not remove them.

was brought back. This toing and froing gave *Endurance* a very unhappy time. But I am sure the prime minister and Lord Carrington were right to take the view that HMS *Endurance*'s movement down to Georgia was important, to demonstrate that we were concerned, that Britain *did* mind about it, and we could not allow this kind of thing to happen. That really was the kind of thinking which led to *Endurance* being despatched very quickly to South Georgia.

Would it be true to say that you received conflicting advice about Davidoff? The ambassador in Buenos Aires is beseeching you not to pay too much attention to what he called 'a trivial and low-level affair', while the governor of the Falkland Islands, Hunt, appears to take a different view of the significance of the Davidoff landing?

Clearly Governor Hunt was concerned about the position, and saw it from a slightly different viewpoint. I do not recall him opposing the advice of the ambassador that we should try and take the sting out of this one.

On 24th of March, in the House of Commons, a motion was put down on Falkland Islands security, which ninety members of Parliament signed. It asked the government to secure the maintenance of a Royal Navy presence of sufficient strength, and for a specific assurance that sovereignty would not be transferred without the 'wishes' of the Islanders. What stays in your mind of this period, immediately before the invasion?

The scene was escalating all the time. I remember, the weekend before the invasion, talking late on the Sunday night[6] on the telephone to Lord Carrington and coming up on the Monday morning with my walking stick. I only take my walking stick with me if I think there is trouble. I stayed with that walking stick until the day I resigned. I talked to one of my ministerial colleagues on the Monday night and he asked, 'Why the walking stick?' I said, 'Because trouble is coming.' I knew, Lord Carrington knew, we all knew, that we were in grave difficulties by that stage.

I was, of course, having to make statements repeatedly, and answer questions, in the House of Commons. When you are in the middle of a crisis, this can make a considerable difference to the scene, and to your handling of the issue. Certainly, I was being pushed to say what action we were taking.

One course of action was to send a nuclear submarine down there. Earlier that week we took that decision.[7] It was too late, because it took fourteen days sailing to get there. But when the dispatch of that

6 That is, 28 March.
7 Franks Report, para. 213, gives the date of this decision as 29 March.

submarine leaked out,[8] in the *Daily Express*, that week, it was very, very unhelpful indeed. We obviously did not want it known, at that stage.

Sending Endurance *to South Georgia was resuming a posture which, as Argentina saw it, led back to the 1960s. You felt you had to move because of Parliamentary opinion?*

Yes. I think there would have been a violent reaction in the House of Commons if we had sat down and done nothing. You have to view it against that understandable feeling in the House and elsewhere. But, again, I do not think that was the cause of the invasion. It was the spark.

And so to war. It is a rueful, but cherished, self-perception of the British that they are an eleventh-hour nation. Stooping to finish the game. Unpredictable, because they are often so late to act. Two days too late to rescue General Gordon, in Khartoum, two years too late in rearming Britain for two world wars, too late in the Falklands. The British reserve a niche in history for those heroes who then make the best of it.

On Wednesday night, forty-eight hours before the actual landing of Friday 2 April, the Argentine Fleet was at sea, invasion imminent, and disaster impending. The defence secretary, John Nott, was briefing the prime minister. It is generally agreed that a sea-change came over all deliberations that night with the arrival, from Portsmouth, of the First Sea Lord and chief of the naval staff, **Admiral Sir Henry Leach**.

I returned to the Ministry of Defence at about 6 p.m., and on my desk I found two sets of briefs; one from intelligence, and the other from the naval staff. The latter was tending to say, 'Well, it is just another "blow-hot" with Argie, and things are going to be very difficult next year anyway', and so on. Perfectly prudent and valid up to a point. The other, from intelligence, indicated to me, for the first time, that they were *really* predicting – which they do not awfully like doing unless they are pretty sure of their ground – that there *would* be an invasion. At the time, they said probably of West Falkland, or one of the outer Islands. But *early*, during the first week in April. The general ethos of that intelligence brief to me meant, for the first time, 'They really mean business', and 'They're going to *do* something.' And if they did something on a bit of British territory, with British citizens on it, then to me it meant that *we* had to do something. And my reaction was, 'What the hell's the point in having a navy if, when you get a requirement like this, you are not prepared to do anything with it?'

8 Cf. Admiral Train quoting Admiral Anaya, and also Rear-Admiral Busser, in Ch. 5.

That being so, and having reached that conclusion, I reckoned that the advice put up by the naval staff was not the right advice. Presumably, as my secretary of state[9] was being briefed even then, he was being briefed *in those terms*. So I went straight along to his room, only to find that he was receiving his briefing in his room at the House of Commons. I grabbed the House of Commons pass from his private secretary and went straight down to the House. I was delayed there, because the only way into the House I then knew was via the public entrance, and I was held up by that splendid policeman in the central lobby, who would not take no for an answer. He could not have been nicer about it, either.

You were in full uniform, weren't you?

Well, I was dressed in ordinary working uniform, yes. Day uniform. Therefore a bit conspicuous, you might say.

A resplendent figure, I think somebody recalled?

Well, it wasn't very resplendent. Anyway, there it was. Various people passed, and I was rescued by one of the whips, and taken to the Whips Room, which was just round the corner, and given a stiff glass of whisky, and I had a long talk to the whips, practically all of whom were soldiers, bless them. In the course of that, they were trying to locate John Nott, which was really the *only* reason I had gone there. Eventually they did, and found that he was, by then, with the prime minister, in her room. Hard on the heels of that, I was asked to step up. So that's how I came to get to the prime minister, which otherwise had never entered my mind. And I simply walked through the door and said, 'Good evening, prime minister. Is there anything I can do to help?'

To which she said?

She replied in the sense that my arrival was 'timely', I think. We immediately got into a discussion.

Ironically, at this meeting Sir Henry Leach was facing the defence secretary, John Nott, he had so bitterly opposed over Nott's defence review the previous year. Nott, in calling for an 'end to the naval task force mentality', as something beyond Britain's resources, believed it also to be nostalgia for the past. What Sir Henry Leach proposed, therefore, was something John Nott's review had intended should come to an end. But that night both national honour, and the traditional Royal Navy, were at issue. To save one was to save both.

9 John Nott.

In these first hours of confusion and shock for the British Government, asking **Sir Henry Leach** for his opinion was tantamount to calling Drake from his hammock 'if the Dons sight Devon'. The First Sea Lord is a man's man, and no bloodless wraith. It is not hard to imagine that the Admiral's arrival at the House of Commons this night was not just 'timely' to the prime minister but, in the words of the old hymn, a case of 'his presence shall my wants supply'.

I think the Prime Minister was very worried, because I think her gut feel was that we were going to *have* to do something. I think that I sensed, when I went in, that the sort of advice she had been getting prior to that had tended to deflect her from doing anything beyond negotiating, and putting the screw on with words again. She had been receiving advice, I think, that under *no* circumstances should she do anything about it, because it was too far away, and much too difficult.

How was that obvious to you?

It was just the atmosphere. When I said really quite the opposite, and even took it a bit outside my terms of reference, nobody else spoke a word. That is why I deduced that this was perhaps different advice from what had been going on.

It did seem to me that *if* this invasion came about, then we would *have* to do something. We would have to do it fast, and we would have to do it with complete success. If we either found it was 'too difficult' or 'too far away' and did not do it, or if we pussy-footed and only *half* did it, and it was a bit of a shambles, either way it would be a disaster. That really would be the end of this country as a force in the world. I do not mean a *military* force, but a national force.

How far should we see you, chief of the naval staff, at the end of a period lasting many years in which Britain's role had diminished, seeing the Royal Navy, to which you were devoted, thereby reduced – the Royal Navy which had been the very instrument of Britain's world position? Therefore, at that moment, to the Prime Minister, you were not just sizing up for her the risks, but you were also seizing the opportunity to demonstrate what the Royal Navy could do?

I'm aware of that and of course it is a possible allegation. People can believe it or not as they wish, but it was *not* actually in my mind at the time. There was no question of, 'Oh, here's an opportunity to put the navy on the map', although patently the whole navy virtually was going to be involved, if it were to be done. With what degree of success, took you back to the risk factor. It *had* to succeed. What *was* in my mind was this broader, bigger, business of *this country*. I reiterate: I think that if we had not done it, or, in the course of doing it, had not done it sufficiently powerfully to achieve complete success, we would never have been the same country again.

All unsuspecting, Britain's political and military leadership was dispersed when the full awakening came. The foreign secretary, Lord Carrington, was in Israel. The chief of the defence staff, Admiral Lewin, was on the other side of the world, in New Zealand. The defence secretary, John Nott, had only just returned from a Nato meeting in Colorado Springs. By the time he left that first meeting with the prime minister and her hastily assembling Cabinet colleagues, Sir Henry Leach had created a vital new fact. A task force would mobilize, and start to sail by the weekend of Argentina's invasion. As the House of Commons rose to express the wounded pride of the nation, Lord Carrington felt consumed by the fires of its accusatory and unanimous emotion, and resigned. It was widely concluded that the Government would have fallen had it stood the task force down.

Lord Carrington's replacement as Foreign Secretary was **Francis Pym**.

There was no hesitation on the part of the Cabinet in preparing that task force, none whatsoever. It was indeed the only possible decision that could be taken.

When Carrington resigned, and you became foreign secretary, how much support was there, in that Cabinet, for a negotiated settlement?

Full support in the Cabinet, if it could be achieved on terms that were acceptable to us. There is absolutely no doubt about that. An awful lot has been written about how Mrs Thatcher, and the war Cabinet, *wanted* to go to war and were not interested in negotiated settlements. I can absolutely disprove that and, without any question of doubt, of *course* we wanted that. Unfortunately, it did not happen, so, in the end, we had to take military action.

Having been shocked by the invasion, how common was the feeling in the Cabinet, from the outset, that now Argentina had actually done it, they were very unlikely to be dislodged by diplomacy?

I always held the hope that something might be achieved, and I spent a number of weeks doing everything that I conceivably could to try and achieve such a result. But I have to tell you that I always thought it was very doubtful. The Argentines had become very excited by what they had achieved. Indeed, it was something they had long wanted. There was Galtieri, exciting the crowds in Argentina. We saw them on television. The square, in Buenos Aires, was absolutely full of cheering people. Very difficult for him then to come along and say he had agreed to something the British could agree, and which would mean their withdrawal. However, I was not going to be put off by that. It was my responsibility to do everything conceivable to try and reach an agreement.

The answer to your question about 'how much support was there in the Cabinet', I think, is really this. On each occasion, and there were three occasions when genuine proposals were on the table, to be agreed or disagreed, in *every* case the Cabinet agreed with *all three proposals*. That has to be remembered. The fact that Argentina did not accept any of them meant that we had to go to war at the end of the day. To arrive at a series of agreements that we thought acceptable to the British people, and which would be far better than military action, was not particularly easy to achieve. I explored every detail that I could.

The evidence is in what happened. The Peruvian proposals, and the final proposals we ourselves laid before the United Nations, were very important parts of the whole process. It is a matter for the utmost regret that Argentina could not agree.

There are, no doubt, many 'decisive' moments you recall. Can I suggest that one of them was Enoch Powell, in the House, saying, upon news of the Argentine invasion, 'We shall now see what metal the prime minister is made of', and then, outside it and at once, 'We've got to go to war!'? You have a long experience in the House. Over Suez, in 1956, a part of the Party was extravagantly warlike, another part more apprehensive. How did the balance lie in the case of the Falklands?

I think the position is entirely clear. If we did not manage to get a settlement, we would go to war. For a week or two it would be fair to say that the hope of reaching a settlement was rather higher than it deserved to be, both in the mind of the members of the Commons, and in the mind of the public. But it gradually became clear, as one proposal after another was rejected by Argentina, that we were going to fight a war, because there would be no other means of achieving our objective *except* military means.

General Haig has told us of his first visit to London after the Argentine invasion, and the 'working dinner' that followed in Downing Street. The prime minister had made a point, he says, of showing him the portraits of Nelson and Wellington. At one point during a discussion of the capabilities of the British task force, then on its way, Haig says, 'Mr Pym murmured, "Maybe we should ask the Falkland Islanders how they feel about a war." Mrs Thatcher heatedly challenged him', says Haig, and, 'Had I been Francis Pym I would not have counted my chances of remaining in the Cabinet as very great if I persisted in suggesting to this prime minister that a retreat from her principles might be desirable. It was evident', says Haig, 'that Mrs Thatcher did not enjoy the full support of other members of the government.' How should we understand that?

I think that is a nonsensical passage. No doubt it is quite true, I don't recall, but in the course of all the numerous discussions in the war Cabinet and the main Cabinet about what terms we would be prepared to agree to, a great many issues were raised. I put forward quite a number of proposals which I thought the Cabinet ought to consider, even if they were not obviously acceptable to British interests, because there was no possibility of any military engagement for weeks after the task force sailed. In the first place they had to get there, and in the meantime the only object of policy was to see whether we could reach a negotiated settlement. It was my job to turn over every stone. On every occasion, with Haig's proposals, the Peruvian proposals, and our own, the whole Cabinet fully agreed. *That* is the answer.

Let me pursue that. Here was something which, over many years, several governments in Britain had tried to settle. How far did you and your advisers see it as a chance, given the full weight of American mediation, to achieve what had eluded us all those years and settle it, once and for all?

I do not think there was the slightest chance of that happening after the invasion by the Argentines. Every proposal we put forward naturally included not only an immediate ceasefire, but an immediate withdrawal. That is what the Argentines were never prepared to do. Against that background there was not the slightest chance of thinking we could solve the problem. But at the time of the Falklands war, the idea *that* could be the key to solving it was no part of our thinking whatsoever.

Unlike Suez, when Eisenhower was neither informed nor consulted, this time Alexander Haig, the secretary of state, was present with the war Cabinet in Downing Street?

The invasion of the Falklands, and the strong and immediate response of the British Cabinet, which had such widespread support, put the United States, with all their major interests throughout South America, in a very difficult position. Al Haig took a very brave decision to put himself in the firing line in trying to mediate between the two. I thought to myself, 'That is a marvellous thing to do. Very dangerous. Might even cost him his job', because the likelihood of achieving success seemed to me to be very remote. But how marvellous that he tried.

It did cost him his job!

And, in the end, it cost him his job. What Al Haig staked his reputation on trying to do was to get an agreement where, perhaps, none was possible. Nevertheless, he tried to do it.

As Argentina had calculated, the ghost of Sir Anthony Eden and what had happened at Suez in 1956 hovered over all, in Cabinet and high command, called upon to decide. The manner in which the British Government's aims and objectives were drawn up, following the invasion, bore the stamp of the Royal Navy. Like light reaching us from a star that is dead, but that we still steer by, these memories of the Suez affair navigated the British task force south. **Admiral Lord Lewin**, the chief of the defence staff, was a member of the war Cabinet.

The attitude of most people of my generation to Suez was that it was a political disaster of major dimensions because the military were not allowed to finish the job. I was in command of a destroyer in the Mediterranean at that time. The military felt that we had been badly let down because, having been told to do the invasion, we were not allowed to finish it off. If we had got right down through the Canal, things might have been different.

Suez entered my thoughts very much more, as the days went by, from the point of view of the relationship between the politicians and the military. I was determined that we should not make the mistakes of Suez. The military must have a clear operational directive from ministers as to what they expected us to do, and we would carry it out. I went to the very first meeting of the war Cabinet determined to get an objective out of it. What was it they wanted to do?

How was the British aim over the Falkland Islands, at that meeting, defined and drafted?

Well, I arrived back at Heathrow,[10] at about half past six or seven, and was met by two or three of my staff officers and went back to the Ministry of Defence; got there I suppose before 8 o'clock, and had a briefing meeting there. We knew the first meeting of the war Cabinet was at half past nine. It emerged from this discussion that we must get the aim straight, which is the first thing any staff college trained officer is taught to do – what any staff college trained officer is determined to do. So we drafted it out. I had the objective typed. The objective was 'To cause the withdrawal of the Argentinian forces, and to restore the British administration'. Remember, by this time Tony Parsons[11] had got Resolution 502 passed, and this more or less put Resolution 502 in terms of a military objective.

I went to the first meeting of the war Cabinet. At some stage in the discussion going on, I said, 'Look, could I know what the

10 From New Zealand.
11 Sir Anthony Parsons, British Ambassador to the UN in New York.

Government's objective is? I think it is very important that the
military know what the objective is, so we can decide what is
required.' Everybody agreed that it was a good thing to have an objective. I said, 'Well, we have written one out, will this do?' I read it out,
and everybody thought that it was splendid. We stuck to it for the next
seventy days. And we achieved it.

*In other words, the views of the war Cabinet were not solicited? You presumably
went armed with your own draft believing they were unlikely to produce a
coherent one?*

Yes I did, because I do not think that the ministerial machine, divided
as it is between the various ministries, is organized to produce
operational directives.

The directives drafted by Admiral Lewin, which were simply stated as
being to bring about the 'withdrawal of the Argentine forces and to restore
the British administration' of the Islands, set down, as he says, in terms of a
military objective the swift and remarkable accomplishment of British
diplomacy at the United Nations, secured by the British ambassador, Sir
Anthony Parsons. This was the adoption by the world body of Resolution
502, calling upon Argentina to withdraw from the Falklands.

As the British task force set out across the deserts of the ocean on its
eight-thousand-mile journey, finally to assemble before that monument
to self-determination, the Falkland Islands, the intervening weeks
belonged to the diplomats. The Foreign Office, in organizing support
for Britain in Europe, at the United Nations, and in America, achieved
striking success in tuning the pulpits of world opinion, at a time when
the American emphasis on 'even-handedness' and friendship towards
Argentina raised palpable fears in London that the United States might
prove as cold-blooded over the Falklands as it had been at Suez. In 1956,
American opposition to the British and French attempt to make Egypt,
in Eden's words, 'disgorge the Suez Canal', was the major factor in
forcing Britain to submit and withdraw. In 1982, the British ambassador
to Washington was **Sir Nicholas Henderson**. In these eerie, hectic
weeks 'Nicko' Henderson proved a masterful nurse and tutor of the
British cause in an atmosphere, at first, rather grimly reminiscent of
Suez.

It certainly was very much in the mind of Secretary of State Haig, and
I think in the mind of the president. It was also in the minds of many
people in the United States who had doubts about our resistance to
the Argentinian invasion, because the feeling exists still, in the
United States, that they must resist the continuation of anything that

they might call 'colonialism', 'imperialism', or the maintenance of positions, in distant parts of the world, on the basis of military force 'against the wills of the people', etcetera. There was a strong feeling that we were doing again what we had done, and the Americans had criticized, at Suez.

That was one side of it. The other side, which was one certainly held by Haig, and I am pretty sure by the president, because Haig told me it was the president's view, was that whatever was going to be done by the Americans, whatever attitude they adopted about our resistance, they would not, what they called, 'repeat Suez'. By which they meant they would not pillory us, even if they did not agree with us. They would not put us in the dock, as they had done in 1956 over Suez, and bring us to our knees. It was a very important decision on their part, because there were many parallels, and it could *look* like maintenance or continuation of a colonial attitude, which is instinctively unpopular in the United States.

When one reflects upon the parallels between Suez in 1956 and the Falklands, Eisenhower simply did not think that the Suez Canal was worth a war. Would you agree that neither did Reagan, over the Falklands? At the outset he referred, to 'That little ice-cold bunch of land down there'. He chose to appear quite baffled by it all?

'Little bunch of ice-cold rock down there', yes, I remember. I think that is completely true. There were very many people who were sceptical in Washington about whether it was worth a great military effort, for distant islands inhabited by less than two thousand British subjects, or whether – it was an equally widely held doubt – we could launch and maintain an attack eight thousand miles away.

But Eisenhower was consistent throughout. Eden could not convince him that the Suez Canal was vital in the eyes of Britain and France. So what convinced President Reagan this time about the Falklands?

I think there was one fundamental difference. Not that I am defending what the Americans did at Suez, but I understand, in retrospect, why they were indignant we went ahead at Suez. The fundamental difference was that, at Suez, *we* took the initiative in military action. In the 1982 Falklands episode, it was the Argentinians who had committed aggression. The Americans acknowledged from the start that it was the Argentinians who had committed aggression, and 'They must not be allowed to get away with it.' That was a phrase that Haig continually used to me, 'Even though', he said, 'we are not going to take sides. For a long time we must persist in the effort to reach a negotiated agreement. But we do acknowledge that aggression has taken place in the American continent, and if that becomes an unchallenged precedent, it could have very dangerous repercussions', given the numbers of frontier disputes and other differences by which the American continent is beleaguered.

In which case, how easy or difficult was it to persuade the United States that Britain saw it as an issue of principle and not just a question, for example, of saving Mrs Thatcher's face?

It was not altogether easy. 'To save the prime minister's face' is an interesting point. Haig often saw it as 'Galtieri, or Mrs Thatcher': one is going to fall, both of them cannot survive.

Two things, I think, were decisive in the American mind. One was the principle which they had, after all, pioneered in the international jungle, that the ideological guiding line must be self-determination. People must have a right to be governed by those they wish to govern them. And, it was perfectly apparent, the people on the Falklands wanted to remain British. The second was, aggression had been culpably committed.

But there is a third one that is relevant, and I don't think it has been adequately explained. It is perhaps a little delicate, I suppose. It is the fact that we are a key member of the Alliance. A very important senator said to me, 'You realize that if it had been, for example, another Latin American country which had been invaded by Argentina, we would not have felt compelled to become so emotionally, deeply and practically involved as we are now. You are our ally. You are British.' It is moments like this when the connection between us has practical results.

How important, over and above the historical Anglo-American partnership, was the relationship between Mrs Thatcher and President Reagan? How important was Mrs Thatcher to the president?

The relationship established between them from the time President Reagan entered the White House was important. I do not, frankly, think it was the decisive thing over the Falklands. It would have made it very difficult for Reagan to have criticized us or come out openly against us. The people pushing for positive action, and indeed sympathy, in support of us were largely Haig himself and the secretary of defence, Caspar Weinberger.

If one goes back again to 1956, after the first 'bellicosity' there was a sharp fall in enthusiasm for a military solution. How far were all responses shaped by that? Were the Americans, for example, 'waiting to see' before they committed themselves over the Falklands?

The Americans were definitely very worried, at the beginning, by our ability to carry out the military operation, and for the British public then to put up with the heavy casualties that were expected. I had to appear many times in public, discussing with high-powered American military and intelligence experts who cast doubts on our ability to do this.

The sinking of HMS *Sheffield*, at the beginning of May, was greeted in the United States with almost as much concern as it was in this country. It was considered deeply shocking and disturbing, because it meant that our forces were in jeopardy from the air or mines and would not be able to carry out their mission. There was, for a very long time, widespread doubt, even among those who sympathized perhaps emotionally with us, whether we could do it.

The first thing you had to contemplate, before the fighting, was Haig's mediation. Why was there an American mediation? Did we seek it? Or was it at American insistence?

It was entirely an American initiative. For reasons you have already hinted at, they did not like the prospect of having to take sides, having to make a choice between their hemispheric neighbours and their close ally in the Atlantic Alliance. So Haig's determination was to try and bring about a negotiated settlement that would *absolve* them from having to commit themselves.

There was another aspect to it. Haig perceived that if, as I think he in his heart of hearts hoped, the outcome of a military action was defeat of the Argentinians, and the reassertion of British sovereignty on those Islands, then this could have long-term consequences but it would not bring about a long-term solution of the problem. I think Haig saw that, and he believed that it would be useful to take advantage of the Argentine invasion, not simply to correct and redress a wrong, but to provide something in terms of a long-term settlement.

The very first American utterance was made by the State Department, by the under-secretary of state, Walter Stoessel. It was that the United States would be 'even-handed'. What became your task then?

That was, as you say, 'utterance'. I am not sure he ever made it public. He said it to me. It did not go down at all well. The Argentine had committed the aggression, and this could not be left, in my view, by the US government as something for 'even-handedness'. They changed. As soon as he took hold of the thing, which he did extremely quickly, Haig said America could not be 'even-handed' on the subject of aggression. What they *could* be 'even-handed' about was trying to bring about a negotiated settlement.

Mrs Jeane Kirkpatrick, America's ambassador to the United Nations, who held Cabinet rank, was among those who felt the United States should not commit itself to Britain. Jeane Kirkpatrick was puzzled by British tenacity over the Falklands, which did not, she thought, accord with the broad sweep of Britain's record in shedding her colonies. In addition, she found it difficult to see why the Alliance was suddenly at stake in the Falklands, when Britain had not found it relevant in American calls for support elsewhere, as, for example, in Central America. Argentina, on the other hand, was becoming an active partner for America there.

A sympathetic response to the invasion, at the United Nations, was central to Argentina's strategy. Over many years United Nations votes had consistently recognized Argentina had a claim to sovereignty. In her belief that the Falklands issue was not worth a war, Kirkpatrick was a potentially formidable, because hostile, obstacle for Britain at the United Nations. In those shoal-filled waters, the British permanent representative, **Sir Anthony Parsons** of the Foreign Office, proved a mighty helmsman. The winning by Parsons of Resolution 502, which called upon Argentina to withdraw, enabled Britain to scramble on to the high ground of the Falklands issue, from which, in the weeks of intense diplomacy that followed, it was never dislodged.

The day before the invasion took place I got the green light from London, at lunch time, to call the Security Council. I started out ringing up all my colleagues, myself, to get the Council into session immediately. It was really rather extraordinary, because it revealed that pretty well nobody on the Security Council had ever *heard* of the Falklands. It had not been in the press, or anything like that. It was April the 1st. Quite a few of them thought I was being my 'jokey' self and I was pulling an April Fool trick on them. In fact, one of my very distinguished colleagues told me, very firmly, that he probably knew our customs better than I did and that as it was after midday April Fool jokes no longer ran, and I was 'offside' in every sense! I do not exaggerate when I say that it took some persuasion to convince them that an emergency meeting of the Security Council *was* going to take place.

I got agreement very quickly that there should be a statement by the president of the Council calling on both sides to exercise restraint and not to do anything to rock the boat in the South Atlantic. All that happened about eight o'clock in the evening. There was a little bit of drama. We gathered around the table, and the Argentine representative, who was not a member of the Council, asked to sit at the table. That was granted, of course. The president read out this statement, there was no debate. I immediately put up my pencil and said, 'My government would, of course, carry out the president's statement to the letter. *We* had no intention of disturbing the peace down there. I challenge my distinguished Argentine colleague to make a similar statement.' He remained silent. I think that it was, at that moment, that the whole Council realized, and the penny dropped, that it *was* going to happen and there would be big trouble in the next few days.

Why was it, given the support there had always been for the Argentine claim at the UN, particularly among the Third World countries and the Afro-Asian bloc, that there was both overt and surreptitious support for Britain from those who had always upheld the Argentine case in vote after vote?

It is very interesting. That same night, April 1st, the night before the invasion, we obviously considered in the British mission how we were going to deal with the situation the following day, assuming the Argentine invasion was going to take place. We came to the conclusion we must avoid the sovereignty issue. We had virtually no support, throughout the whole system, for that. We must concentrate on the fact there had been an unprovoked act of aggression. Particularly among the non-aligned Third World countries, a large number of whom have suffered, themselves, such acts of aggression, that rang a very loud bell indeed.

In the first debate, when we were working up to the first Resolution, 502, a number of non-aligned states made the point that they adhered to non-aligned summit declarations on the Falklands that sovereignty rested with Argentina, but this was nothing to do with it. This was a matter of *aggression*. Therefore a wrong had been committed, and it had to be put right.

How much interest had there been among the foreign delegations at the UN over the Falklands?

Before the crisis, very little. It actually made the whole evolution of the crisis, in the United Nations, far more interesting. Almost for the first time in my UN experience, the debates were really *live* debates. People were learning from those who knew something about it, like myself, the Argentine colleague, the Americans and the Latin Americans. One could actually sense, in the debate, people changing their minds according to how the debate was going. That is virtually unique in my experience at the UN.

How far could it be said Mrs Kirkpatrick was hostile to the British position? How keen was she not to be seen standing up alongside Britain at the UN?

Mrs Kirkpatrick had been one of the authors of the new American policy towards Latin America and she is an academic, and a Latin American expert. She had put a lot of time and trouble, and her personal prestige, into this whole Latin American business, so her choice was extremely difficult.

I got to know her very well indeed. We worked together closely for a long time at the UN and got on extremely well. I would be the last person to suggest that Jeane Kirkpatrick is in any way anti-British, in the sense that some Americans are – on the contrary, very 'pro', I think. Her problem was that she saw what seemed to her a kind of factitious quarrel was going to upset many things. It was going to shake, if it did not destroy, this whole policy she was trying to put together. She also feared that the infection of the Falklands dispute with Britain would spread throughout Latin America. She thought it would become a pan-Latin American issue, and that Latin America, because of the Falklands, would range itself against the West, including the United States.

There were the Latin American people in the State Department who felt very much as she did, and there were the secretary of state, Al Haig, and the defence secretary, Caspar Weinberger, who felt differently. This debate was going on not only in New York, but in Washington also.

It is said that Mrs Kirkpatrick thought you were 'mad' to take it to the Security Council, and said that she would 'block you' if you did. Was there such an exchange between you?

Yes, we did have an exchange on those lines. I think, you see, she was taken as much by surprise as anybody by the way things started to unfold and the imminence of the invasion. She was very reluctant to see the thing get into the international arena. I think she still felt that it could be settled bilaterally, with American help. Of course we felt totally differently, and I was determined to go ahead.

What was your response to her, when she said she would 'block you' if you tried to take it to the Council?

My response, on that particular occasion, was that I was calling an emergency session of the Security Council and I was determined to get into the building, as it were, into the Security Council Chamber, and to inscribe an item on the Security Council Agenda. And if she was disposed to oppose me, I would demand a vote, a procedural vote on whether we actually discussed the problem. She would have to oppose me on the vote, in public, underneath the television cameras and all the rest of it.

You were determined to see that her blocking of you would not be something that took place in the corridor? Mrs Kirkpatrick, for the United States, would have to do it publicly?

Certainly. I was absolutely determined that we were going to get an emergency meeting of the Security Council that afternoon, and that if it was blocked, it would only be blocked in a formal way, by a vote. It would have looked extremely odd if the Americans had not supported us.

What is to be said of the Argentine performance at the United Nations?

In getting that first resolution, getting the maximum number of votes for it, I think we were to some extent rather lucky in the actual composition of the Security Council and lucky also in the Argentine diplomatic performance. When the Foreign Minister, Costa Méndez, arrived – and we agreed to postpone the debate for one day to allow him to get there – I think he was convinced that, because Argentina was a non-aligned country and Britain was an ex-imperial power, and because all those non-aligned summits had endorsed Argentina's view of sovereignty, the non-aligned members of the Security Council would be *bound* to support Argentina. When he got there, the non-aligned Council members asked to talk to him and they retired into one of the consultation rooms. They came out rather quickly. I sensed that it had not been a very successful meeting. I think he had rather taken them for granted, and perhaps he had not been all that diplomatic, or persuasive, with them. This crossed my mind as the debate began, that it was going to be helpful to me.

Then, during the debate, he made one enormous mistake. I was really basing all my arguments, and I spoke again and again, on the breach of Article 2 of the Charter, about 'peaceful settlement of disputes' and non-use of force. He asked to speak in right of reply to me at one stage. He said he thought that I, the British representative, did not realize that this provision only applied to disputes which had come into existence *after* 1945, when the Charter came into effect. When he said this, I could feel the whole atmosphere in the Security Council changing – because just about every delegation came from a country which was embroiled in disputes going back to the nineteenth century, if not the eighteenth century. Try and tell the Arabs, or the Israelis, or the black Africans that the Charter applied only after 1945, and what had happened before that had nothing to do with the Charter! It was an enormous mistake.

Of course, I put my hand up immediately, and said I thought this was an extremely dangerous doctrine, and if it was generally adopted the world would be an even more dangerous place than it is now . . . and all the rest of it. That error of judgement on his part was very helpful to my cause.

And, for a great footballing nation like Argentina, a diplomatic 'own goal'?

Absolutely. I would have said a *rasping* own goal, yes.

Why did the Russians not use the veto against you at the United Nations?

A question we were asking ourselves at the time, and I have asked myself frequently since. The Soviet delegation spent a great deal of the day of the vote on the first resolution running backwards and forwards to the telephone to Moscow. They too had been taken totally by surprise. I simply don't think they had their act together at the beginning and then found it very difficult to get one together.

To start with, the Soviet Union regards the UN as a forum in which to capture the hearts and minds of the Third World majority. This does not mean, as so many people think, that the non-aligned majority meekly follows the Soviet Union into the voting chamber. It is the other way round: the Soviet Union, normally, likes to be seen to be supporting the non-aligned majority. I think they saw, as the debate developed, that with the exception of Panama all the non-aligned states on the Security Council were going to vote in favour of the resolution Britain had put down. They realized they were going to sail across the bows of their non-aligned chums if they vetoed. I think that was the reason they did not.

Again, the impression I got from the Soviet delegation and, of course, we used to discuss this in the background as things went on, is that they found it very difficult to believe that we would, actually, follow through *with military action*. They expected us to make a fuss internationally, of course, in the United Nations. But even when it became more and more obvious that Argentina was *not* going to withdraw, and that we were going to have to take the military tack to redeem the aggression, I think they still found it very difficult to believe we *would* actually go through with it, to the end.

On what was that judgement founded?

I am guessing now, but from the bits and pieces I picked up from them, my impression is that they felt Britain had been trying for years to *divest* itself of the Falklands problem. Argentina had done it for us, in an extremely rude and offensive way, and although we had to react very strongly to that, diplomatically, we would be unlikely to re-impale ourselves on the Falklands hook.

An awful lot of people were in the same boat. One of the things I found very frustrating, after the invasion had taken place, and after the task force had set out, was the difficulty in persuading my colleagues in the Security Council, not just the Soviet Union, but pretty well *all* of them, that this *was* really serious. If we could not bring about a peaceful Argentine withdrawal from the Islands, then we were going to recover them by military action.

There were many instances of this totally unrealistic attitude among my Security Council colleagues. When actual hostilities were beginning, as the task force was getting closer to the Islands, and there were air attacks by our aircraft on Port Stanley, the Security Council kept on wanting to issue declarations calling on both sides 'to exercise restraint'. As if it were some kind of game! I remember saying, very heatedly, in these consultations, 'How do you translate a request to exercise restraint to the pilot of a British aircraft who sees himself attacked by an Argentine aircraft? Does he think "I must exercise restraint", or does he think "I am fighting a war"?' It was very difficult to persuade them that *the real thing* was going on down there. It was not until pretty late in the day that people realized this.

Sir Anthony Parsons bestowed the dramatically important United Nations victory on Mrs Thatcher as the task force set out. It was a reversal of what had happened at Suez.

As the British fleet sailed for the Falklands, no matchless opportunity was seen. Quite the opposite. Sir Nicholas Henderson, hurtling back and forth by Concorde[12] as occasion demanded between Washington and London, had been taken aside by Sir John Fieldhouse, the commander-in-chief of the fleet, and soberly told 'I suppose you realize that this is the most difficult thing we have attempted since the Second World War?'

Suez was the last time an enterprise of this character had been tried. It had ended in unmitigated disaster. In 1956 the derisory mood of humiliation and restlessness in Britain had been caught by *Punch* with a cartoon of the prime minister. Its caption was, 'The Grand Old Anthony Eden, he had ten thousand men, he marched them up to the top of the hill, and he marched them down again.' How strong in the war Cabinet, of which **Admiral Lewin** was a member, was the feeling born of the Suez experience, that this time there could be no turning back?

Very strong. Very strong, particularly in ministerial minds. Suez was mentioned, in the early days, on a number of occasions. I was pleased about that, because what Suez lacked was coherent ministerial resolve. There were too many changes of mind, and changes of course, whereas I think the background to success of the Falklands was that we set our objective, and we stuck to it, absolutely, throughout.

12 British diplomats and Cabinet ministers alike attest to the benefits of this new instrument in the conduct of diplomacy and in the management of the Falklands crisis.

Of what significance was it that, this time, there was a prime minister who did not know war – almost unique in recent history? How did that alter relationships with her advisers?

Well, I have thought about this a great deal. I think that it made my job much easier. The important thing is the relationship between ministers, and particularly the *prime* minister, who ultimately has to take the decision, and the military adviser. It is important there should be confidence between the two. This had to be built up, because Mrs Thatcher did not know me all that well. She certainly did not know whether she could rely on me in an operational crisis. So the confidence had to be built up.

Now she had, as you say, no knowledge of war or of military affairs, which a male equivalent, or contemporary, might well have done – even if it was only National Service. For example, Lord Whitelaw,[13] and Francis Pym[14] and John Nott[15] had all served at various levels in the services, and had all experienced action. I think it would have been much more difficult to get *some* decisions, quickly, from people with that experience, than it was from the prime minister. Because, once she had got confidence, and you were able to explain to her why you needed a change in the rules of engagement, or something like that, she understood it very quickly, and then gave tremendous support. I think that a *male* contemporary might have argued rather more.

It is recorded that when William the Conqueror landed at Pevensey, he fell over as he stepped ashore. The omens and prophetic signs in the Falklands were similarly daunting. Long after the Falklands conflict was over, a member of Mrs Thatcher's war Cabinet was asked why she had succeeded when the hazards of such a conflict, without adequate command of the air, have long been acknowledged to be so very great. He returned this answer: 'Only a woman would have attacked the Golden Temple in Amritsar.[16] Only a woman would have gone on in the Falklands.' But it was the Nelson touch, and it proved not the least of Argentina's misjudgements. 'That woman wouldn't dare', as General Galtieri had told Haig's emissary Vernon Walters, before the fighting began.

Haig, who believed that Argentina should not be rewarded for its aggression, also thought, as Sir Nicholas Henderson has told us, it would be useful to take adantage of the Argentine invasion, 'not simply

13 Home secretary and deputy prime minister: in the Scots Guards in World War II.
14 Foreign secretary: in the 9th Lancers in World War II, and holder of the MC.
15 Defence secretary: regular officer in the Gurkha Rifles, 1952–6.
16 Prime Minister Indira Gandhi. The Golden Temple was stormed in 1984.

to correct and redress a wrong, but to provide something in terms of a long-term settlement'. The Foreign Office advice was that Britain could not ignore, but had to finesse, the American interest. In addition, it was surely right to have in mind that had a troop-carrying ship been sunk, *Canberra* or *QE2* (and the Argentine submarines hunting them were never found by British forces), then the cry would very likely have gone up from ministers, 'Get us out of this!'

How was Britain's attitude to negotiations affected by the fact that the Foreign Office was not numbered among Mrs Thatcher's warmest enthusiasms, and was often suspected of infirmity of purpose? **Sir Nicholas Henderson** was then British ambassador to Washington.

The Foreign Office is accustomed to unpopularity, particularly in Whitehall. I once said about Mrs Thatcher's attitude towards it that, 'It is like her attitude towards the Church of England, in reverse.' She likes the people in the Foreign Office, and dislikes the institution. With the Church of England, she likes the institution, but she does not like the leaders of it.

So she was in touch with people from the Foreign Office, and I hope she read the endless telegrams I sent from Washington. But what underlies your question is perfectly true. The Foreign Office was holding out the need to show a readiness to negotiate, maximum readiness to negotiate, and the prime minister's emphasis always was, 'We cannot put up with this intolerable aggression.' Of course, there was room for agreement on some sort of middle ground between those two. Eventually, that is what we did reach. But I expect Mrs Thatcher thought the Foreign Office, and certainly thought that *I* was, unnecessarily soft in saying, 'We must take the American wish to have a negotiated settlement seriously.'

There is an old jibe by those deeply suspicious of the diplomatic arts in any case, and the period of decolonization in which they were applied, which says the Foreign Office is 'a hotbed of cold feet'. How far was the prime minister persuaded of that, in the immediate aftermath of the Argentine invasion?

I think you're right. I think she *does* think that. It is her nature to go for outright victory, rather than compromise. As the whole life of international affairs involves various forms of compromise, she is not instinctively, emotionally, particularly enamoured of the Foreign Office approach to things.

The secretary of state at the time was Francis Pym, and I don't think he had a very easy time in trying to keep on board with Haig, on one side of the Atlantic, and keeping faith with, or retaining the confidence of, the prime minister on the other. It was not easy riding, as it were, those twin horses in the circus. Francis Pym did not last long.

On the other hand, here was a problem that we had wished to be rid of, if possible, for many years. The whole thrust of our policies had been to diminish our interests, visibly, in the South Atlantic. How far did you see what had happened, together with the American mediation, as offering hope of a real negotiation, the chance for which ministers had so often hoped, of settling it 'once and for all'?

Now you are slightly trespassing beyond the particular objectives of what we were trying to persuade the American Government to do during the days of the Falklands war. You are looking at the longer term. But I entirely share the view behind your question, that, if it could have led to a negotiated settlement that somehow provided for a long-term agreement, then that would have been to our advantage, and to the advantage of the United States and Argentina. I think that was possible, and I think it was extraordinarily blind of the Argentinians not to see that.

Haig's mediation failed when apparent Argentine agreement to his peace proposals was, in Haig's words, 'withdrawn at the last moment as though by some hidden hand'. In the pessimism following Argentina's rejection of Haig, the issue of war had now to be faced.

The American secretary of state had not in fact yielded, but continued his diplomacy by drafting a set of proposals which were then put forward by President Belaunde of Peru. America had come down on Britain's side on 30 April 1982. The sinking of the Argentine cruiser, *Belgrano*, two days later on 2 May coincided with the genesis of the so-called 'Peruvian initiative'. It also coincided with the arrival in America to see Haig, 'this time as an ally', as he said, of the foreign secretary, **Francis Pym**.

Having failed with this initiative of his own, Al Haig was naturally very keen to try another. So was I. Either Peru put itself in the position of a go-between, or was invited to do so by Al Haig, it doesn't much matter which. Obviously they tried to put together another collection of proposals that might be a possibility of agreement between the two countries.

The story of those proposals has become ludicrously confused by the *Belgrano*, and all the allegations that have been made about the *Belgrano*. But the point is that those proposals were refined, between the 1st May and the 6th of May, to the *second* set of proposals, which the Cabinet was prepared to go along with, and which were put to Argentina, and which they refused. That happened five days or six days *after* the *Belgrano* went down.

How right are we to suppose that with Haig's failure, two days before the Peruvian initiative, the British Government could imagine no one else succeeding where all the resource of the United States had failed? Therefore when you arrive in Washington, on the evening of Saturday May 1st, you bring with you a sort of 'We've reached the end of the road' feeling?

I did not feel that at all, actually. I went there because, after the rejection of the Haig proposals, and the president's decision to come down on our side, I wanted to go over and talk over the whole situation with Al Haig, and see what other steps we could take, what other work we could do. He was thinking on the same lines, and had already had his first conversation with the president of Peru. This was the beginning of what turned out to be the second series of proposals.

On the Sunday morning, May 2nd, you had two hours with Mr Haig. What did he say to you about the proposals of President Belaunde of Peru?

He said that they had been in touch with each other, and that he'd come up with a series of *ideas* – not *proposals*, but *ideas* – for another possible negotiated settlement. From my point of view it made no difference whether it had started from Peru itself or whether Al Haig had inspired it. Here was another initiative being taken. The question was, was it going to help the British Government? So I said, 'Yes, I am quite certain that it is something we ought to pursue.' There were certain aspects of it, I remember thinking, that would be extremely difficult for us. But these ideas were not worked out.

In all the argument about the *Belgrano*, everybody tries to represent that here was some tremendous peace proposal which, in some curious way, was not properly addressed. The truth is completely different. As I have already said, these ideas, which is all they were on Sunday 2nd May, *were developed*, over the next few days, to such a point that they were actually put to Argentina, the British Government having accepted them. So that is the answer to that.

That same afternoon, on Sunday May 2nd, you leave Washington and fly to New York to see the UN secretary general. Just before you go, Haig rings you again, it is said to stress the importance of the Peruvian proposals. But you did not take the call. The ambassador, Sir Nicholas Henderson, did. Why was that?

Well, not only had I had a couple of *hours* with Al Haig in the morning, he had come to lunch. We talked over the whole thing. The gravamen of Al Haig's telephone message, when I was just getting into the car, was to stress the importance of this.[17] Well, do you think I *needed* to be told that?

17 That is, of 'the Peruvian initiative'.

I think we ought to consider Al Haig's position then. He had just put his reputation, and his office, on the line in trying to negotiate a settlement. It was totally admirable but it failed. He had his own political position to bear in mind. It is perfectly obvious that if there was something of *real substance* coming out, some *worked out* series of proposals, the circumstances would have been quite different. They were not, of course. The evidence is conclusive on this point.

Why did our ambassador in Lima go to see the foreign minister of Peru at your request on the morning of May 1st?

Because having heard of these *ideas*, not *proposals*, coming out I thought it would be a good idea if our ambassador went and had a talk with them. In fact he had already done so. The whole scene was discussed, and the president of Peru never mentioned any ideas that he was preparing, never *mentioned* any conversation with Al Haig, or in any way indicated that any initiative at all was being taken. It was when I heard about it that I said, 'We must send in our ambassador and get another line on this from Peru', and he did that.

'Undeveloped' though these proposals were, from Peru, why did you conclude that they were perhaps capable of development?

I was very positive from the outset with Al Haig. I said, 'Yes, work on them, work on them, tell me more. Let's see what they look like.' This of course happened. We had a lot of exchanges of telegrams, and talks, to the extent that it *was* agreed later that very week. Al Haig thought that the position we were taking was quite reasonable. Then the Peruvians put it to the Argentines, who turned it down. So we went on for several days after the *Belgrano* was sunk. This is the whole point. It may well be that the Argentines had decided that *no* proposals should be agreed. But we got to a position where the British Cabinet had agreed a series of proposals that were acceptable from Britain's point of view and would not have made military action necessary. Those were turned down.

To say that the *Belgrano* completely scuppered all chances of a negotiated settlement is, I think, not borne out by the facts.

The sinking of the *Belgrano* was, thus, preceded by a diplomacy which became confused between two initiatives at a critical time. The British had anticipated the rejection by Argentina of Haig's mediation. When that happened, they quickly switched the focus of their diplomacy to the United Nations. At the UN, Britain had firm support, expressed in Parsons's achievement of Resolution 502, for an immediate Argentine withdrawal.

Two hours before Pym's meeting with Haig in Washington on 2 May, where the Peruvian proposals were first talked over, the war Cabinet in London had given the Royal Navy permission to alter the rules of engagement, which authorized the submarine *Conqueror* to attack the *Belgrano*. Nothing was then known in London of the nature of Peru's involvement. By the time the *Belgrano* was sunk, seven hours later, Francis Pym had flown to New York for his working dinner with the secretary general of the United Nations.

How, therefore, should we see the context that weekend, in which this Peruvian initiative had surfaced, and as it was inherited by the secretary general of the United Nations, **Javier Pérez de Cuéllar**, himself a Peruvian?

It was not an easy heritage. Although I was secretary general of the UN, I had followed this situation very carefully from the very beginning. As soon as I got this mission I thought it my first duty to show a perfect impartiality. I had some kind of handicap at the beginning of the exercise because, as a Latin American, I might be suspected of some kind of bias, I suppose. I must say that I got, from the British government, immediate expressions of confidence. I had a very good personal relationship with Ambassador Parsons and so I was in a position to embark on the process of 'good offices' with the full confidence of both sides.

There seems to have been a sense of anticipation that you would, *in the end, take over negotiations. Is it correct to suppose that you felt it right to wait until Haig admitted failure?*

I am a career diplomat and I believe very much in preventive diplomacy. That is why, as soon as the problem started, I set up a small group of officers working on a kind of framework for negotiations. When I received General Haig's letter,[18] I was already prepared.

But then, just as you were about to launch the UN effort, comes the initiative from Peru. How did you understand the context in which those Peruvian proposals emerged?

I am glad that you are asking me such a question, because I was never informed about the Peruvian efforts. I think it must sound to you, to everybody, extremely odd that, being a Peruvian, I was not informed of the Peruvian effort. I had some indications. I can remember that once, I think, the foreign minister of Peru called me, but not in order to brief me on what they were doing, but in order to know what *I* was doing. It was the only time we had any contact.

18 Upon the failure of Haig's mediation.

The British felt, as you know, that those Peruvian proposals were 'undeveloped', a series of headings only, skeletal proposals. The British view at the time was that they were much the same as those which had been canvassed by Haig himself, and which had been rejected by Argentina.

That was also my impression after I learnt that the Peruvians had embarked on an effort. But, as I told you, I was not informed. I never had official information about it either from the Peruvians, or the British, or the Argentinians. There was no coordination between the efforts of the Peruvian government, the Peruvian president himself, and my own efforts.

When the Peruvian proposals did become known, surprised as you were by them, did you have the impression that they were under direct and active consideration by both Britain and Argentina?

I do not know, because I must tell you that neither the British nor Argentina ever referred them to me. They never mentioned to me this Peruvian involvement.

Mr Secretary General, as you have reminded me, you are a Peruvian. You had followed these events closely. Had you felt that the Peruvian proposals were in such a form, or of such a nature, that they stood a chance of producing a result, would you have put forward your own proposals?

At the United Nations we always try not to compete with member countries, when member countries are interested in the solution of a problem. It would have been ridiculous for me to embark in a kind of competition with the Peruvian government.

Just to be quite clear: are we right to assume that at that long working dinner, on that Sunday night, May 2nd, with Francis Pym and Sir Anthony Parsons[19] in New York, all of you were focusing on the United Nations *initiative, your own initiative, not the Peruvian initiative?*

Exactly. And excluding any other involvement. Because it was not in the interests of the parties to have two exercises at the same time.

The 'Peruvian' initiative, far from offering an eleventh-hour chance of agreement, added confusion at a crucial moment, and perhaps made all-out conflict even more certain. Had there been a serious prospect of agreement, it seems unlikely that President Belaunde of Peru would have mutely stood aside with Pérez de Cuéllar, himself a Peruvian, over-took or supplanted Peru's attempt.

The British were convinced that after the three weeks of negotiations which ended with the rejection of Haig's own peace settlement, Argentina

19 Britain's permanent representative to the UN.

was prevaricating. The secretary general says Francis Pym, at their working dinner together in New York that Sunday night after Pym had met Haig earlier the same day in Washington, did not mention the Peruvian proposal. The separation between military and diplomatic action was now rapidly widening.

On Sunday 2 May, the war Cabinet, at Chequers, agreed to a change in the rules of engagement around the Falklands. The military imperatives as seen by the chief of the defence staff, **Lord Lewin**, a member of the War Cabinet, were straightforward. The Argentine cruiser *Belgrano* was torpedoed on the night of Sunday 2 May, at 8 p.m. London time, 3 p.m. Washington time.

The whole of the *Belgrano* thing is a nonsense. There was never any doubt that this was the right political and military thing to do. There was never any chance whatsoever of the Peruvian initiative being successful. It was a half-baked proposal, nowhere near as detailed as the one that Haig had failed with. And, of course, we knew nothing of it until *after* the *Belgrano* had been sunk.[20]

Sir Nicholas Henderson, the ambassador, wrote retrospectively, 'It was widely thought that if negotiations were going to lead to anything, this would only be as a result not of conciliatory noises, but of direct and heavy military pressure.' Did the decision to sink the Belgrano *incorporate that element?*

No, not at all. What people continue to forget is that there had been a great deal of military action *before* the *Belgrano* was sunk. The day before the *Belgrano* was sunk we bombed Port Stanley. There was an air battle in which four Argentinian aircraft were shot down. They bombed our ships, near-missed the *Glamorgan* with two one-thousand-pound bombs, about fifty yards on either side. They might both have hit the *Glamorgan* and sunk her. This was the day before the *Belgrano* was sunk. That night, the night of the 1st May, Argentinian television and radio were claiming that they had set the *Hermes* on fire, they had sunk a destroyer and damaged three others, and shot down six Harriers. Well now, that was in our minds on the morning of May 2nd.[21]

Was there not also a thought that there was 'a need to concentrate the mind', as Pym had said, to convince the Argentinians that we were serious? The sinking of

20 The war Cabinet authorized the attack on the *Belgrano* on 2 May at 1300 London time, 0800 Washington time. The first meeting between Pym and Haig on 2 May was at 1000 Washington time, 1500 London time. The *Belgrano* was hit at 2000 London time, 1500 Washington time.

21 When the war Cabinet authorized attacks on Argentine warships.

the Belgrano *followed the crucial event of Haig's failure. Was there a feeling,* *'negotiations are over, the war begins'?*

No. The decision was taken because this was a military threat, which could be eliminated. It was *only* the submarines that were not allowed to attack. All the *other* elements down there, the carriers with the Harriers and guided missiles, all these were free, under the control of Admiral Woodward, to attack anything they found. We had put an extra restriction on the submarines because of the task they had been carrying out earlier on. We had not, at that time, lifted it. If the *submarines* had been detected by *Belgrano*'s escort, and a submarine had thought it was being attacked, it too had the right to retaliate. It was entirely to remove a military threat that we changed the rule of engagement.

I should make it clear that we did not order the submarine to sink the *Belgrano*. We told all submarines down there that they were now free to attack Argentinian warships when they had an opportunity to do so. We did not say, to *Conqueror*, 'Sink the *Belgrano*', although we knew that was going to be the effect. We *hoped* it would be the effect. By the time she got the signal, she might possibly have lost contact. I remember saying to ministers, 'Look, we will send this signal, but don't think that this will necessarily mean the sinking of the *Belgrano*, because, by the time she gets it, she may have lost her.'

It is said that permission was given in the porch at Chequers?

We got a report that *Conqueror* was in contact with the *Belgrano*, and Woodward,[22] during the night, had sent a signal saying, 'Please change the rules of engagement because this chap is a threat to me and I cannot carry out my mission.' His mission was to prepare for a landing on the Falkland Islands, which required him to land intelligence parties. He had to get close in, he had to put helicopters in, had to carry out bombardment. He could not carry out his mission with a couple of destroyers, armed with Exocet, hanging around the Falkland Islands. So he asked for the rules of engagement to be changed.

Because of the risk of the submarine losing contact with *Belgrano*, I took the earliest opportunity to get a change in the rules of engagement. I was not prepared to wait until after lunch to raise it at a war Cabinet.

How was it raised?

I took Admiral Fieldhouse with me and, when I arrived, I told the prime minister that we were in contact, we would like a change in the

22 Admiral Woodward, the task force commander.

rules of engagement, and could she get ministers together and give us the approval.

To sink this ship?

No. To change the rules of engagement, which *allowed* the sinking of the ship. We said that she[23] is not allowed at the moment to attack those things outside the exclusion zone. We do not know if it[24] will come in, but the time has come to change the rules of engagement for the submarines. Everything *else* has got freedom.

This, you see, had actually come up before. We had thought, earlier on, that one of our submarines was about to get in touch with the aircraft carrier,[25] a long way from the Falklands, and we asked for a change in the rules of engagement then. It was not granted because, at that time, we had not set up the total exclusion zone and also, at that time, the Americans had not tilted towards us. There was still just the vaguest chance of a negotiated settlement. I was prepared to accept that, because of where the submarine was, and where the aircraft carrier was. Our forces had not yet arrived down there, and this was an acceptable risk. In the event, that submarine did not get in contact with the aircraft carrier.

Critics of the decision to sink the Belgrano *at that time, which coincides with the 'Peruvian' initiative . . .*

Which we knew nothing about.

. . . also point out that the Argentine Navy transmitted 'return' signals to surface units some fifteen hours before Belgrano *was sunk. You say, in effect, 'We could not wait', but the critics suggest that may have been because you knew the opportunity might not occur again. Were events, that weekend, being hastily handled?*

No. Not in the slightest. It is quite untrue to say we knew the force had turned back before the *Belgrano* was sunk, or certainly before the signal changing the rules of engagement was sent. Even if we *had* known, it would not have changed our minds. They could have turned back because the weather was unsuitable for launching their aircraft.[26]

There is nothing like *responsibility* for concentrating the mind. Most of those people who criticize the sinking of the *Belgrano* are those who have never had responsibility for the lives of our people. I hope they never will do.

23 The submarine *Conqueror*.
24 The *Belgrano* and her escorts.
25 The *Veinticinco de Mayo*.
26 Admiral Allara, commander of Task Force 79, which included the *Belgrano*, confirms the weather as a factor in this decision. See p. 216.

Such diplomatic reverses as Britain suffered because of the sinking of the Belgrano *were due, would you agree, to the very high casualties on that ship?*

Entirely. I was shocked at the number of casualties. They showed a remarkable lack of professionalism or preparedness. In our aircraft carriers, for example, no one slept below 4 deck, which is below the water line, *for the whole of the time they were down there*, with the chance of being torpedoed or sunk. Everybody carried a lifebelt, as we did during the last war. Everybody had a survival suit if they went into the water. All the watertight doors were closed below the water line. My understanding of the *Belgrano* is that a large number of the watertight doors were open. They were not at any level of 'damage control', some of the men were in their bunks in underpants and nothing else. I believe that their casualties would have been very much less if they had exhibited a higher standard of professionalism. I am sorry to say it, but I think that is so.

One cannot foretell what is going to happen. In my view there was something like a 75 per cent chance that *Conqueror* would be successful. There was a 25 per cent chance that she would not, that she would lose contact. In my view we could have expected one torpedo hit. She fired three torpedoes and got two hits. This is really quite dramatic. It is about a 10 or 15 per cent chance that you will get two hits out of three.

What led to your seeking permission for extending the 'total exclusion zone'? On the face of it there is not much point in establishing such a zone if it is not to be maintained.

There is this confusion in the public mind between the 'total exclusion zone' and a war in the South Atlantic. It was called a 'maritime exclusion zone' and was set up initially because the first force to arrive there was the nuclear submarine. A nuclear submarine is very limited in what it can do. By international law it cannot sink merchant ships without first stopping them, warning them, and giving the crew a chance to abandon ship. A nuclear submarine will not expose itself on the surface, because it is then at its most vulnerable. So, under international law, submarines can only attack warships, and then only with some sort of general warning.

We first set up the maritime exclusion zone at two hundred miles, which is where the submarines were operating to try and dissuade the Argentinians from reinforcing the Falklands. It was not going to have much effect because merchant ships could still get in and out and so, of course, could aircraft. When the task force got down there we could turn this maritime exclusion zone into a blockade, which applied to *everything* of all nations, whether Russian, Polish, Argentinian or

Brazilian, or whether aircraft, merchant ships, or warships. Anything within that zone, we claimed we had a right to sink. By this time, we had *surface* ships which could stop a merchant ship and ask, 'Where are you going?', and, 'Have you got troops on board? If so, you either turn round or I will sink you!' This, then was a blockade.

From April 23rd onwards, when the task force got south of the equator, and we were overflown by Argentinian Boeing 707s fitted with radar capable of reporting their position, all our ships were under threat from Argentine long-range aircraft: Canberras with a range of seven hundred miles, and submarines which could have attacked us at any moment, and surface ships which could 'sortie' out and attack us with Exocet missiles, which they fire from over the horizon. At that stage, I got permission from the Cabinet to attack *first* any Argentinian forces we met. You cannot wait until *they* fire first with an Exocet missile.

We then issued that warning to Argentina that, if we met any of their forces on the high seas who appeared to be interfering, or were in a position to interfere, with the mission of our task forces, they would be treated as hostile and dealt with accordingly. I am quite certain that all the Argentinian naval commanders knew exactly what that meant.

The sinking of the *Belgrano* changed dramatically all perceptions of the Falklands struggle. There were many to proclaim Britain wrong. The Argentine cruiser was sunk outside the ring drawn round the Falklands and announced by Britain as a zone of exclusion.

The *Belgrano* was attached to Task Force 79 under the Command of **Admiral Gualter Allara**, flying his flag in the aircraft carrier, *Veinticinco de Mayo*. Allara is a former chief of Argentine intelligence. He had previously been a minister in the military government, and as such was the man who negotiated over the Falklands with Labour's Foreign Office Minister, Ted Rowlands, in the 1970s.

For those who, like Adam, nibble guiltily on the fruits of victory, here is Admiral Allara's evidence. He gave the *Belgrano* her orders.

When the plan was made for the recovery of the Malvinas we took into account the naval strength Great Britain could command in the area of the Malvinas, and reached the conclusion that it would be impossible for us to enter into battle with the full strength of British forces. That is to say, it was a case of finding the right conditions, when groups of British forces were separated from the main one, when our strength would be about the same, in order to mount an attack. For that reason, the mission of Task Force 79, which I commanded, was to attack British forces under favourable conditions.

On May 1st, the Argentine High Command told us the British were disembarking on the northern part of the Falklands. That evidently meant most of their ships would be concentrated, for a prolonged period of time, in that area. This, therefore, was a favourable opportunity for the mission of Task Force 79.

In the afternoon of May 1st a second spotter plane from our aircraft carrier, *Veinticinco de Mayo*, where I was in command, detected a group of eight British ships. At that moment, I decided this group made a good target for our forces, and I gave the order to prepare an air attack. Unfortunately our aircraft-carrier cannot launch aircraft by night. As it was late already, I postponed the attack until dawn the next day, May 2nd. As the hours passed, two things made me decide to call it off. First was confirmation the British were not landing, and so not preoccupied with that operation. Second, the weather conditions. There was absolutely no wind. It was, therefore, not possible for our planes to take off from the carrier with the weapons, and fuel, needed. These weather conditions were forecast for the whole day of May 2nd. Therefore we called it off, and pulled the carrier back to shallower waters, in order to avoid or diminish the chance of submarine attack.

In this context you have just described, how is the historian to judge the sinking of the cruiser Belgrano*?*

The cruiser, *General Belgrano*, together with two destroyers, had been sent by me to the southern zone of the theatre of operations. They had two missions. The first was to intercept British supply convoys that might be coming from the Pacific. We had some information on that. Secondly, at the time, there was our country's continuing dispute with Chile, which was still unresolved. We thought it advisable to station ships in that area as a counter to Chilean forces. The *General Belgrano* was attacked and sunk outside the exclusion zone.

As far as I'm concerned, from a strictly professional point of view, I cannot criticize that action. She was a ship carrying out a war mission, and this military mission was connected with the conflict. On the other hand, at the time of the sinking, negotiations were still in progress concerning a solution to the conflict, both at a political and diplomatic level, and the sinking of the *Belgrano* diminished, without a doubt, their chance of success.

Admiral, you appear to have placed a good deal of reliance upon a literal interpretation of the maritime exclusion zone. Do you agree that, on April 23, a week before, the British had told the Argentine Government and the Security Council, and had circulated this notice widely through diplomatic channels, that the British fleet and British forces would undertake operations outside the total exclusion zone, if they were considered necessary in defence of British forces?

I am in no way disregarding that. I can assure you it was always present in our minds. Again, I would just say that, as a professional naval officer, I do not criticize the British attack on a warship with a war fighting capability, and on a military mission, when she was in the area of the conflict.

The ships of that Argentine force, as we now know, were sailing away from the area at the time. But ships that sail away can always come back. The real problem seems to me that by this time any trust or confidence had deteriorated to the point where this kind of incident, and conflict, were inevitable?

I fully agree with you. That is why I said that although, in my country and abroad, many voices condemned the sinking of the *Belgrano*, I repeat that as a professional, and especially from a military point of view, I do not condemn it. That ship was in the area of operations.

Admiral Allara's reflections are those of the man on the bridge of the flagship of the Argentine Navy, and in command of the *Belgrano* task group, Task Force 79. For the reasons explained earlier,[27] Admiral Jorge Anaya, the driving force behind the Falklands invasion as the naval member of the Argentine Junta, speaks to us through that informed interlocutor the Supreme Allied Commander Atlantic, **Admiral Harry Train** USN. Admiral Train spent a good deal of time with Anaya, who was in detention after the Junta's fall, going over Anaya's views concerning the *Belgrano* episode for the classified American study of the Falklands conflict.

That's almost an essay in itself. He believed that when the British established and announced the maritime exclusion zone, they meant it, and that the zone would have a certain size and shape. As you know, it was circular and described around Port Stanley. The Argentine leadership thought the British would not fight outside the maritime exclusion zone.

Despite the fact that, on April 23rd, eight days before the Belgrano, *the British had said they* would *if they felt British interests were in danger?*

Yes, notwithstanding that. As far as Anaya and Vice-Admiral Lombardo were concerned, they saw the maritime exclusion zone as a *cordon sanitaire*, and as long as they stayed outside it they would be safe.[28] The maritime exclusion zone has a definition in international law based on the principle of the *cordon sanitaire*. When the British announced subsequently that they would operate *outside* the zone,

27 See Ch. 5.
28 Cf Admiral Allara's opinion, given above.

they did not modify the maritime exclusion zone. They were, in effect, merely modifying their own rules of engagement, which do not have status in international law.

Vice-Admiral Lombardo then planned an operation to divert attention away from the beachhead at Port Stanley. His operation was to sail the *Belgrano* task group to the east, south of the maritime exclusion zone, then swing north, following the boundary of the maritime exclusion zone up to the channel, or the space, between the Falklands and South Georgia. At the same time the *Veinticinco de Mayo* was ordered to come in from the north, also outside the exclusion zone, to execute a pincer movement into that space between South Georgia and the Falklands.

Now bear in mind that, at this time, Sandy Woodward[29] had pulled *his* ships way back into the eastern portion of the maritime exclusion zone, in order to keep them away from land-based air. He was favouring the eastern portion of that zone. He recognized that if the *Veinticinco de Mayo* and *Belgrano* came into the vicinity, he could have a problem. He would be threatened by sea-based tactical air on one hand, and land-based tactical air on the other, and he could not get back in the middle.

Does Admiral Anaya, therefore, have any complaint about the sinking of the Belgrano?

No. None. As a politician he should have realized that the British had the capability to attack it and that the nuclear submarines were there. Remember, Anaya was filling the role of both military and political leader. Argentina did not have the luxury of having civilian political leaderships superimposed over accountable military leadership, as we do in the United States and Britain. He did not have that check and balance. He was trying to play both roles simultaneously. He was ultra-cautious in some instances, and as it turned out, he was fool-hardy on other occasions.

The three weeks which passed between the sinking of the *Belgrano* and the British landing to repossess the Falklands saw the last and best-organized attempt to solve the Falklands question short of war. This was the mediation of the United Nations secretary general, Pérez de Cuéllar. Hundreds of telegrams flashed back and forth with different drafts of different articles, of a draft treaty. The final British concessions, handed by Sir Anthony Parsons to Pérez de Cuéllar in New York, were substantial. They included the non-reintroduction of a British administration

29 Admiral Woodward, the commander of the British Task force.

on the Islands, an interim United Nations administration and a specified target date for the end of negotiations, and they abandoned the demand that Argentina recognize British sovereignty over the Islands. But Argentina could not face the question of withdrawal. In the end, Haig's experience, that the Argentine Junta was incapable of coming to a proper decision, was repeated by **Pérez de Cuéllar**.

I must say that, as far as I am concerned, all the time my efforts lasted, I felt I had the full involvement of both the British and the Argentinians. When the British decided to present the most flexible proposal, they presented it through the United Nations exercise. Unfortunately, it was not accepted by the other side, but that is another problem. The impression I had was that the parties were much more involved in the United Nations exercise than in the Peruvian one.

You said the British came up with a 'most flexible' response. Right at the very end, when the British presented those final proposals of theirs to you, what view did you take as to whether they formed a reasonable basis for a peaceful settlement?

I do believe that it was a sensible proposal. It would have allowed the Argentinian position to be completely different to what it is now. The proposal was a flexible proposal which, in my opinion, was a very good basis for proceeding with substantive, constructive negotiations.

Can you remember what your reactions were when Parsons handed it to you?

My reaction was, I must say, optimistic. I thought that these proposals could be considered favourably by the Argentinian government. And now I am going to be very frank with you: the fact that there were two exercises at the same time was really misleading. From Argentina's point of view, perhaps they thought, while they were playing on the United Nations 'board', 'Why should we accept this idea when perhaps we can achieve a better outcome through the Peruvians?' That is why I think, as a technician – and I am supposed to be, as secretary general, a technician on international negotiations – it was a tremendous mistake: this mistake of playing on two different boards.

Right at the very end, Argentina was still saying, here in New York, that they were prepared to make progress with ideas proposed by you as secretary general. That does not fit, does it, with the charge made that the sinking of the Belgrano ended all such possibilities of a negotiated settlement?

No, I do not think so. I think it is not because of that Argentina did not accept the last British ideas. I think it was because they were expecting *more* than that. And that was very unfortunate. The

situation today would be completely different, from an Argentinian
point of view, if the Galtieri government had accepted to work on the
basis of the British ideas.

When Pérez de Cuéllar put down the phone after his last talk with
General Galtieri, it was the final defeat for diplomacy. It left no arbiter
other than war.

From the 1960s onwards, Britain had decided that Suez was a
watershed and it would no longer equip itself for a post-colonial war. Sir
John Nott's defence review in 1981, the year before the conflict, confirmed
that decision and incorporated his belief that 'the task force mentality' was
'nostalgia for the days of empire', the days when the ships of the Royal
Navy had been the key to the lock of the world. Presented with that fundamental change of circumstance, **Admiral Lord Lewin** makes answer.

> I wish politicians had a marvellous crystal ball which enabled them to
> see into the future. The Falklands was the war they told us we would
> never have to fight. The chiefs of staff, I think, would have been
> perfectly within their rights to have said, 'I'm sorry, prime minister,
> this is the war you told us we would not have to fight, and there is
> nothing we can do to help you.'

Britain fought a war in the Falklands for islands it had spent the better
part of twenty years suggesting it did not want. It therefore had no
coherent strategic policy. The British return to Europe after empire has
not been accompanied by an unequivocal sense of direction or purpose.
In the 1960s British policy had set out, after years of neglect, to re-
invigorate the old relationship in trade with Argentina, and with the
South American continent as a whole. It is an odd but important fact
that, in addressing her changed circumstances after the Second World
War, Britain had a Falklands 'lobby' but never a Latin America lobby.

How to persuade the unwilling to accept the unavoidable, the
dilemma over the Islanders, has a wonderful continuity in this post-war
era. The lesson of the Falklands seems commonplace. Political leaders
who avoid the difficult choices face harder ones in the end.

The Falklands was a national war for an international principle of the
United Nations: aggression is not admissible. In upholding the rights of
a tiny minority in those circumstances, Britain convinced the international community, and showed that to do right is generally the right
thing to do. In going to the defence of the Islanders, Britain was lit by its
own hearth fire. It defended the first principle of democracy as laid
down by Edmund Burke – attachment to the subdivision, the small case
that cannot be overlooked, Burke's 'little platoon'.

Index